Expert Cube Development with Microsoft SQL Server 2008 Analysis Services

Design and implement fast, scalable, and maintainable cubes

Chris Webb

Alberto Ferrari

Marco Russo

BIRMINGHAM - MUMBAI

Expert Cube Development with Microsoft SQL Server 2008 Analysis Services

First published: July 2009

Production Reference: 1100709

Published by Packt Publishing Ltd.
32 Lincoln Road
Olton
Birmingham, B27 6PA, UK.

ISBN 978-1-847197-22-1

www.packtpub.com

Cover Image by Vinayak Chittar (vinayak.chittar@gmail.com)

Credits

Authors
Chris Webb
Alberto Ferrari
Marco Russo

Reviewers
Stephen Gordon Christie
Deepak Puri

Acquisition Editor
James Lumsden

Development Editor
Dhiraj Chandiramani

Technical Editors
Abhinav Prasoon
Gaurav Datar
Chaitanya Apte
Ishita Dhabalia
Gagandeep Singh

Editorial Team Leader
Gagandeep Singh

Project Team Leader
Lata Basantani

Copy Editor
Leonard D'Silva

Project Coordinator
Joel Goveya

Proofreader
Laura Booth

Indexer
Rekha Nair

Production Coordinator
Aparna Bhagat

Cover Work
Aparna Bhagat

About the Authors

Chris Webb (chris@crossjoin.co.uk) has been working with Microsoft Business Intelligence tools for almost ten years in a variety of roles and industries. He is an independent consultant and trainer based in the UK, specializing in Microsoft SQL Server Analysis Services and the MDX query language. He is the co-author of *MDX Solutions for Microsoft SQL Server Analysis Services 2005 and Hyperion Essbase, Wiley, 0471748080,* is a regular speaker at conferences, and blogs on Business Intelligence (BI) at http://cwebbbi.spaces.live.com. He is a recipient of Microsoft's Most Valuable Professional award for his work in the SQL Server community.

First and foremost, I'd like to thank my wife Helen and my two daughters Natasha and Amelia for putting up with me while I've been working on this book. I'd also like to thank everyone who's helped answer all the questions I came up with in the course of writing it: Deepak Puri, Darren Gosbell, David Elliott, Mark Garner, Edward Melomed, Gary Floyd, Greg Galloway, Mosha Pasumansky, Sacha Tomey, Teo Lachev, Thomas Ivarsson, and Vidas Matelis. I'm grateful to you all.

Alberto Ferrari (alberto.ferrari@sqlbi.com) is a consultant and trainer for the BI development area with the Microsoft suite for Business Intelligence. His main interests are in the methodological approaches to the BI development and he works as a trainer for software houses that need to design complex BI solutions.

He is a founder, with Marco Russo, of the site www.sqlbi.com, where they publish many whitepapers and articles about SQL Server technology. He co-authored the *SqlBI Methodology*, which can be found on the SQLBI site.

My biggest thanks goes to Caterina, who had the patience and courage to support me during all the hard time in book writing and my son, Lorenzo, is just a year old but he's an invaluable source of happiness in my life.

Marco Russo (marco.russo@sqlbi.com) is a consultant and trainer in software development based in Italy, focusing on development for the Microsoft Windows operating system. He's involved in several Business Intelligence projects, making data warehouse relational, and multidimensional design, with particular experience in sectors such as banking and financial services, manufacturing and commercial distribution.

He previously wrote several books about .NET and recently co-authored *Introducing Microsoft LINQ*, 0735623910, and *Programming Microsoft LINQ*, 0735624003, both published by Microsoft Press. He also wrote *The many-to-many revolution*, a mini-book about many-to-many dimension relationships in Analysis Services, and co-authored the *SQLBI Methodology* with Alberto Ferrari. Marco is a founder of SQLBI (http://www.sqlbi.com) and his blog is available at http://sqlblog.com/blogs/marco_russo.

About the Reviewers

Stephen Christie started off in the IT environment as a technician back in 1998. He moved up through development, to become a Database Administrator — Team Lead, which is his current position.

Stephen was hired by one of South Africa's biggest FMGC companies to start off their BI environment. When he started at the company, they were still working on SQL Server 7; he upgraded all the servers to SQL Server 2000 and started working on Analysis services, this challenged him daily as technology was still very ne. When the first cube was signed off, he got involved with ProClarity 5 so that the BA's could use the information in the Cubes. This is where Stephen became interested in the DBA aspect of SQL 2000 and performance tuning. After working for this company for 5 years all the information the company required was put into cubes and Stephen moved on.

Stephen has now been working as a Team lead for a team of database administrators in Cape Town South Africa for an online company. He has specialized in performance tuning and system maintenance.

Deepak Puri is a Business Intelligence Consultant, and has been working with SQL Server Analysis Services since 2000. Deepak is currently a Microsoft SQL Server MVP with a focus on OLAP. His interest in OLAP technology arose from working with large volumes of call center telecom data at a large insurance company. In addition, Deepak has also worked with performance data and Key Performance Indicators (KPI's) for new business processes. Recent project work includes SSAS cube design, and dashboard and reporting front-end design for OLAP cube data, using Reporting Services and third-party OLAP-aware SharePoint Web Parts.

Deepak has helped review the following books in the past:

- *MDX Solutions* (2nd Edition) *978-0-471-74808-3*.
- *Applied Microsoft Analysis Services 2005, Prologika Press, 0976635305.*

Table of Contents

Preface

Microsoft SQL Server Analysis Services ("Analysis Services" from here on) is now ten years old, a mature product proven in thousands of enterprise-level deployments around the world. Starting from a point where few people knew it existed and where those that did were often suspicious of it, it has grown to be the most widely deployed OLAP server and one of the keystones of Microsoft's Business Intelligence (BI) product strategy. Part of the reason for its success has been the easy availability of information about it: apart from the documentation Microsoft provides there are white papers, blogs, newsgroups, online forums, and books galore on the subject. So why write yet another book on Analysis Services? The short answer is to bring together all of the practical, real-world knowledge about Analysis Services that's out there into one place.

We, the authors of this book, are consultants who have spent the last few years of our professional lives designing and building solutions based on the Microsoft Business Intelligence platform and helping other people to do so. We've watched Analysis Services grow to maturity and at the same time seen more and more people move from being hesitant beginners on their first project to confident cube designers, but at the same time we felt that there were no books on the market aimed at this emerging group of intermediate-to-experienced users. Similarly, all of the Analysis Services books we read concerned themselves with describing its functionality and what you could potentially do with it but none addressed the practical problems we encountered day-to-day in our work—the problems of how you should go about designing cubes, what the best practices for doing so are, which areas of functionality work well and which don't, and so on. We wanted to write this book to fill these two gaps, and to allow us to share our hard-won experience. Most technical books are published to coincide with the release of a new version of a product and so are written using beta software, before the author has had a chance to use the new version in a real project. This book, on the other hand, has been written with the benefit of having used Analysis Services 2008 for almost a year and before that Analysis Services 2005 for more than three years.

What this book covers

The approach we've taken with this book is to follow the lifecycle of building an Analysis Services solution from start to finish. As we've said already this does not take the form of a basic tutorial, it is more of a guided tour through the process with an informed commentary telling you what to do, what not to do and what to look out for.

Chapter 1 shows how to design a relational data mart to act as a source for Analysis Services.

Chapter 2 covers setting up a new project in BI Development Studio and building simple dimensions and cubes.

Chapter 3 discusses more complex dimension design problems such as slowly changing dimensions and ragged hierarchies.

Chapter 4 looks at measures and measure groups, how to control how measures aggregate up, and how dimensions can be related to measure groups.

Chapter 5 looks at issues such as drillthrough, fact dimensions and many-to-many relationships.

Chapter 6 shows how to add calculations to a cube, and gives some examples of how to implement common calculations in MDX.

Chapter 7 deals with the various ways we can implement currency conversion in a cube.

Chapter 8 covers query performance tuning, including how to design aggregations and partitions and how to write efficient MDX.

Chapter 9 looks at the various ways we can implement security, including cell security and dimension security, as well as dynamic security.

Chapter 10 looks at some common issues we'll face when a cube is in production, including how to deploy changes, and how to automate partition management and processing.

Chapter 11 discusses how we can monitor query performance, processing performance and usage once the cube has gone into production.

What you need for this book

To follow the examples in this book we recommend that you have a PC with the following installed on it:

- Microsoft Windows Vista, Microsoft Windows XP
- Microsoft Windows Server 2003 or Microsoft Windows Server 2008
- Microsoft SQL Server Analysis Services 2008
- Microsoft SQL Server 2008 (the relational engine)
- Microsoft Visual Studio 2008 and BI Development Studio
- SQL Server Management Studio
- Excel 2007 is an optional bonus as an alternative method of querying the cube

We recommend that you use SQL Server Developer Edition to follow the examples in this book. We'll discuss the differences between Developer Edition, Standard Edition and Enterprise Edition in chapter 2; some of the functionality we'll cover is not available in Standard Edition and we'll mention that fact whenever it's relevant.

Who this book is for

This book is aimed at Business Intelligence consultants and developers who work with Analysis Services on a daily basis, who know the basics of building a cube already and who want to gain a deeper practical knowledge of the product and perhaps check that they aren't doing anything badly wrong at the moment.

It's not a book for absolute beginners and we're going to assume that you understand basic Analysis Services concepts such as what a cube and a dimension is, and that you're not interested in reading yet another walkthrough of the various wizards in BI Development Studio. Equally it's not an advanced book and we're not going to try to dazzle you with our knowledge of obscure properties or complex data modelling scenarios that you're never likely to encounter. We're not going to cover all the functionality available in Analysis Services either, and in the case of MDX, where a full treatment of the subject requires a book on its own, we're going to give some examples of code you can copy and adapt yourselves, but not try to explain how the language works.

One important point must be made before we continue and it is that in this book we're going to be expressing some strong opinions. We're going to tell you how we like to design cubes based on what we've found to work for us over the years, and you may not agree with some of the things we say. We're not going to pretend that all advice that differs from our own is necessarily wrong, though: best practices are often subjective and one of the advantages of a book with multiple authors is that you not only get the benefit of more than one person's experience but also that each author's opinions have already been moderated by his co-authors.

Think of this book as a written version of the kind of discussion you might have with someone at a user group meeting or a conference, where you pick up hints and tips from your peers: some of the information may not be relevant to what you do, some of it you may dismiss, but even if only 10% of what you learn is new it might be the crucial piece of knowledge that makes the difference between success and failure on your project.

Analysis Services is very easy to use—some would say too easy. It's possible to get something up and running very quickly and as a result it's an all too common occurrence that a cube gets put into production and subsequently shows itself to have problems that can't be fixed without a complete redesign. We hope that this book helps you avoid having one of these "If only I'd known about this earlier!" moments yourself, by passing on knowledge that we've learned the hard way. We also hope that you enjoy reading it and that you're successful in whatever you're trying to achieve with Analysis Services.

Conventions

In this book, you will find a number of styles of text that distinguish between different kinds of information. Here are some examples of these styles, and an explanation of their meaning.

Code words in text are shown as follows: "We can include other contexts through the use of the `include` directive."

A block of code will be set as follows:

```
CASE WHEN Weight IS NULL OR Weight<0 THEN 'N/A'
WHEN Weight<10 THEN '0-10Kg'
WHEN Weight<20 THEN '10-20Kg'
ELSE '20Kg or more'
END
```

When we wish to draw your attention to a particular part of a code block, the relevant lines or items will be shown in bold:

```
SCOPE([Measures].[Sales Amount]);
    THIS = TAIL(
            NONEMPTY(
                {EXISTING [Date].[Date].[Date].MEMBERS}
                * [Measures].[Sales Amount])
            ,1).ITEM(0);
END SCOPE;
```

New terms and **important words** are shown in bold. Words that you see on the screen, in menus or dialog boxes for example, appear in our text like this: "clicking the **Next** button moves you to the next screen".

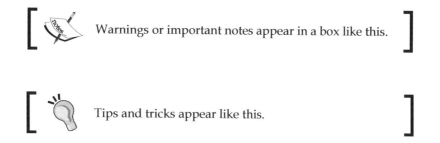

Warnings or important notes appear in a box like this.

Tips and tricks appear like this.

Reader feedback

Feedback from our readers is always welcome. Let us know what you think about this book—what you liked or may have disliked. Reader feedback is important for us to develop titles that you really get the most out of.

To send us general feedback, simply drop an email to feedback@packtpub.com, and mention the book title in the subject of your message.

If there is a book that you need and would like to see us publish, please send us a note in the **SUGGEST A TITLE** form on www.packtpub.com or email suggest@packtpub.com.

If there is a topic that you have expertise in and you are interested in either writing or contributing to a book, see our author guide on www.packtpub.com/authors.

Customer support

Now that you are the proud owner of a Packt book, we have a number of things to help you to get the most from your purchase.

Downloading the example code and database for the book

Visit http://www.packtpub.com/files/code/7221_Code.zip to directly download the example code and database.

The downloadable files contain instructions on how to use them.

All of the examples in this book use a sample database based on the Adventure Works sample that Microsoft provides, and which can be downloaded from http://tinyurl.com/SQLServerSamples. We use the same relational data source data to start but then make changes as and when required for building our cubes, and although the cube we build as the book progresses resembles the official Adventure Works cube it differs in several important respects so we encourage you to download and install it.

Errata

Although we have taken every care to ensure the accuracy of our contents, mistakes do happen. If you find a mistake in one of our books—maybe a mistake in text or code—we would be grateful if you would report this to us. By doing so, you can save other readers from frustration, and help us to improve subsequent versions of this book. If you find any errata, please report them by visiting http://www.packtpub.com/support, selecting your book, clicking on the **let us know** link, and entering the details of your errata. Once your errata are verified, your submission will be accepted and the errata added to any list of existing errata. Any existing errata can be viewed by selecting your title from http://www.packtpub.com/support.

Piracy

Piracy of copyright material on the Internet is an ongoing problem across all media. At Packt, we take the protection of our copyright and licenses very seriously. If you come across any illegal copies of our works in any form on the Internet, please provide us with the location address or website name immediately so that we can pursue a remedy.

Please contact us at copyright@packtpub.com with a link to the suspected pirated material.

We appreciate your help in protecting our authors, and our ability to bring you valuable content.

Questions

You can contact us at questions@packtpub.com if you are having a problem with any aspect of the book, and we will do our best to address it.

1
Designing the Data Warehouse for Analysis Services

The focus of this chapter is how to design a data warehouse specifically for Analysis Services. There are numerous books available that explain the theory of dimensional modeling and data warehouses; our goal here is not to discuss generic data warehousing concepts but to help you adapt the theory to the needs of Analysis Services.

In this chapter we will touch on just about every aspect of data warehouse design, and mention several subjects that cannot be analyzed in depth in a single chapter. Some of these subjects, such as Analysis Services cube and dimension design, will be covered in full detail in later chapters. Others, which are outside the scope of this book, will require further research on the part of the reader.

The source database

Analysis Services cubes are built on top of a database, but the real question is: what kind of database should this be?

We will try to answer this question by analyzing the different kinds of databases we will encounter in our search for the best source for our cube. In the process of doing so we are going to describe the basics of dimensional modeling, as well as some of the competing theories on how data warehouses should be designed.

The OLTP database

Typically, a BI solution is created when business users want to analyze, explore and report on their data in an easy and convenient way. The data itself may be composed of thousands, millions or even billions of rows, normally kept in a relational database built to perform a specific business purpose. We refer to this database as the **On Line Transactional Processing (OLTP)** database.

The OLTP database can be a legacy mainframe system, a CRM system, an ERP system, a general ledger system or any kind of database that a company has bought or built in order to manage their business.

Sometimes the OLTP may consist of simple flat files generated by processes running on a host. In such a case, the OLTP is not a real database but we can still turn it into one by importing the flat files into a SQL Server database for example. Therefore, regardless of the specific media used to store the OLTP, we will refer to it as a database.

Some of the most important and common characteristics of an OLTP system are:

- The OLTP system is normally a complex piece of software that handles information and transactions; from our point of view, though, we can think of it simply as a database.

  We do not normally communicate in any way with the application that manages and populates the data in the OLTP. Our job is that of exporting data from the OLTP, cleaning it, integrating it with data from other sources, and loading it into the data warehouse.

- We cannot make any assumptions about the OLTP database's structure.

  Somebody else has built the OLTP system and is probably currently maintaining it, so its structure may change over time. We do not usually have the option of changing anything in its structure anyway, so we have to take the OLTP system "as is" even if we believe that it could be made better.

- The OLTP may well contain data that does not conform to the general rules of relational data modeling, like foreign keys and constraints.

  Normally in the OLTP system, we will find historical data that is not correct. This is almost always the case. A system that runs for years very often has data that is incorrect and never will be correct.

  When building our BI solution we'll have to clean and fix this data, but normally it would be too expensive and disruptive to do this for old data in the OLTP system itself.

- In our experience, the OLTP system is very often poorly documented. Our first task is, therefore, that of creating good documentation for the system, validating data and checking it for any inconsistencies.

The OLTP database is not built to be easily queried, and is certainly not going to be designed with Analysis Services cubes in mind. Nevertheless, a very common question is: "do we really need to build a dimensionally modeled data mart as the source for an Analysis Services cube?" The answer is a definite "yes"!

As we'll see, the structure of a data mart is very different from the structure of an OLTP database and Analysis Services is built to work on data marts, not on generic OLTP databases. The changes that need to be made when moving data from the OLTP database to the final data mart structure should be carried out by specialized ETL software, like SQL Server Integration Services, and cannot simply be handled by Analysis Services in the Data Source View.

Moreover, the OLTP database needs to be efficient for OLTP queries. OLTP queries tend to be very fast on small chunks of data, in order to manage everyday work. If we run complex queries ranging over the whole OLTP database, as BI-style queries often do, we will create severe performance problems for the OLTP database. There are very rare situations in which data can flow directly from the OLTP through to Analysis Services but these are so specific that their description is outside the scope of this book.

Beware of the temptation to avoid building a data warehouse and data marts. Building an Analysis Services cube is a complex job that starts with getting the design of your data mart right. If we have a dimensional data mart, we have a database that holds dimension and fact tables where we can perform any kind of cleansing or calculation. If, on the other hand, we rely on the OLTP database, we might finish our first cube in less time but our data will be dirty, inconsistent and unreliable, and cube processing will be slow. In addition, we will not be able to create complex relational models to accommodate our users' analytical needs.

The data warehouse

We always have an OLTP system as the original source of our data but, when it comes to a data warehouse, it can be difficult to answer this apparently simple question: "Do we have a data warehouse?" The problem is not the answer, as every analyst will happily reply, "*Yes, we do have a data warehouse*"; the problem is in the meaning of the words "data warehouse".

There are at least two major approaches to data warehouse design and development and, consequently, to the definition of what a data warehouse is. They are described in the books of two leading authors:

- **Ralph Kimball**: if we are building a Kimball data warehouse, we build fact tables and dimension tables structured as data marts. We will end up with a data warehouse composed of the sum of all the data marts.

- **Bill Inmon**: if our choice is that of an Inmon data warehouse, then we design a (somewhat normalized), physical relational database that will hold the data warehouse. Afterwards, we produce departmental data marts with their star schemas populated from that relational database.

If this were a book about data warehouse methodology then we could write hundreds of pages about this topic but, luckily for the reader, the detailed differences between the Inmon and Kimball methodologies are out of the scope of this book. Readers can find out more about these methodologies in *Building the Data Warehouse* by Bill Inmon and *The Data Warehouse Toolkit* by Ralph Kimball. Both books should be present on any BI developer's bookshelf.

A picture is worth a thousand words when trying to describe the differences between the two approaches. In Kimball's bus architecture, data flows from the OLTP through to the data marts as follows:

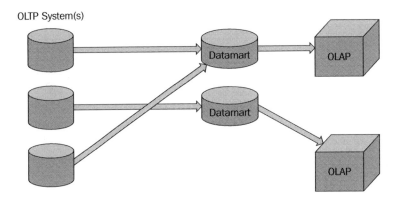

In contrast, in Inmon's view, data coming from the OLTP systems needs to be stored in the enterprise data warehouse and, from there, goes to the data marts:

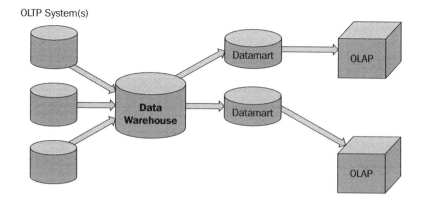

What is important is to understand is that the simple phrase "data warehouse" has different meanings in each of these methodologies.

We will adopt Inmon's meaning for the term "data warehouse". This is because in Inmon's methodology the data warehouse is a real database, while in Kimball's view the data warehouse is composed of integrated data marts. For the purposes of this chapter, though, what is really important is the difference between the data warehouse and the data mart, which should be the source for our cube.

The data mart

Whether you are using the Kimball or Inmon methodology, the front-end database just before the Analysis Services cube should be a data mart. A data mart is a database that is modeled according to the rules of Kimball's dimensional modeling methodology, and is composed of fact tables and dimension tables.

As a result we'll spend a lot of time discussing data mart structure in the rest of this chapter. However, you will not learn how to build and populate a data mart from reading this chapter; the books by Kimball and Inmon we've already cited do a much better job than we ever could.

Data modeling for Analysis Services

If you are reading this book, it means you are using Analysis Services and so you will need to design your data marts with specific features of Analysis Services in mind. This does not mean you should completely ignore the basic theory of data warehouse design and dimensional modeling but, instead, adapt the theory to the practical needs of the product you are going to use as the main interface for querying the data.

For this reason, we are going to present a summary of the theory and discuss how the theoretical design of the data warehouse is impacted by the adoption of Analysis Services.

Fact tables and dimension tables

At the core of the data mart structure is the separation of the entire database into two distinct types of entity:

- **Dimension**: a dimension is the major analytical object in the BI space. A dimension can be a list of products or customers, time, geography or any other entity used to analyze numeric data. Dimensions are stored in dimension tables.

  Dimensions have attributes. An attribute of a product may be its color, its manufacturer or its weight. An attribute of a date may be its weekday or its month.

  Dimensions have both natural and surrogate keys. The natural key is the original product code, customer id or real date. The surrogate key is a new integer number used in the data mart as a key that joins fact tables to dimension tables.

  Dimensions have relationships with facts. Their reason for being is to add qualitative information to the numeric information contained in the facts. Sometimes a dimension might have a relationship with other dimensions but directly or indirectly it will always be related to facts in some way.

- **Fact**: a fact is something that has happened or has been measured. A fact may be the sale of a single product to a single customer or the total amount of sales of a specific item during a month. From our point of view, a fact is a numeric value that users would like to aggregate in different ways for reporting and analysis purposes. Facts are stored in fact tables.

  We normally relate a fact table to several dimension tables, but we do not relate fact tables directly with other fact tables.

  Facts and dimensions are related via surrogate keys. This is one of the foundations of Kimball's methodology.

When we build an Analysis Services solution, we build Analysis Services dimension objects from the dimension tables in our data mart and cubes on top of the fact tables. The concepts of facts and dimensions are so deeply ingrained in the architecture of Analysis Services that we are effectively obliged to follow dimensional modeling methodology if we want to use Analysis Services at all.

Star schemas and snowflake schemas

When we define dimension tables and fact tables and create joins between them, we end up with a star schema. At the center of a star schema there is always a fact table. As the fact table is directly related to dimension tables, if we place these dimensions around the fact table we get something resembling a star shape.

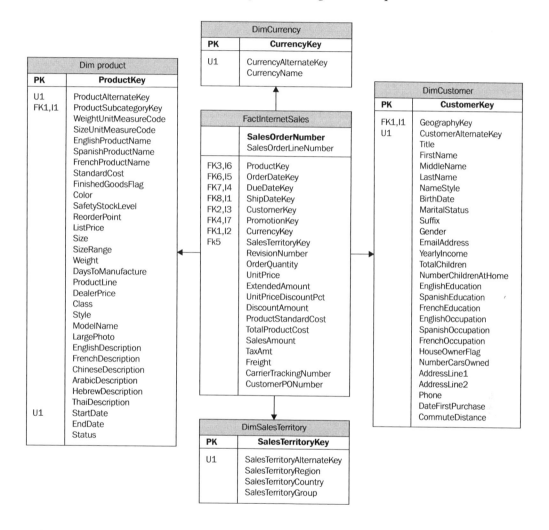

In the diagram above we can see that there is one fact table, FactInternetSales, and four dimension tables directly related to the fact table. Looking at this diagram, we can easily understand that a Customer buys a Product with a specific Currency and that the sale takes place in a specific Sales Territory. Star schemas have the useful characteristic that they are easily understandable by anybody at first glance.

Moreover, while the simplicity for human understanding is very welcome, the same simplicity helps Analysis Services understand and use star schemas. If we use star schemas, Analysis Services will find it easier to recognize the overall structure of our dimensional model and help us in the cube design process. On the other hand, snowflakes are harder both for humans and for Analysis Services to understand, and we're much more likely to find that we make mistakes during cube design – or that Analysis Services makes incorrect assumptions when setting properties automatically – the more complex the schema becomes.

Nevertheless, it is not always easy to generate star schemas: sometimes we need (or inexperience causes us) to create a more complex schema that resembles that of a traditional, normalized relational model. Look at the same data mart when we add the Geography dimension:

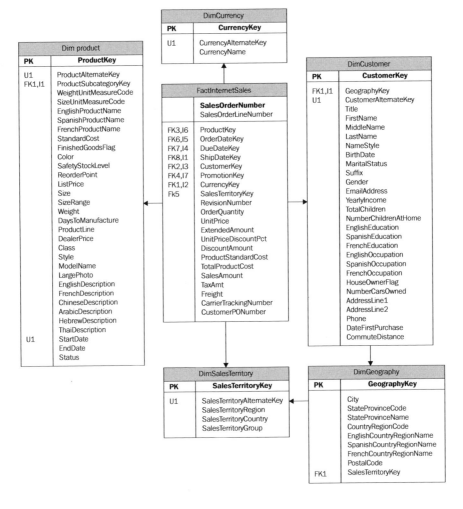

This is as a "snowflake" schema. If you imagine more tables like DimGeography appearing in the diagram you will see that the structure resembles a snowflake more than the previous star.

The snowflake schema is nothing but a star schema complicated by the presence of intermediate tables and joins between dimensions. The problem with snowflakes is that reading them at first glance is not so easy. Try to answer these simple two questions:

- Can the Geography dimension be reached from FactInternetSales?
- What does the SalesTerritoryKey in FactInternetSales mean?
    - Is it a denormalization of the more complex relationship through DimCustomer, or
    - Is it a completely separate key added during ETL?

The answers in this case are:

- DimGeography is not used to create a new dimension, but is being used to add geographic attributes to the Customer dimension.
- DimSalesTerritory is not the territory of the customer but the territory of the order, added during the ETL phase.

The problem is that, in order to answer these questions, we would have to search through the documentation or the ETL code to discover the exact meaning of the fields.

So the simplicity of the star schema is lost when we switch from a star schema to a snowflake schema. Nevertheless, sometimes snowflakes are necessary, but it is very important that – when a snowflake starts to appear in our project – we explain how to read the relationships and what the fields mean.

It might be the case that a snowflake design is mandatory, due to the overall structure of the data warehouse or to the complexity of the database structure. In this case, we have basically these options:

- We can use views to transform the underlying snowflake into a star schema. Using views to join tables, it's possible to hide the snowflake structure, persist our knowledge of how the tables in the snowflake should be joined together, and present to Analysis Services a pure star schema. This is—in our opinion—the best approach.

- We can use Analysis Services to model joins inside the Data Source View of the project using Named Queries. By doing this, we are relying on Analysis Services to query the database efficiently and recreate the star schema. Although this approach might seem almost equivalent to the use of views in the relational database, in our opinion there are some very good reasons to use views instead of the Data Source View. We discuss these in the section later on in this chapter called *Views versus the Data Source View*.

- We can build Analysis Services dimensions from a set of snowflaked tables. This can have some benefits since it makes it easier for the Dimension Wizard to set up optimal attribute relationships within the dimension, but on the other hand as we've already noted it means we have to remember which columns join to each other every time we build a dimension from these tables. It's very easy to make mistakes when working with complex snowflakes, and to get the error message "the '[tablename]' table that is required for a join cannot be reached based on the relationships in the Data Source View" when we try to process the dimension.

- We can leave the snowflake in place and create one Analysis Services dimension for each table, and then use referenced relationships to link these dimensions back to the fact table. Even if this solution seems an interesting one, in our opinion it is the worst.

  First of all, the presence of reference dimensions may lead, as we will discuss later, to performance problems either during cube processing or during querying. Additionally, having two separate dimensions in the cube does not give us any benefits in the overall design and may make it less user friendly. The only case where this approach could be advisable is when the dimension is a very complex one: in this case it might be useful to model it once and use reference dimensions where needed. There are some other situations where reference dimensions are useful but they are rarely encountered.

In all cases, the rule of thumb we recommend is the same: keep it simple! This way we'll make fewer mistakes and find it easier to understand our design.

Junk dimensions

At the end of the dimensional modeling process, we often end up with some attributes that do not belong to any specific dimension. Normally these attributes have a very limited range of values (perhaps three or four values each, sometimes more) and they seem to be not important enough to be considered dimensions in their own right, although obviously we couldn't just drop them from the model altogether.

We have two choices:

- Create a very simple dimension for each of these attributes. This will lead to rapid growth in the number of dimensions in the solution, something the users will not like because it makes the cube harder to use.

- Merge all these attributes in a so-called "Junk dimension". A junk dimension is simply a dimension that merges together attributes that do not belong anywhere else and share the characteristic of having only a few distinct values each.

The main reasons for the use of a junk dimension are:

- If we join several small dimensions into a single junk dimension, we will reduce the number of fields in the fact table. For a fact table of several million rows this can represent a significant reduction in the amount of space used and the time needed for cube processing.

- Reducing the number of dimensions will mean Analysis Services performs better during the aggregation design process and during querying, thereby improving the end user experience.

- The end user will never like a cube with 30 or more dimensions: it will be difficult to use and to navigate. Reducing the number of dimensions will make the cube less intimidating.

However, there is one big disadvantage in using a junk dimension: whenever we join attributes together into a junk dimension, we are clearly stating that these attributes will never have the rank of a fully-fledged dimension. If we ever change our mind and need to break one of these attributes out into a dimension on its own we will not only have to change the cube design, but we will also have to reprocess the entire cube and run the risk that any queries and reports the users have already created will become invalid.

Degenerate dimensions

Degenerate dimensions are created when we have columns on the fact table that we want to use for analysis but which do not relate to any existing dimension. Degenerate dimensions often have almost the same cardinality as the fact table; a typical example is the transaction number for a point of sale data mart. The transaction number may be useful for several reasons, for example to calculate a "total sold in one transaction" measure.

Moreover, it might be useful if we need to go back to the OLTP database to gather other information. However, even if it is often a requested feature, users should not be allowed to navigate sales data using a transaction number because the resulting queries are likely to bring back enormous amounts of data and run very slowly. Instead, if the transaction number is ever needed, it should be displayed in a specifically-designed report that shows the contents of a small number of transactions.

Keep in mind that, even though the literature often discusses degenerate dimensions as separate entities, it is often the case that a big dimension might have some standard attributes and some degenerate ones. In the case of the transaction number, we might have a dimension holding both the transaction number and the Point Of Sale (POS) number. The two attributes live in the same dimension but one is degenerate (the transaction number) and one is a standard one (the POS number). Users might be interested in slicing sales by POS number and they would expect good performance when they did so; however, they should not be encouraged to slice by transaction number due to the cardinality of the attribute.

From an Analysis Services point of view, degenerate dimensions are no different to any other dimension. The only area to pay attention to is the design of the attributes: degenerate attributes should not be made query-able to the end user (you can do this by setting the attribute's `AttributeHierarchyEnabled` property to **False**) for the reasons already mentioned. Also, for degenerate dimensions that are built exclusively from a fact table, Analysis Services has a specific type of dimension relationship type called **Fact**. Using the **Fact** relationship type will lead to some optimizations being made to the SQL generated if ROLAP storage is used for the dimension.

Slowly Changing Dimensions

Dimensions change over time. A customer changes his/her address, a product may change its price or other characteristics and – in general – any attribute of a dimension might change its value. Some of these changes are useful to track while some of them are not; working out which changes should be tracked and which shouldn't can be quite difficult though.

Changes should not happen very often. If they do, then we might be better off splitting the attribute off into a separate dimension. If the changes happen rarely, then a technique known as **Slowly Changing Dimensions (SCDs)** is the solution and we need to model this into our dimensions.

SCDs come in three flavors:

- **Type 1**: We maintain only the last value of each attribute in the dimension table. If a customer changes address, then the previous one is lost and all the previous facts will be shown as if the customer always lived at the same address.

- **Type 2**: We create a new record in the dimension table whenever a change happens. All previous facts will still be linked to the old record. Thus, in our customer address example the old facts will be linked to the old address and the new facts will be linked to the new address.

- **Type 3**: If what we want is simply to know the "last old value" of a specific attribute of a dimension, we can add a field to the dimension table in order to save just the "last value of the attribute" before updating it. In the real world, this type of dimension is used very rarely.

The SCD type used is almost never the same across all the dimensions in a project. We will normally end up with several dimensions of type 1 and occasionally with a couple of dimensions of type 2. Also, not all the attributes of a dimension have to have the same SCD behavior. History is not usually stored for the date of birth of a customer, if it changes, since the chances are that the previous value was a mistake. On the other hand, it's likely we'll want to track any changes to the address of the same customer. Finally, there may be the need to use the same dimension with different slowly changing types in different cubes. Handling these changes will inevitably make our ETL more complex.

- Type 1 dimensions are relatively easy to handle and to manage: each time we detect a change, we apply it to the dimension table in the data mart and that is all the work we need to do.

- Type 2 dimensions are more complex: when we detect a change, we invalidate the old record by setting its "end of validity date" and insert a new record with the new values. As all the new data will refer to the new record, it is simple to use in queries. We should have only one valid record for each entity in the dimension.

The modeling of SCDs in Analysis Services will be covered later but, in this theoretical discussion, it might be interesting to spend some time on the different ways to model Type 2 SCDs in the relational data mart.

A single dimension will hold attributes with different SCD types since not all the attributes of a single dimension will need to have historical tracking. So, we will end up with dimensions with some Type 1 attributes and some Type 2 attributes. How do we model that in the data mart?

We have basically these choices:

- We can build two dimensions: one containing the Type 2 attributes and one containing the Type 1 attributes. Obviously, we will need two different dimension tables in the data mart to do this.

  This solution is very popular and is easy to design but has some serious drawbacks:

  - The number of dimensions in the cube is much larger. If we do this several times, the number of dimensions might reach the point where we have usability problems.

  - If we need to run queries that include both Type 1 and Type 2 attributes, Analysis Services has to resolve the relationship between the two dimensions via the fact table and, for very big fact tables, this might be very time-consuming. This issue is not marginal because, if we give users both types of attribute, they will always want to use them together in queries.

- We can build a complex dimension holding both the Type 1 and Type 2 values in a single dimension table. This solution will lead to much more complex ETL to build the dimension table but solves the drawbacks of the previous solution. For example, having both the Type 1 and Type 2 attributes in a single dimension can lead to better query performance when comparing values for different attributes, because the query can be resolved at the dimension level and does not need to cross the fact table. Also, as we've stressed several times already, having fewer dimensions in the cube makes it much more user-friendly.

Bridge tables, or factless fact tables

We can use the terms **bridge table** and **factless fact table** interchangeably – they both refer to the same thing, a table that is used to model a many-to-many relationship between two dimension tables. Since the name **factless fact table** can be misleading, and even if the literature often refers to these tables as such, we prefer the term **bridge table** instead.

All fact tables represent many-to-many relationships between dimensions but, for bridge tables, this relationship is their only reason to exist: they do not contain any numeric columns – facts – that can be aggregated (hence the use of the name 'factless fact table'). Regular fact tables generate many-to-many relationships as a side effect, as their reason for being is the nature of the fact, not of the relationship.

Now, let us see an example of a bridge table. Consider the following situation in an OLTP database

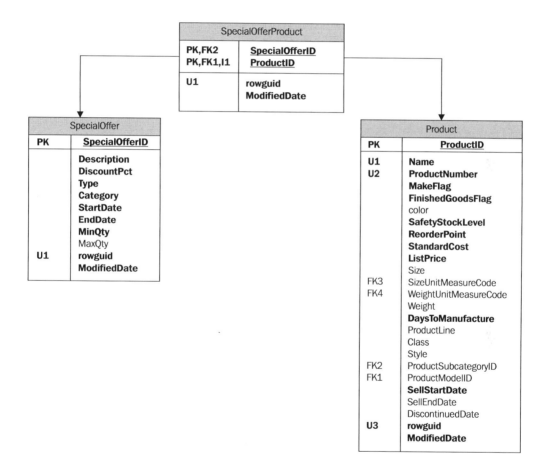

In any given period of time, a product can be sold on special offer. The bridge table (SpecialOfferProduct) tells us which products were on special offer at which times, while the SpecialOffer table tells us information about the special offer itself: when it started, when it finished, the amount of discount and so on.

A common way of handling this situation is to denormalize the special offer information into a dimension directly linked to the fact table, so we can easily see whether a specific sale was made under special offer or not. In this way, we can use the fact table to hold both the facts and the bridge. Nevertheless, bridge tables offer a lot of benefits and, in situations like this, they are definitely the best option. Let's take a look at the reasons why.

It is interesting to consider whether we can represent the relationship in the example above only using fact tables (that is, storing three types of data for each sale: product, sale and special offer) or whether a bridge table is necessary. While the first option is certainly correct, we need to think carefully before using it because if we do use it all data on special offers that did not generate any sales will be lost. If a specific special offer results in no product sales, then we aren't storing the relationship between the special offer and the product anywhere—it will be exactly as though the product had never been on special offer. This is because the fact table does not contain any data that defines the relationship between the special offers and the products, it only knows about this relationship when a sale is made. This situation may lead to confusion or incorrect reports. **We always need to remember that the absence of a fact may be as important as its presence is**. Indeed, sometimes the absence of a fact is more important than its presence.

We recommend using bridge tables to model many-to-many relationships that do not strictly depend on facts to define the relationship. The relationships modeled by many-to-many relationships are often not bound to any fact table and exist regardless of any fact table. This shows the real power of bridge tables but, as always, the more power we have the bigger our responsibilities will be, and bridge tables will sometimes cause us headaches.

Bridge tables are modeled in Analysis Services as measure groups that act as bridges between different dimensions, through the **many-to-many** dimension relationship type, one of the most powerful features of Analysis Services. This feature will be analyzed in greater detail in Chapter 6.

Snapshot and transaction fact tables

Now that we have defined what a fact table is, let us go deeper and look at the two main types: transaction fact tables and snapshots.

A transaction fact table records events and, for each event, certain measurements are recorded or values recorded. When we record a sale, for example, we create a new row in the transaction fact table that contains information relating to the sale such as what product was sold, when the sale took place, what the value of the sale was, and so on.

A snapshot fact table records of the state of something at different points in time. If we record in a fact table the total sales for each product every month, we are not recording an event but a specific situation. Snapshots can also be useful when we want to measure something not directly related to any other fact. If we want to rank out customers based on sales or payments, for example, we may want to store snapshots of this data in order to analyze how these rankings change over time in response to marketing campaigns.

Using a snapshot table containing aggregated data instead of a transaction table can drastically reduce the number of rows in our fact table, which in turn leads to smaller cubes, faster cube processing and faster querying. The price we pay for this is the loss of any information that can only be stored at the transaction level and cannot be aggregated up into the snapshot, such as the transaction number data we encountered when discussing degenerate dimensions. Whether this is an acceptable price to pay is a question only the end users can answer.

Updating fact and dimension tables

In an ideal world, data that is stored in the data warehouse would never change. Some books suggest that we should only support insert operations in a data warehouse, not updates: data comes from the OLTP, is cleaned and is then stored in the data warehouse until the end of time, and should never change because it represents the situation at the time of insertion.

Nevertheless, the real world is somewhat different to the ideal one. While some updates are handled by the slowly changing dimension techniques already discussed, there are other kinds of updates needed in the life of a data warehouse. In our experience, these other types of update in the data warehouse are needed fairly regularly and are of two main kinds:

- **Structural updates**: when the data warehouse is up and running, we will need to perform updates to add information like new measures or new dimension attributes. This is normal in the lifecycle of a BI solution.

- **Data updates**: we need to update data that has already been loaded into the data warehouse, because it is wrong. We need to delete the old data and enter the new data, as the old data will inevitably lead to confusion. There are many reasons why bad data comes to the data warehouse; the sad reality is that bad data happens and we need to manage it gracefully.

Now, how do these kinds of updates interact with fact and dimension tables? Let's summarize briefly what the physical distinctions between fact and dimension tables are:

- Dimension tables are normally small, usually with less than 1 million rows and very frequently much less than that.

- Fact tables are often very large; they can have up to hundreds of millions or even billions of rows. Fact tables may be partitioned, and loading data into them is usually the most time-consuming operation in the whole of the data warehouse.

Structural updates on dimension tables are very easy to make. You simply update the table with the new metadata, make the necessary changes to your ETL procedures and the next time they are run the dimension will reflect the new values. If your users decide that they want to analyze data based on a new attribute on, say, the customer dimension, then the new attribute can be added for all of the customers in the dimension. Moreover, if the attribute is not present for some customers, then they can be assigned a default value; after all, updating one million rows is not a difficult task for SQL Server or any other modern relational database. However, even if updating the relational model is simple, the updates need to go through to Analysis Services and this might result in the need for a full process of the dimension and therefore the cube, which might be very time consuming.

On the other hand, structural updates may be a huge problem on fact tables. The problem is not that of altering the metadata, but determining and assigning a default value for the large number of rows that are already stored in the fact table. It's easy to insert data into fact tables. However, creating a new field with a default value would result in an UPDATE command that will probably run for hours and might even bring down your database server. Worse, if we do not have a simple default value to assign, then we will need to calculate the new value for each row in the fact table, and so the update operation will take even longer. We have found that it is often better to reload the entire fact table rather than perform an update on it. Of course, in order to reload the fact table, we need to have all of our source data at hand and this is not always possible.

Data updates are an even bigger problem still, both on facts and dimensions. Data updates on fact tables suffer from the same problems as adding a new field: often, the number of rows that we need to update is so high that running even simple SQL commands can take a very long time.

Data updates on dimensions can be a problem because they may require very complex logic. Suppose we have a Type 2 SCD and that a record was entered into the dimension table with incorrect attribute values. In this situation, we would have created a new record and linked all the facts received after its creation to the new (and incorrect) record. Recovering from this situation requires us to issue very precise UPDATE statements to the relational database and to recalculate all the fact table rows that depend – for any reason – on the incorrect record. Bad data in dimensions is not very easy to spot, and sometimes several days – if not months – pass before someone (in the worst case the user) discovers that something went wrong.

There is no foolproof way for stopping bad data getting into the data warehouse. When it happens, we need to be ready to spend a long time trying to recover from the error. It's worth pointing out that data warehouses or data marts that are rebuilt each night ("one shot databases") are not prone to this situation because, if bad data is corrected, the entire data warehouse can be reloaded from scratch and the problem fixed very quickly. This is one of the main advantages of "one shot" data warehouses, although of course they do suffer from several disadvantages too such as their limited ability to hold historic data.

Natural and surrogate keys

In Kimball's view of a data mart, all the natural keys should be represented with a surrogate key that is a simple integer value and that has no meaning at all. This gives us complete freedom in the data mart to add to or redefine a natural key's meaning and, importantly, the usage of the smallest possible integer type for surrogate keys will lead to a smaller fact table.

All this is very good advice. Nevertheless, there are situations in which the rules surrounding the usage of surrogate keys should be relaxed or to put it another way—there can be times when it's useful to make the surrogate keys meaningful instead of meaningless. Let's consider some of the times when this might be the case:

- **Date**: we can use a meaningless key as a surrogate key for the Date dimension. However, is there any point in doing so? In our opinion, the best representation of a date surrogate key is an integer in the form YYYYMMDD, so 20080109 represents January 9th 2008. Note that even the Kimball Group, writing in the book *The Microsoft Data Warehouse Toolkit*, accept that this can be a good idea. The main reason for this is that it makes SQL queries that filter by date much easier to write and much more readable – we very often want to partition a measure group by date, for instance. The reason that it's safe to do this is that the date dimension will never change. You might add some attributes to a date dimension table and you might load new data into it, but the data that is already there should never need to be altered.

All invalid dates may be easily represented with negative numbers, so -1 may be the unknown date, -2 may be the empty date and so on. We will have plenty of space for all the dummy dates we will ever need.

A word of warning about the type of the key: we sometimes face situations where the `DateTime` type has been used for the key of the Date dimension. This is absolutely the wrong thing to do, as not only is a `DateTime` representation going to be bigger than the `INT` representation, the `DateTime` type does not let us add dummy values to the dimension easily.

- **Ranges**: Suppose we want a dimension that will rank the sales based on the amount of the specific sale. We want to analyze information based on a range, not on each single amount.

  If we define a "Range Amount" dimension and an `ID_RangeAmount` key in the fact table, this will solve our modeling problem. However, what will happen when the customer wants to change the ranges? We will have to re-compute the whole fact table because the `ID_RangeAmount` key will become useless.

  On the other hand, if you decide that $100 will be the granularity of the range dimension, you can use `FLOOR` (Amount / 100) as `ID_RangeAmount` and, in doing so, you will be able to update the attributes of the RangeAmount dimension that will lead to hierarchies without updating the fact table. The advantages of doing this are discussed in more detail in the following blog entry: `http://tinyurl.com/rangedims`, and we discuss how to model this in Analysis Services in Chapter 4.

- The surrogate key of a dimension will be surfaced in MDX in the unique names generated for members on the key attribute of the dimension. Since all Analysis Services client tools save their queries using these unique names, this means that if for any reason we change the surrogate key of a member in the future (for example, because we have a "one shot" data warehouse that is reloaded each night), the saved queries will no longer work.

- **Junk dimensions**: junk dimensions, when defined at the conformed dimension level, can cause problems when there is the need to update data. If, for example, we need a new attribute on a junk dimension, this can involve a change in the meaning of the existing members of the junk dimension. This will invalidate the older facts, requiring a careful rebuilding of the junk dimension. In our opinion it is better to maintain the junk dimensions as separate dimensions in the relational data mart and then merge them into a single dimension for Analysis Services, creating a key attribute that uses a composite key made up of the keys of all the dimension tables that make up the junk dimension.

Therefore, the conclusion is that although surrogate keys are very useful and we are not saying that there is something wrong with them, in some well-defined situations it makes sense to deviate from the standard recommendations for surrogate keys and use different forms instead.

The last consideration is that – even in cases where we deviate from the standard – the usage of surrogate keys of the smallest integer type possible is always strongly advised. The Analysis Services engine is optimized for the handling of integer values and does not handle string and date values anywhere near as well.

Unknown members, key errors, and NULLability

When designing a data mart, questions often arise about the relationship between the fact table and the dimensions. Should the foreign keys be NULLable or not? Should we use the built-in foreign keys of SQL Server to handle the relationship? What about key errors?

Since these are very interesting topics, let us discuss them in more detail.

- Can we use NULLable foreign keys columns? The answer is definitely no. If we do, when the data is moved into the cube, there will be no relationship between the dimension and the facts containing the NULL key, leading to either processing errors or situations where the user will see partial data. It is much better to add a new member to the dimension, and relate the facts with missing key values to that member in our ETL. Although the Unknown Members feature in Analysis Services does this for us, we will have more flexibility if we handle the issue ourselves.

- Should we use SQL Server FOREIGN KEYS? The correct technique to adopt here is as follows: we should define the foreign keys in the data model and activate them during debugging, in order to detect errors. When the system is in production, the foreign key can be disabled in order to speed up the ETL code.

- Key errors: there should be no key errors at all. If we enable foreign key checking then we will end up with a table without key errors. This is important: even though we can leverage Analysis Services' key error handling functionality during processing, we advise not using it because the presence of a key error should be detected and resolved during the ETL process, as with NULL keys.

Physical database design for Analysis Services

Apart from the issue of modeling data in an appropriate way for Analysis Services, it's also important to understand how details of the physical implementation of the relational data mart can be significant too.

Multiple data sources

All of the dimension and fact tables we intend to use should exist within the same relational data source, so for example if we're using SQL Server this means all the tables involved should exist within the same SQL Server database. If we create multiple data sources within Analysis Services then we'll find that one is treated as the 'primary data source'; this has to point to an instance of SQL Server (either SQL Server 2000 or above) and all data from other data sources is fetched via the primary data source using the SQL Server OPENROWSET function, which can lead to severe processing performance problems.

Data types and Analysis Services

When we design data marts, we need to be aware that Analysis Services does not treat all data types the same way. The cube will be much faster, for both processing and querying, if we use the right data type for each column. Here we provide a brief table that helps us during the design of the data mart, to choose the best data type for each column type:

Fact column type	Fastest SQL Server data types
Surrogate keys	tinyint, smallint, int, bigint
Date key	int in the format yyyymmdd
Integer measures	tinyint, smallint, int, bigint
Numeric measures	smallmoney, money, real, float
	(Note that decimal and vardecimal require more CPU power to process than money and float types)
Distinct count columns	tinyint, smallint, int, bigint
	(If your count column is char, consider either hashing or replacing with surrogate key)

Clearly, we should always try to use the smallest data type that will be able to hold any single value within the whole range of values needed by the application.

This is the rule for relational tables. However, you also need to remember that the equivalent measure data type in Analysis Services must be large enough to hold the largest aggregated value of a given measure, not just the largest value present in a single fact table row.

Always remember that there are situations in which the rules must be overridden. If we have a fact table containing 20 billion rows, each composed of 20 bytes and a column that references a date, then it might be better to use a SMALLINT column for the date, if we find a suitable representation that holds all necessary values. We will gain 2 bytes for each row, and that means a 10% in the size of the whole table.

SQL queries generated during cube processing

When Analysis Services needs to process a cube or a dimension, it sends queries to the relational database in order to retrieve the information it needs. Not all the queries are simple SELECTs; there are many situations in which Analysis Services generates complex queries. Even if we do not have space enough to cover all scenarios, we're going to provide some examples relating to SQL Server, and we advise the reader to have a look at the SQL queries generated for their own cube to check whether they can be optimized in some way.

Dimension processing

During dimension processing Analysis Services sends several queries, one for each attribute of the dimension, in the form of SELECT DISTINCT ColName, where ColName is the name of the column holding the attribute.

Many of these queries are run in parallel (exactly which ones can be run in parallel depends on the attribute relationships defined on the Analysis Services dimension), so SQL Server will take advantage of its cache system and perform only one physical read of the table, so all successive scans are performed from memory. Nevertheless, keep in mind that the task of detecting the DISTINCT values of the attributes is done by SQL Server, not Analysis Services.

We also need to be aware that if our dimensions are built from complex views, they might confuse the SQL Server engine and lead to poor SQL query performance. If, for example, we add a very complex WHERE condition to our view, then the condition will be evaluated more than once. We have personally seen a situation where the processing of a simple time dimension with only a few hundred rows, which had a very complex WHERE condition, took tens of minutes to complete.

Dimensions with joined tables

If a dimension contains attributes that come from a joined table, the JOIN is performed by SQL Server, not Analysis Services. This situation arises very frequently when we define snowflakes instead of simpler star schemas. Since some attributes of a dimension are computed by taking their values from another dimension table, Analysis Services will send a query to SQL Server containing the INNER JOIN between the two tables.

 Beware that the type of JOIN requested by Analysis Services is always an INNER JOIN. If, for any reason, you need a LEFT OUTER JOIN, then you definitely need to avoid using joined tables inside the DSV and use, as we suggest, SQL VIEWS to obtain the desired result.

As long as all the joins are made on the primary keys, this will not lead to any problems but, in cases where the JOIN is not made on the primary key, bad performance might result. As we said before, if we succeed in the goal of exposing to Analysis Services a simple star schema, we will never have to handle these JOINs. As we argue below, if a snowflake is really needed we can still hide it from Analysis Services using views, and in these views we will have full control over, and knowledge of, the complexity of the query used.

Reference dimensions

Reference dimensions, when present in the cube definition, will lead to one of the most hidden and most dangerous types of JOIN. When we define the relationship between a dimension and a fact table, we can use the Referenced relationship type and use an intermediate dimension to relate the dimension to the fact table. Reference dimensions often appear in the design due to snowflakes or due to the need to reduce fact table size.

A referenced dimension may be **materialized** or not. If we decide to materialize a reference dimension (as BI Development Studio will suggest) the result is that the fact table query will contain a JOIN to the intermediate dimension, to allow Analysis Services to get the value of the key for the reference dimension.

If JOINs are a problem with dimension processing queries, they are a serious problem with fact table processing queries. It might be the case that SQL Server needs to write a large amount of data to its temporary database before returning information to Analysis Services. It all depends on the size of the intermediate table and the number of reference dimensions that appear in the cube design.

We are not going to say that referenced dimensions should not be used at all, as there are a few cases where reference dimensions are useful, and in the following chapters we will discuss them in detail. Nevertheless, we need to be aware that reference dimensions might create complex queries sent to SQL server and this can cause severe performance problems during cube processing.

Fact dimensions

The processing of dimensions related to measure group with a fact relationship type, usually created to hold degenerate dimensions, is performed in the same way as any other dimension. This means that a SELECT DISTINCT will be issued on all the degenerate dimension's attributes.

Clearly, as the dimension and the fact tables are the same, the query will ask for a DISTINCT over a fact table; given that fact tables can be very large, the query might take a long time to run. Nevertheless, if a degenerate dimension is needed and it is stored in a fact table, then there is no other choice but to pay the price with this query.

Distinct count measures

The last kind of query that we need to be aware of is when we have a measure group containing a DISTINCT COUNT measure. In this case, due to the way Analysis Services calculates distinct counts, the query to the fact table will be issued with an ORDER BY for the column we are performing the distinct count on.

Needless to say, this will lead to very poor performance because we are asking SQL Server to sort a fact table on a column that is not part of the clustered index (usually the clustered index is built on the primary key). The pressure on the temporary database will be tremendous and the query will take a lot of time.

There are some optimizations, mostly pertinent to partitioning, that need to be done when we have DISTINCT COUNT measures in very big fact tables. What we want to point out is that in this case a good knowledge of the internal behavior of Analysis Services is necessary in order to avoid bad performance when processing.

Indexes in the data mart

The usage of indexes in data mart is a very complex topic and we cannot cover it all in a simple section. Nevertheless, there are a few general rules that can be followed both for fact and dimension tables.

- Dimension tables
    - Dimension tables should have a primary clustered key based on an integer field, which is the surrogate key.

- ○ Non clustered indexes may be added for the natural key, in order to speed up the ETL phase for slowly changing dimensions. The key might be composed of the natural key and the slowly changing dimension date of insertion. These indexes might be defined as UNIQUE, but, like any other constraint in the data mart, the uniqueness should be enforced in development and disabled in production.

- Fact tables

  - ○ It is questionable whether fact tables should have a primary key or not. We prefer to have a primary clustered key based on an integer field, because it makes it very simple to identify a row in the case where we need to check for its value or update it.

  - ○ In the case where the table is partitioned by date, the primary key will be composed of the date and the integer surrogate key, to be able to meet the needs of partitioning.

  - ○ If a column is used to create a DISTINCT COUNT measure in a cube, then it might be useful to have that column in the clustered index, because Analysis Services will request an ORDER BY on that column during the process of the measure group. It is clear that the creation of a clustered index is useful in large cubes where data is added incrementally, so processing will benefit from the ordered data. If, on the other hand, we have a one-shot solution where all tables are reloaded from scratch and the cube is fully processed, then it is better to avoid the creation of a clustered index since the sorting of the data is performed only once, during cube processing.

Once the cube has been built, if MOLAP storage is being used, no other indexes are useful. However if the data mart is queried by other tools like Reporting Services, or if ROLAP partitions are created in Analysis Services, then it might be necessary to add more indexes to the tables. Remember, though, that indexes slow down update and insert operations so they should be added with care. A deep analysis of the queries sent to the relational database will help to determine the best indexes to create.

Usage of schemas

The data warehouse is normally divided into subject areas. The meaning of a subject area really depends on the specific needs of the solution. Typical subject areas include:

- Sales
- Accounts
- Warehouses
- Suppliers
- Personnel and staff management

Clearly, this list is far from complete and is different for every business. SQL Server 2005 and 2008 provide schemas to arrange tables and – in our experience – the usage of schemas to assign database objects to subject areas leads to a very clear database structure.

Some tables will inevitably have no place at all in any subject area, but we can always define a "COMMON" subject area to hold all these tables.

Naming conventions

A clear and consistent naming convention is good practice for any kind of relational database and a data mart is no different. As well as making the structure more readable, it will help us when we come to build our cube because BI Development Studio will be able to work out automatically which columns in our dimension and fact tables should join to each other if they have the same names.

Views versus the Data Source View

The **Data Source View (DSV)** is one of the places where we can create an interface between Analysis Services and the underlying relational model. In the DSV we can specify joins between tables, we can create named queries and calculations to provide the equivalent of views and derived columns. It's very convenient for the cube developer to open up the DSV in BI Development Studio and make these kind of changes.

This is all well and good, but nevertheless our opinion about the DSV is clear: it is almost too powerful and, using its features, we risk turning a clean, elegant structure into a mess. It is certainly true that there is the need for an interface between the relational model of the database and the final star schema, but we don't think it's a good idea to use the DSV for this purpose.

SQL Server gives us a much more powerful and easy-to-use tool to use instead: SQL Views. Here's a list of some of the reasons why we prefer to use views instead of the DSV:

- Views are stored where we need them.

  When we need to read the specification of an interface, we want to be able to do it quickly. Views are stored in the database, exactly where we want them to be. If we need to modify the database, we want to be able to find all of the dependencies easily and, using views, we have a very easy way of tracking dependencies.

  If we use the DSV, we are hiding these dependencies from the database administrator, the person who needs to be able to update and optimize the data mart. In addition, there are tools on the market that can analyze dependencies between table and views. It is not easy to do this if information on the joins between tables is stored outside the database.

- We can easily change column names in views.

  In the database, we might have SoldQty as a field in a table. This is good because it is concise and does not contain useless spaces. In the cube, we want to show it as "Quantity Sold" simply because our user wants a more descriptive name.

  Views are a very useful means of changing names when needed. In turn, with views we are publicly declaring the name change so that everybody will easily understand that a specific field with a name in one level is – in reality – a field that has another name in the previous level.

  Clearly we should avoid the practice of changing names at each level. As always, having the opportunity to do something does not mean that we need to do it.

- We can perform simple calculations in views easily.

  If we need to multiply the value of two columns, for example Qty * Price, to use in a measure in our cube we have two options. We can perform the calculation in the DSV but, as before, we are hiding the calculation in a Visual Studio project and other people will not be able to see what we're doing easily. If we perform the calculation in a view then other developers can reuse it, and tracking dependencies is more straightforward.

  This is certainly true for simple calculations. On the other hand, if we're performing complex calculations in views then we are probably missing some transformation code in our ETL. Moreover, performing this calculation will waste time when we execute the view. Performing the calculation during ETL will mean we perform the calculation only once; from then it will always be available.

- Views are made up of plain text.

  We can easily search for all the occurrences of a specific column, table or any kind of value using a simple text editor. We do not need any specialized development tools, nor need we to dive into unreadable XML code to have a clear view of how a specific field is used.

  If we need to update a view we can do it without opening BI Development Studio. This means that nearly everybody can do it, although, as it is very easy to update a view, some sort of security does need to be applied.

  Furthermore, as views are simple text, a source control system can handle them very easily. We can check who updated what, when they did it and what they changed very easily.

- Views can be updated very quickly.

  A view can be updated very quickly as it does not require any kind of processing, we just ALTER it and the work is done. We do not need to use an UPDATE statement if we want to make simple (and possibly temporary) changes to the data.

- Views can reduce the number of columns we expose.

  There is really no need to expose more columns to a cube than it needs. Showing more columns will only lead to confusion and a chance that the wrong column will be used for something.

- Views can provide default values when needed.

  When we have a NULLable column that contains NULL values, we can easily assign a default value to it using views. We shouldn't really have a NULLable column in a data mart, but sometimes it happens.

- Views can expose a star schema even if the relational model is more complex.

  As we've already mentioned, sometimes we end up with a relational design that is not a perfectly designed star schema. By removing unused columns, by creating joins when necessary and in general by designing the appropriate queries, we can expose to Analysis Services a star schema, even when the relational model has a more complex structure.

- Views are database objects.

  As views are database objects they inherit two important properties:
  - We can configure security for views, and so stop unauthorized access to data very easily.
  - Views can belong to a schema. If we are using schemas for the definition of subject areas, we can assign views to subject areas. This will lead to a very clean project where each object belongs to the subject area that is relevant to it.

- Views can be optimized.

  With views we can use hints to improve performance. For example we can use the NOLOCK hint to avoid locking while reading from tables – although of course removing locking leads to the possibility of dirty reads, and it is up to the developer to decide whether doing this is a good idea or not. Moreover, we can analyze the execution path of a view in order to fine tune it. All this can be done without affecting in any way the Analysis Services project.

> One very important point needs to be stressed: views should not be used as a substitute for proper ETL. Whenever views are used to feed Analysis Services they should not contain complex calculations or WHERE clauses as this can lead to serious processing performance and maintenance problems. We can use a view instead of ETL code for prototyping purposes but this is very bad practice in a production system.

Summary

In this chapter we've learned a bit about the theory of data warehouse and data mart design and how it should be applied when we're using Analysis Services. We've found out that we definitely do need to have a data mart designed according to the principles of dimensional modeling, and that a star schema is preferable to a snowflake schema; we've also seen how certain common design problems such as Slowly Changing Dimensions, Junk Dimensions and Degenerate Dimensions can be solved in a way that is appropriate for Analysis Services. Last of all, we've recommended the use of a layer of simple views between the tables in the data mart and Analysis Services to allow us to perform calculations, change column names and join tables, and we've found out why it's better to do this than do the same thing in the Data Source View.

2
Building Basic Dimensions and Cubes

Having prepared our relational source data, we're now ready to start designing a cube and some dimensions. This chapter covers the steps you need to go through in order to create simple dimensions and cubes, and although you may be confident that you know how to do this already, we encourage you to read through this chapter nonetheless. You may be familiar with the overall process, but some of the detailed recommendations that we make may be new to you, and they could save you a lot of time and effort later on in your project.

In this chapter, we'll be taking a look at the following topics:

- Creating Data Sources and Data Source Views
- Creating dimensions, setting up user hierarchies and configuring attribute relationships
- Creating a simple cube
- Deployment and processing

From a methodology point of view, this chapter represents the creation of the first draft of your cube. In subsequent chapters we'll look at how you tackle the more advanced modeling problems. However, there are a lot of advantages in taking an iterative and incremental approach to cube development. If you're unfamiliar with your data or Analysis Services, it will allow you to get something up and running quickly so that you can be sure that it works properly. It will also allow you to show your end-users something quickly too, so that they can ensure it meets their expectations and that they can check over it for problems. That doesn't mean you shouldn't concentrate on getting what you do build at this stage right first time, though, far from it, but it is easier to get the details correct when you're concentrating on a small subset of the solution you hope to build eventually. We therefore recommend you to pick the most important fact table in your data warehouse plus a few of the more straightforward dimensions that join to it, one of which should be the Time dimension, and open up BI Development Studio.

Choosing an edition of Analysis Services

Before we start developing with Analysis Services, we need a clear idea of which edition of Analysis Services we're going to be developing for. There are two choices: Standard Edition, which is cheaper but missing some features, and Enterprise Edition, which is more expensive but feature complete. Licensing cost is likely to be the major factor in this decision. If money is no object, then you should use Enterprise Edition. If it is an issue, then you'll just have to live with the limitations of Standard Edition. Of course, if we install Analysis Services on a server that already has SQL Server installed then there are no extra license costs involved, but as we'll see in Chapter 11, we have to be careful they don't compete for resources. This document on the Microsoft website gives a detailed breakdown of which features are available in each edition: `http://tinyurl.com/sqlstdvsent`.

Don't worry about having to use the Standard Edition though. Some of the features it lacks can be recreated with a little bit of extra work. The key features in Enterprise Edition are in the area of performance for very large or complex cubes, and you can go a long way with Standard Edition before you really need to use Enterprise Edition. The Deployment Server Edition project property, which is described below, will help you make sure you only use the features available in the edition of your choice.

Setting up a new Analysis Services project

The first step towards creating a new cube is to create a new Analysis Services project in BIDS. Immediately after doing this, we strongly recommend putting your new project into source control. It's easy to forget to do this, or not bother, because building a cube doesn't seem like a traditional development project, but you'll be glad that you did it when you receive your first request to rollback a change to a complex MDX calculation.

As you're probably aware, there are two ways of working with Analysis Services projects in BIDS:

- **Project mode**: where you work with a local Visual Studio project and deploy to your Analysis Services server only when you're happy with all the changes you've made
- **Online mode**: where you edit your Analysis Services database live on the server and commit changes every time you click on the **Save** button

You'll only be able to use source control software effectively if you work in the project mode. Therefore, it's a good idea to resist the temptation to work in online mode unless you're only making temporary changes to your cube, even though online mode often seems to be the most convenient way of working.

With all new Analysis Services projects, there are a few useful project properties that can be set. You can set project properties by right-clicking on the **Project** node in the **Solution Explorer** pane and selecting **Properties**.

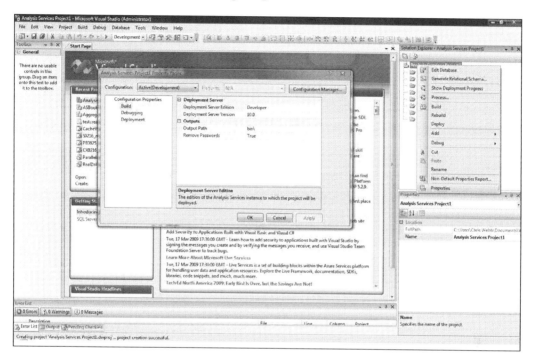

Here is a list of properties you may want to change:

- Build
  - ○ Deployment Server Edition: If you plan to deploy Standard Edition in production, but you're using Developer Edition in development, you will want to set this property to **Standard**. This will make BIDS raise errors when you build a project if you accidentally use features that aren't available in the Standard Edition.

- Deployment
  - Processing Option: This property allows you to process your database automatically whenever you deploy a project. The **'Default'** option will perform a Process Default, but in many cases, when you deploy a change that doesn't need any cube processing at all, a Process Default can still waste 10 or 20 seconds, and if you've made more substantial changes to an object you will still want to control when processing takes place. Setting this property to **Do Not Process** instead will stop all automatic processing. This means that you have to remember to manually process any objects yourself if you make changes to them but it will save you time in the long run by preventing a lot of unintentional processing.
  - Server: This contains the name of the server you're deploying to and defaults to `localhost`. If you're not developing on a local Analysis Services instance, then you'll need to change this anyway. Even if you are, it's a good idea to enter the name of the target server, rather than use `localhost`, in case anyone wants to work on the project on another machine.
  - Database: This contains the name of the database that you're deploying to. It defaults to the name of the Visual Studio project. Of course, you can change it if you want your project and database to have different names.

We'll be looking again at how Visual Studio project configurations can help you when you need to deploy your project to your production environment in Chapter 10.

 It is good to install BIDS Helper, an award-winning free community-developed tool that adds a lot of useful functionality to BIDS. You can download it from `http://www.codeplex.com/bidshelper`. We'll be referring to some of its features later on in this chapter.

Creating data sources

Once we've created a new project and configured it appropriately, the next step is to create a data source object. Even though you can create multiple data sources in a project, you probably shouldn't. If you've read the previous chapter, then you'll know that we recommend that all of the data needed for your cube should already be present in a single data mart.

You are then faced with the choice of which OLE DB provider to use, since there are often several different options for any given relational database. For SQL Server data sources, you have the option of using the SQLClient .NET data provider, the Microsoft OLE DB provider for SQL Server and the SQL Server Native Client (often referred to as SNAC). You should always choose the SQL Server Native Client since it offers the best performance. For Oracle data sources, the choice is more complicated since, even though Oracle is a supported data source for Analysis Services, there is a long list of bugs and issues. Some are addressed in the white paper at `http://tinyurl.com/asdatasources`, but if you do run into problems, the best approach is to try using Microsoft's Oracle OLE DB Provider, Oracle's own OLE DB Provider, the .NET Provider for Oracle or any of the third-party OLE DB Providers on the market to see which one works. Access, DB2, Teradata and Sybase are the other officially supported relational data sources, and if you need to load data from another source, you can always use SQL Server Integration Services to push data into the cube by using the Dimension Processing and Partition Processing destinations in a Data Flow.

Remember to install the same version of any OLE DB provider you're using on all of your development, test and production machines. Also, while BIDS is a 32-bit application and needs a 32-bit version of the driver to connect to a relational database, if your Analysis Services instance is 64-bit, it will need the 64-bit version of the same driver to process cubes successfully.

Analysis Services must also be given permission to access the data source, and how it does so depends on the type of data source you're using and how its security is set up. If you're using Windows authentication to connect to SQL Server, as Microsoft recommends you to, then you should set up a new Windows domain account specifically for Analysis Services, and then use the SQL Server Configuration Manager tool to set the Analysis Services service to run under that account. You should then give that account any permissions it needs in SQL Server on the tables and views you'll be using. Most of the time 'Read' permissions will be sufficient. However, some tasks, such as creating Writeback fact tables, will need more. You'll notice on the **Impersonation Information** tab in the Data Source Designer dialog in BI Development Studio there are some other options for use with Windows authentication, such as the ability to enter the username and password of a specific user. However, we recommend that you use the **Use Service Account** option so that Analysis Services tries to connect to the relational database under the account you've created.

If you need to connect to your data source using a username and a password (for example, when you're using SQL Server authentication or Oracle), then Analysis Services will keep all sensitive information, such as passwords, in an encrypted format on the server after deployment. If you try to script the data source object out you'll find that the password is not returned, and since opening an Analysis Services project in online mode essentially involves scripting out the entire database, you'll find yourself continually re-entering the password in your data source whenever you want to reprocess anything when working this way. This is another good reason to use project mode rather than online mode for development and to use Windows authentication where possible.

Creating Data Source Views

In an ideal world, if you've followed all of our recommendations so far, then you should need to do very little work in your project's Data Source View—nothing more than selecting the views representing the dimension and fact tables and setting up any joins between the tables that weren't detected automatically. Of course, in the real world, you have to compromise your design sometimes and that's where a lot of the functionality available in Data Source Views comes in useful.

When you first create a new **Data Source View (DSV)**, the easiest thing to do is to go through all of the steps of the wizard, but not to select any tables yet. You can then set some useful properties on the DSV, which will make the process of adding new tables and relationships much easier. In order to find them, right-click on some blank space in the diagram pane and click on **Properties**. They are:

- Retrieve Relationships—by default, this is set to **True**, which means that BIDS will add relationships between tables based on various criteria. It will always look for foreign key relationships between tables and add those. Depending on the value of the NameMatchingCriteria property, it may also use other criteria as well.

- SchemaRestriction—this property allows you to enter a comma-delimited list of schema names to restrict the list of tables that appear in the **Add/Remove Tables** dialog. This is very useful if your data warehouse contains a large number of tables and you used schemas to separate them into logical groups.

- NameMatchingCriteria—if the RetrieveRelationships property is set to **True**, then BIDS will try to guess relationships between tables by looking at column names. There are three different ways it can do this:

  1. by looking for identical column names in the source and destination tables (for example, FactTable.CustomerID to Customer.CustomerID)

2. by matching column names to table names (for example, `FactTable.Customer` to `Customer.CustomerID`)

3. by matching column names to a combination of column and table names (for example, `FactTable.CustomerID` to `Customer.ID`).

This is extremely useful if the tables you're using don't actually contain foreign key relationships, or if you've used views on top of your dimension and fact tables in the way we suggested in the previous chapter. You'll also see an extra step in the **New Data Source View** wizard allowing you to set these options if no foreign keys are found in the Data Source you're using.

Now, you can go ahead and right-click on the DSV design area and select the **Add/Remove Tables** option and select any tables or views you need to use. It might be a good idea not to select everything you need initially, but to select just one fact table and a few dimension tables so you can check the relationships and arrange the tables clearly, then add more. It's all too easy to end up with a DSV that looks like a plate of spaghetti and is completely unreadable. Even though you don't actually need to add every single relationship at this stage in order to build a cube, we recommend that you do so, as the effort will pay off later when BIDS uses these relationships to automatically populate properties such as dimension-to-measure group relationships.

Creating multiple diagrams within the DSV, maybe one for every fact table, will also help you organize your tables more effectively. The Arrange Tables right-click menu option is also invaluable.

Named Queries and Named Calculations allow you to add the equivalent of views and derived columns to your DSV, and this functionality was added to help cube developers who needed to manipulate data in the relational database, but didn't have the appropriate permissions to do so. However, if you have the choice between, say, altering a table and a **SQL Server Integration Services (SSIS)** package to fix a modeling problem or creating a Named Query, then we recommend that you always choose the former one—only do work in the DSV if you have no other choice. As we've already said several times, it makes much more sense to keep all of your ETL work in your ETL tool, and your relational modeling work in the relational database where it can be shared, managed and tuned more effectively. Resist the temptation to be lazy and don't just hack something in the DSV! One of the reasons why we advocate the use of views on top of dimension and fact tables is that they are as easy to alter as named queries and much easier to tune. The SQL that Analysis Services generates during processing is influenced heavily by what goes on in the DSV, and many processing performance problems are the result of cube designers taking the easy option early on in development.

If you make changes in your relational data source, those changes won't be reflected in your DSV until you click the **Refresh Data Source View** button or choose **Refresh** on the right-click menu.

Problems with TinyInt

Unfortunately, there's a bug in Analysis Services 2008 that causes a problem in the DSV when you use key columns of type `TinyInt`. Since Analysis Services doesn't support this type natively, the DSV attempts to convert it to something else—a `System.Byte` for foreign keys to dimensions on the fact table and a `System.Int32` for primary keys on dimension tables which have Identity set to true. This in turn means you can no longer create joins between your fact table and dimension table. To work around this, you need to create a named query on top of your dimension table containing an expression that explicitly casts your `TinyInt` column to a `TinyInt` (for example using an expression like `cast(mytinyintcol as tinyint)`), which will make the DSV show the column as a `System.Byte`. It sounds crazy, but for some reason it works.

Designing simple dimensions

Next, let's build some dimensions. As this is one of the more complicated steps in the cube design process, it's a topic we'll return to again in future chapters when we need to deal with more advanced modeling scenarios. Right now we'll concentrate on the fundamentals of dimension design.

Using the 'New Dimension' wizard

Running the **New Dimension** wizard will give you the first draft of your dimension, something you'll then be able to tweak and tidy up in the Dimension Editor afterwards. The first question you'll be asked, on the **Select Creation Method** step, is how you want to create the new dimension and there are effectively two choices:

- Create the dimension from an existing table or view in your data source (the **Use an Existing Table** option)
- Have BIDS create a dimension automatically for you and optionally fill it with data (the other three options)

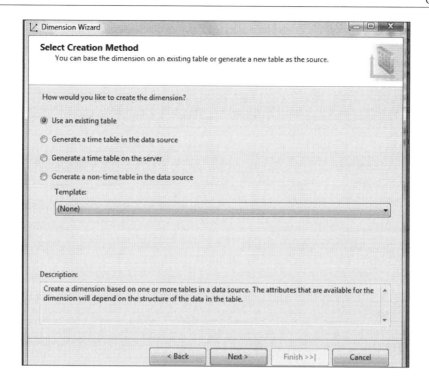

In keeping with our line of argument that all relational modeling work should be done outside BIDS, we recommend you to use the **Use an existing table** option. If you're trying to build a cube before you have prepared any dimension tables, you're probably running ahead of yourself and you need to go back and think about your data modeling in more detail.

In the next step of the wizard, you have to choose the main table for your dimension—the table or view that contains the lowest level of granularity of data for your dimension, and which joins directly to a fact table in your DSV. You also need to define the key attribute for the dimension, the attribute that represents the lowest level of granularity in the dimension and to which all other attributes have a one-to-many relationship. For example, on a Product dimension, the key attribute could represent the **Stock Keeping Unit** (**SKU**), and on a Customer dimension, the key attribute could represent the Customer itself. To define the key attribute, as with any attribute, you have to specify two extremely important properties:

- The Key. This is the column or collection of columns in your dimension table that uniquely identifies each individual member on the attribute, and for the key attribute, this is usually the dimension's surrogate key column. This will set the value of the KeyColumns property of the attribute.

- The Name. This is the column in your dimension table that contains the name or description that the end user expects to see on screen when they browse the dimension. This will set the `NameColumn` property of the attribute. The Name may or may not uniquely identify each member on the attribute. For example, on your Customer dimension there may be many members on the key attribute—many individual customers—with the name "John Smith". Member uniqueness is determined by the value of the Key property of the attribute but the end user may well be happy seeing multiple members with the same name, so long as they can distinguish between them using other dimension attributes such as Address.

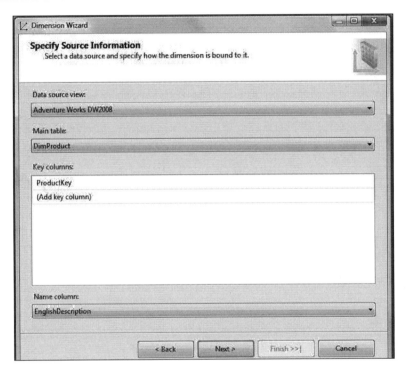

Click **Next** and, if you are building your dimension from a set of snowflaked tables, you get to the Select Related Tables set, where you have the option of selecting other tables you want to use to build this dimension. After this, you move onto the **Select Dimension Attributes** step, where you have the option of creating other new attributes on the dimension by checking any columns that you'd like to turn into attributes. You can also rename the attribute, uncheck the **Enable Browsing** option (which controls the value of the `AttributeHierarchyEnabled` property—for more details on this see below) and set the Attribute Type—a property that has a bewildering array of possible values, most of which are pointless, and which can be ignored unless you're designing a Time or an Account dimension.

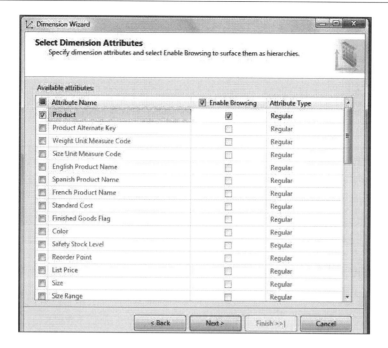

Now that we are into the final step of the wizard, all there is to do is to confirm the name of the dimension and click **Finish**.

A Note About Naming

At various points in the **New Dimension** wizard you have the chance to rename the dimension and attributes on it from whatever the wizard has guessed at as the default. It's a good idea to take naming seriously even at this early stage and discuss with your end users what the names of dimensions and attributes should be. Changing object names later in the development cycle can break any calculations or queries that you've already defined. Also, when you create an object for the first time, its `Object ID` property is set to its name, and even though you can subsequently change the name, the ID (which you'll see if you script the object out to XMLA for example) can never change, which can be confusing if you ever need to work directly with XMLA code. Object names should also be as end-user-friendly as possible, as they're going to be the names that appear in the reports the end-users want to build. The corollary of this is that object names are unlikely to be in a format that anyone with database design experience would choose. You might be happy with a dimension called `DimProduct` or an attribute called `Usr_Addr_FrstLn` but when the CEO gets his sales report, he's not going to want to see these names. Think of designing a cube as designing a user interface for data access by non-technical business people.

Using the Dimension Editor

Once you've completed the wizard, you'll arrive in the Dimension Editor for your new dimension.

Adding new attributes

It's likely that you'll want to add some more attributes to your dimension, and to do so, you can simply drag columns from the tables displayed in the Data Source View pane on the right hand side of the screen, into the Attributes pane on the left hand side. Once again, there are a couple of important properties you'll want to set on each of your attributes once you've created them:

- KeyColumns, NameColumn—the column or columns that represent the key and the name of this attribute. It's common for non-key attributes to be based on just one column which represents both the key and the name. For example, a Year attribute on a Time dimension might have values such as '2001' and '2002'. In this situation it's sufficient to set the KeyColumns property and not set the NameColumn. Analysis Services will display the key of the member as its name. For attributes with a very large number of members, you should always try to use a column of the smallest possible numeric data type as the key to an attribute and set the name separately. Using strings as keys can have a performance overhead, as can using composite keys (that is, when you use more than one column in the KeyColumns collection).

- AttributeHierarchyEnabled—this property controls whether a hierarchy is built for this attribute, that is, whether the user can actually see this attribute when they browse the cube and use it in their queries. By default it is **true**. If you set it to **false**, the attribute still exists, but is only visible in the dimension as a property of another attribute. A good example of when you would do this would be if you were building a Customer dimension. You'd never want to be able to see a hierarchy containing phone numbers and email addresses. However, if you were looking at a specific customer, it might be good to see this information as a property of that customer. Setting this property to **false** also has the benefit of reducing the amount of time needed to process the dimension.

- AttributeHierarchyOptimizedState—For attributes that have their AttributeHierarchyEnabled property set to **true**, this property controls whether indexes are built for the resulting attribute hierarchy. Setting this property to **false** can improve dimension processing times, since building an index for an attribute can take some time. However, the penalty you pay in terms of query performance can be quite significant so you should only consider setting this to false for attributes that are rarely used in queries and which are large enough to have an impact on dimension processing times.

- `OrderBy`, `OrderByAttribute`—The order that members appear in an attribute hierarchy can be important. For example, you would expect days of the week to appear in the order of Sunday, Monday, Tuesday and so on rather than in alphabetical order. The `OrderBy` attribute allows you to order the members on an attribute either alphabetically by name, by the value of the key of the attribute, by the value of the name, or by the key of another attribute that has a relationship with the attribute being ordered (which attribute is used is controlled by the value of the `OrderByAttribute` property). It is only possible to sort in ascending order. As a result, you may end up creating new numeric columns in your dimension table to use as the key of an attribute in order to ensure the type of sorting you want.

- `AttributeHierarchyOrdered`—In some situations, where the order of members on a very large attribute hierarchy doesn't matter much, disabling sorting by setting the `AttributeHierarchyOrdered` property to **false** can save a significant amount of time during dimension processing, as this blog entry shows: `http://tinyurl.com/attributeordered`.

- `IsAggregatable`, `DefaultMember`—For attributes that have their `AttributeHierarchyEnabled` property set to **true**, the `IsAggregatable` property controls whether an attribute's hierarchy contains an **All Member** as the root of the hierarchy. In general, you should not set this property to **false**, even for something like a Year attribute on a Time dimension where you might think it makes no sense to display an aggregated value, because it can have all kinds of confusing consequences for the user. Without an All Member, another member on the hierarchy will be automatically selected every time a query is run, and the user may not know which member this is. You can control which member is selected automatically by setting the `DefaultMember` property, for example, making the default selection on the 'Year' attribute the last year on the hierarchy. However, in our experience it's better to let the user make a selection themselves. The only time you should consider setting `IsAggregatable` to **false** is when `DefaultMember` is used and you have members in an attribute that should never be aggregated together. For instance, in a Budget Scenario attribute, you would get meaningless values if you showed the value of actuals and several different budget scenarios aggregated together. Usually, this situation arises when you only have one attribute on the dimension with `AttributeHierarchyEnabled` set to **true**.

Configuring a Time dimension

Building a Time dimension is really just the same as building a regular dimension, although there are a few extra properties that need to be set. Going back to the **Select Creation Method** step of the **New Dimension** wizard, you'll see that several of the available options are specifically for building Time dimensions, but we still recommend that you do not use them and construct a Time dimension yourself: they're only really useful for proof-of-concepts. Getting BIDS to build and populate a Time dimension table in your data source can be useful as a quick way to get started on building your own dimension. However, it's very likely that you'll want to make changes to what the wizard creates, not just because it uses a `DateTime` column as a primary key rather than an integer. The option to generate a Time dimension on the server—so that there is no relational data source needed—suffers from the same problems but is even more inflexible since there's no way to customize things such as member name formats beyond the options the wizard gives you.

The important thing to do with a Time dimension is to tell Analysis Services that it is in fact a Time dimension, so you can access some of the special functionality that Analysis Services has in this area. You can do this by setting the dimension's Type property to **Time** and then setting attributes' Type property to the nearest approximation of what they represent, so for a Year attribute you would set Type to 'Years', a Month attribute to 'Months' and so on.

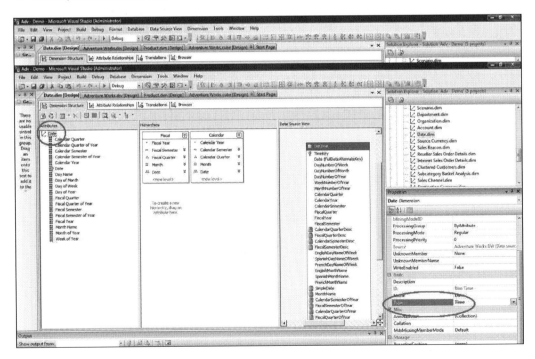

The benefits of doing this are:

- Certain MDX functions such as **Year To Date (YTD)** are 'time aware', and will not need you to specify certain parameters if you have a dimension marked as type Time

- Semi-additive measures, that is, those with their `AggegationFunction` set to **AverageOfChildren, FirstChild, LastChild, FirstNonEmpty** or **LastNonEmpty,** will perform their special types of aggregation on the first Time dimension related to a measure group

Creating user hierarchies

User hierarchies, the multilevel hierarchies that you create in the central 'Hierarchies' pane in the dimension editor, can best be described as being something like views on top of attribute hierarchies. They allow you to take two or more attribute hierarchies and combine them into a more complex drillpath. For example, you could take your Year, Month and Date attributes and combine them into a single hierarchy with Year, Month and Date levels, so that the user could easily drill from a year down to see all the months in that year, and from a month down to all the dates in that month.

When Analysis Services 2005 was first released and developers started coming to grips with the concept of attribute hierarchies and user hierarchies, one question that came up quite frequently was, "Should I expose attribute hierarchies or user hierarchies to my users?" As usual, the answer is that it depends. There are pros and cons to each and you'll probably end up using a mixture of both types of hierarchy. User hierarchies are more user-friendly because drilling down is just a matter of a double-click. On the other hand, rigidly defined drillpaths might be too limiting, and users might prefer the flexibility of being able to arrange attribute hierarchies whichever way they want. Certainly there are some things you can't do with user hierarchies, such as putting different levels of the same hierarchy on different axes in a query. For you as a developer, user hierarchies have some benefits. They make writing the MDX for certain types of calculation easier (members in a multilevel user hierarchy have meaningful 'parents' and 'children'), and 'natural' user hierarchies, which we'll talk about next, are materialized on disk and so offer query performance benefits and also make the aggregation design process much easier.

If you do create a user hierarchy, you should definitely set the **Visible** property of its constituent attribute hierarchies to **false**. If you have too many hierarchies available for a user to choose from in a dimension, then you run the risk of confusing the user, and having the same members appear more than once in attribute hierarchies and user hierarchies will make matters worse. Simplicity is a virtue when it comes to dimension design.

Configuring attribute relationships

Attribute relationships allow you to model one-to-many relationships between attributes. For example, you might have Year, Month and Date attributes on your Time dimension, and you know that there are one-to-many relationships between Year and Month and Month and Date, so you should build the attribute relationships between these three attributes to reflect this. Why? The short answer is performance. Setting attribute relationships optimally can make a very big difference to query performance, and the importance of this cannot be overstated – they drastically improve Analysis Services' ability to build efficient indexes and make use of aggregations. However, attribute relationships do not have anything to do with how the dimension gets displayed to the end user, so don't get them confused with user hierarchies.

It's very likely that there will be many different ways to model attribute relationships between the same attributes in a dimension, so the important thing is to find the best way of modeling the relationships from a performance point of view. When you first build a dimension in BIDS, you will get a set of attributes relationships that, while correct, are not necessarily optimal. This default set of relationships can be described as looking a bit like a bush. Every non-key attribute has a relationship defined either with the key attribute, or with the attribute built on the primary key of the source table in a snowflaked dimension. You can visualize these relationships on the Attribute Relationships tab of the dimension editor as in the first screenshot below or, if you have BIDS Helper installed, by right-clicking on the dimension in the Solution Explorer window and selecting **Visualize Attribute Lattice** you'll see something like what's shown in the second screenshot below. The built-in functionality, in our opinion, sacrifices clarity in favour of saving space, and BIDS Helper visualization is easier to understand. BIDS Helper displays each attribute as a separate node in its relationship diagram, whereas on the Attribute Relationships tab, two attributes are displayed in the same node when there are relationships between them, but no onward relationship.

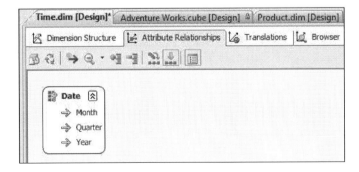

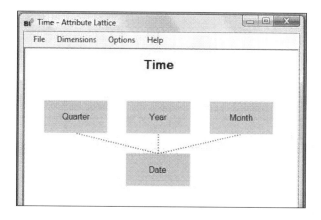

You can see that, in our example using Year, Quarter, Month and Date attributes on a Time dimension, Analysis Services knows that a Year is made up of many Dates, a Quarter is made up of many Dates, and a Month is made up of many Dates, but not that Years are made up of Quarters or that Quarters are made up of Months. Changing the attribute relationships to reflect these facts gives you something resembling a long chain, and in general the more long chains you see in your attribute relationships the better. As Analysis Services understands transitory relationships, there's no need to define a relationship between Year and Date, for example, because it can see that there is an indirect relationship via Quarter and Month. In fact defining such redundant relationships can be a bad thing from a performance point of view.

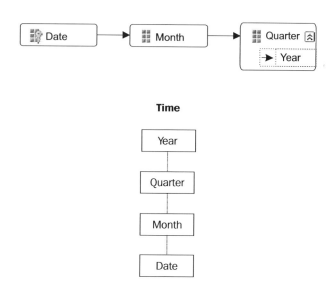

You will also notice a change in how some user hierarchies are displayed once you've optimized your attribute relationships in this way. User hierarchies which have one-to-many relationships defined between the attributes that make up each level are called **natural** user hierarchies. User hierarchies that don't are called **unnatural** user hierarchies and display an amber warning triangle in their top left hand corner. This warning triangle does not signify that the hierarchy is broken or incorrectly configured, just that you should check your attribute relationships to see whether they be optimized. You may actually want to build an unnatural user hierarchy, and it may not be possible to set up the attribute relationships to make it into a natural user hierarchy, and so long as you are aware that unnatural user hierarchies may not perform as well as natural user hierarchies, you should not be put off by the warning.

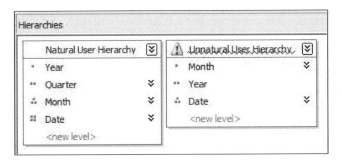

It is very important to understand your data before you set up any attribute relationships, because if you set them up incorrectly then it could result in Analysis Services returning incorrect data. The 'Dimension Health Check' functionality in BIDS Helper, available when you right-click on a dimension in the Solution Explorer, checks whether the attribute relationships you've defined actually reflect the data in your dimension table. Here's an example of a common mistake that is made: your Year attribute has members 2001, 2002, 2003 and 2004; your Quarter attribute has four members from Quarter 1 to Quarter 4. Is there a one-to-many relationship between Year and Quarter? The answer is in fact no, despite what common sense tells you, because, for example, a quarter called Quarter 1 appears in every Year. What you can and should do here is modify your data so that you can build an attribute relationship: a quarter called 'Quarter 1 2001' only exists in the year 2001. There are two ways to do this:

- By modifying the data in your dimension table (the best option)
- By using a composite key in the `KeyColumns` property of the Quarter attribute that is made up of both the keys for the quarter and the year

You can read a more detailed discussion of these techniques at the end of this article: `http://tinyurl.com/attributerelationships`. You should not make changes like this at the expense of the users' requirements, but in most cases they will not mind minor modifications like this and will appreciate the increased query performance.

The `RelationshipType` property of an attribute relationship indicates whether the relationship between any two members on two related attributes is ever likely to change or not. For example, you would hope that the Date 'January 1st 2001' would always appear under the Month 'January 2001' in your dimension. If it moved to the Month 'March 2002', something would be very wrong with your source data. In this case, you should set the `RelationshipType` property of the Month-Date attribute relationship to **Rigid**. On the other hand, it may be true that the relationship between a Customer attribute and a City attribute may change over time if a customer changes his/her residence. In that case, the `RelationshipType` property should be set to **Flexible**. Setting `RelationshipType` to **Rigid** where possible increases the chances that aggregations will not need to be rebuilt when a dimension undergoes a `ProcessUpdate`, something that will be discussed in more detail in Chapter 10. Our advice is never to set the `RelationshipType` property to **Rigid** unless you are absolutely sure that no UPDATE or DELETE statement is ever run on the underlying dimension table. If a rigid relationship does change, dimension processing will fail.

Finally, attribute relationships also have a second function, and that is to act as member properties. If a Month has many Dates, you can think of the relationship in reverse as a Date having a property which is its Month. A better example might be a Customer having an Address, and if the Address attribute has its `AttributeHierarchyEnabled` property set to **false** then it may only be visible as a property of Customer. Every attribute relationship is visible by default as a member property in most client tools. If you want to hide the member property, you can set the relationship's `Visible` property to **false**.

Building a Simple Cube

With some dimensions built, the next step is to run the cube wizard to create the cube itself. Remember that at this stage all we want to do is build a very simple cube so that we can test-drive the data, so we're not going to do anything other than run the wizard. You'll be doing a lot of work in the Cube Editor in the next stage of development, but if you've set up the DSV in the way we recommend, then you'll find that when you've finished running the wizard, you will have something that you can deploy, process and browse immediately with no changes required.

Using the 'New Cube' wizard

On the **Select Creation Method** step of the wizard, as with the same step of the **New Dimension** wizard, choose the **Use an Existing table** option—the **Create an Empty Cube** and the **Generate Tables in the Data Source** options can be ignored for now. The former is useful in more advanced scenarios but regarding the latter, we'll repeat what we said earlier: you should model your data properly in the data warehouse before you start building anything in Analysis Services. On the **Select Measure Group Tables** step, just select the fact table you chose earlier as the basis for the simple cube you want to build. Then on the **Select Measures** step, select one or two columns from that fact table that represents commonly used measures, which can be aggregated by summation. On the **Select Existing Dimensions,** select all the dimensions that you've just built that join to the fact table you've chosen. Don't bother creating any new dimensions on the **Select New Dimensions** step. Finally, on the **Completing the Wizard** Step, enter the name of the cube and click **Finish**. When you're As was the case when creating dimensions, it's worth putting some thought into the name of your cube. Try to make the name reflect the data the cube contains, make sure the name is meaningful to the end users, and keep it short as you'll probably have to type this name hundreds of times over the lifetime of the project.

Deployment

With the wizard complete, go to the **Build** menu in the main Visual Studio menu bar and select '**Deploy** <MyProjectName>'. Deployment is actually a two-stage process:

- First the project is built. You can think of this as being similar to compiling some .NET code, except instead of an executable or a dll the end result is four files containing the XMLA representation of the objects in your project, and information on how the project should be deployed. You can find these files in the bin directory of your Visual Studio project directory.

- Then the project is deployed. This takes the XMLA created in the previous step, wraps it in an XMLA Alter command and then executes that command against your Analysis Services server. Executing this command either creates a new Analysis Services database if one did not exist before, or updates the existing database with any changes you've made.

It's quite common for deployment to fail as a result of you making a mistake somewhere in your cube or dimension designs. If this happens, you should see all of the errors you need to correct in the Error List window. When you go to the appropriate editor to correct the error, you should also see a red squiggly line underneath whichever object it is that needs fixing as with the Month attribute in the following screenshot:

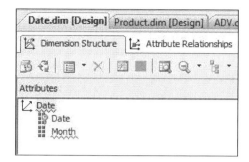

Warnings and Blue Squiggly Lines

Even if you don't see any red squiggly lines anywhere and your project deploys successfully, it's likely that you'll see warnings in the Error List window and blue squiggly lines in various places in BIDS (see for example the Date dimension node in the screenshot above). These design warnings will occur where you have built something that works but does not reflect best practice. A few of the warnings concern quite trivial things but, in general, it's a good idea to pay attention to them. If you want to, though, you can dismiss warnings by right-clicking on them in the Error List window and clicking **Dismiss**, while leaving a comment explaining why you've done this for future reference. You can also manage which warnings appear, and see which ones have been dismissed by right-clicking on the project in the Solution Explorer, by clicking on **Edit Database** to open the Database Editor and going to the **Warnings** tab.

Processing

Assuming you've set the **Processing Option** project property to **Do Not Process**, then the result of deployment will be a new Analysis Services database on the server containing a cube and several dimensions. You won't be able to browse the cube yet though, as all that has been created are empty structures which need to be loaded with data from your data warehouse. In order to load the data, you have to process the objects and you can do this easily from within BIDS by going to the Database menu and clicking **Process**. Once you've done this, the Process Database dialog appears. Leave the **Process** Options column showing **Process Full**, click **Run**, and everything in the database should be processed.

As an Analysis Services database is nothing more than a collection of objects, processing a database involves nothing more than processing all of the cubes and dimensions in the database. In turn, cubes are made up of measure groups, which are made up of partitions, and dimensions are made up of attributes, and all of these objects have their own discrete processing operations. As a result, processing a database can kick off a lot of individual processing jobs and by default, Analysis Services will try to do a lot of this processing in parallel to reduce the overall time taken. A **Process Full** will always drop any data currently in an object and reload its data from scratch. It's the most time-consuming form of processing and there are a lot of other different options here that we can use to reduce processing time which we'll discuss in Chapter 10.

You can watch all of these processing jobs executing in the Process Progress window that appears after you click **Run** in the Process Database dialog. You'll see each object that is being processed listed, as well as the time processing started and ended. If you expand each object, you'll eventually find the SQL queries run to retrieve data from the data warehouse. If you select any node and click the **View Details** button, you'll see a new window appear, containing all of the text for the node, and this is very important when it comes to viewing long SQL queries or messages.

As you can't do anything else in BIDS while processing is taking place, it can be a good idea to just do a Deploy from there, and then start processing separately in SQL Management Studio. This way you can carry on developing while processing is taking place.

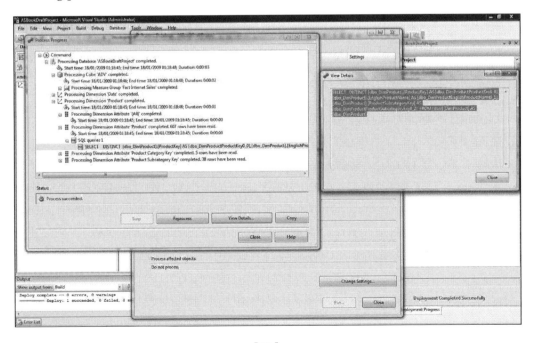

Processing errors are unfortunately as common as deployment errors, and they are caused by four basic types of problem:

- Changes in the underlying relational schema mean that Analysis Services contains invalid references. For example, you might build a measure from a column in a fact table that is subsequently renamed. You'd only find this out if you refreshed your DSV or at processing time when Analysis Services generated SQL that used the old name.

- **Key errors**—You can think of Analysis Services as performing an inner join between tables in a snowflaked dimension, or between dimension tables and fact tables, although it very rarely does so in the SQL it generates. For example, if it finds a dimension key value in a fact table that doesn't exist in the dimension table, by default, it will raise an error and the processing will fail. As mentioned in Chapter 1, you should try to ensure this never happens in your ETL, even if some accidents are inevitable. You can configure processing so that key errors are ignored, or unknown keys are assigned to a special unknown member on a dimension by clicking the **Change Settings** button in the Process dialog to show the Change Settings dialog and going to the **Dimension Key Errors** tab. However, we do not recommend you do this except as insurance against these accidents. You'll get a lot more flexibility with a custom solution. That said, at this stage of the cube development process, it can be useful to ignore errors just to get the cube to process so you can show it to your users.

- Processing objects in the wrong order— For example, if you process a dimension, then update the underlying relational data so that there are new rows in the dimension table and new rows related to them in the fact table, and then process your cube without reprocessing the dimension again first, you'll again run into key errors.

- MDX Script errors—it's very often the case that when you make structural changes to a cube or a dimension, these changes break MDX calculations on the cube. For example, you might rename a dimension but still have MDX code where the old dimension name is referenced. When a cube is processed, the last thing that happens is that all of the code on the MDX Script is executed and if it now contains syntax errors, the whole processing operation will fail. This is extremely frustrating when it happens, and it can lead to a lot of wasted time. If you are making a lot of structural changes it can be a good idea to comment out the whole of the MDX Script before you do any processing, and only uncomment it when you have successfully processed your cube.

Summary

With processing complete, you can take a look at your cube for the first time, either in the Browser tab of the Cube Editor or in your client tool of choice. Now is a good time to reflect on what we've seen of the cube development process so far:

- We've created a very basic cube from a single fact table and a few dimensions rather than attempting to build something more complex. This has allowed us to get a feel for our data and have something to show our users quickly so that they can check if we're on the right track.

- We built a single Data Source and Data Source View. Since we spent time getting our data modeling right earlier, there is very little to do here other than connect to our data warehouse and select the tables or views we want to work with.

- We built a few of the less complex dimensions we need, configuring attribute relationships and creating user hierarchies as necessary.

- We ran the 'New Cube' wizard to build our basic cube, then deployed and processed it so that it can be queried.

In the next chapter we'll go on to look at how we can add more measure groups and measures to the cube, in order to handle more complex modeling problems.

3
Designing More Complex Dimensions

At this point in the cube design process we should now have a simple cube deployed and processed, and our users will be telling us what they like and don't like. Once we've taken their feedback on board, it's time to move on to tackle some of the more complex problems. In this chapter, we'll take a look at some specific issues related to dimension design:

- Grouping and Banding
- Handling the different types of Slowly Changing Dimension
- Junk dimensions
- Modeling ragged hierarchies with parent/child hierarchies and the `HideMemberIf` property

Grouping and Banding

Often, we'll need to create groups of some kind on a dimension either to group long lists of members up into more user-friendly groups, or to group numeric attributes such as Age or measure values into bands or ranges. Analysis Services offers some functionality to help us do this. But as usual, we'll get much more flexibility if we design these groups into the dimension ourselves.

Grouping

First of all let's consider why we might want to group members on a large attribute hierarchy. Some dimensions are not only very large – there are a lot of rows in the dimension table – but they are also very flat, so they have very few attributes on them that are related to each other and have very few natural hierarchies. We might have a **Customer** dimension with millions of individual customers on it, and we might also have **City** and **Country** attributes, but even then it might be the case that for a large city, a user might drill down and see hundreds or thousands of customers. In this situation, a user looking for an individual Customer might have problems finding the one they want if they need to search through a very long list; some client tools might also be slow to respond if they have to display such a large number of members in a dialog or dimension browser. Therefore, it makes sense to create extra attributes on such dimensions to group members together to reduce the chance of this happening.

Analysis Services can automatically create groups for you, using the `DiscretizationMethod` and `DiscretizationBucketCount` properties on an attribute. The `DiscretizationMethod` property allows you to choose how groups should be created: the **EqualAreas** option will try to create groups with a roughly equal number of members in them, the **Clusters** option will use a data mining algorithm to create groups of similar members, and the **Automatic** option will try to work out which of the preceding two options fits the data best; the `DiscretizationBucketCount` property specifies the number of groups that should be created. Full details of how this functionality works can be found at `http://tinyurl.com/groupingatts` and while it does what it is supposed to do, it rarely makes sense to use it. The reason why can be seen from the following screenshot that shows the result of using the **EqualAreas** option to group a Weight attribute:

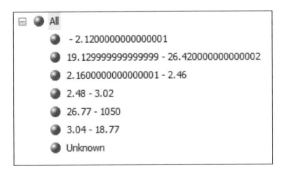

Clearly, this isn't very user-friendly, and while you could try to tweak property values to get the groups and group names you want, frankly, it is much easier to create new columns in the views we're building our dimensions from to get exactly the kind of grouping that you want. Nothing is going to be more flexible than SQL for this job, and writing the necessary SQL code is not hard—usually a simple CASE statement will be sufficient. An expression such as this in TSQL, when used to create a new column in a view or a named calculation:

```
CASE WHEN Weight IS NULL OR Weight<0 THEN 'N/A'
WHEN Weight<10 THEN '0-10Kg'
WHEN Weight<20 THEN '10-20Kg'
ELSE '20Kg or more'
END
```

This yields much better results in the dimension when you build an attribute from it:

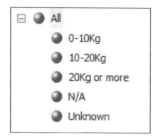

In this case, the names happen to sort in the order you'd want to see them, and you might need an additional column to use as the key for the new attribute. The point is that in this situation, as in many others, a little extra time spent modeling the relational data to get it the way you want it pays dividends even when Analysis Services seems to offer you a quicker way of getting things done.

Banding

Similarly, we might need to create an entire dimension that acts as a way of grouping measure values on a fact table. For example, we might have a measure that gives us the total value of an order, and we might want to find the total number of orders whose values fall into some predefined bandings such as 'High Value', 'Medium Value' or 'Low Value'. In this case, again we would need to create a dimension table to hold these bandings, but one problem we might have to face is that the ranges used for the bandings might change frequently as the users' requirements change—one day a 'High Value' order might be one for more than €10000, the next it might be more than €15000.

If we modeled our new dimension using meaningless surrogate keys, we would have to perform a lookup during our ETL to find out which band each row in the fact table fell into and assign it the appropriate surrogate key:

ID	Order Value	OR
1	9,815	2
2	890	1
3	25,000	3

OR	RANGE
1	LOW
2	MEDIUM
3	HIGH

But what would happen if the user changed the bandings? If a user does this, then we would have to reload our entire fact table, because potentially any order might now fall into a new banding. A more flexible approach is to hardcode only the granularity of the bandings into the fact table: for example, we could say that our bandings could only have boundaries divisible by €1000. This would then allow us to use an expression in our fact table ETL such as Floor(OrderValue/100) to create a meaningful key; in our dimension, we would then create one row per €100 up to what we think the maximum value of an order might be, and then group these €100 ranges into the bandings our users wanted as follows:

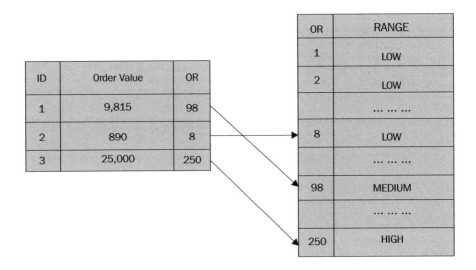

ID	Order Value	OR
1	9,815	98
2	890	8
3	25,000	250

OR	RANGE
1	LOW
2	LOW
	... ...
8	LOW
	... ...
98	MEDIUM
	... ...
250	HIGH

The advantage of this is that so long as the granularity of the bandings doesn't change, we will never need to reload our fact table. In Analysis Services terms, this dimension would have two attributes: one built from the meaningful key, and one to hold the name of the band; a Process Update would be all that was necessary when the banding boundaries changed because only the dimension table would have been changed.

Slowly Changing Dimensions

Slowly Changing Dimensions (SCD) are a fact of life in almost all data warehouses; we discussed how to deal with them in our relational model in Chapter 1 and we'll now look at the issues that arise with each different type when building Analysis Services dimensions. In many cases, of course, different attributes on the same dimension can be subject to different types of change and we'll will use a combination of the techniques outlined below, but it's helpful to discuss each type of change separately for the sake of clarity.

Type I SCDs

Since changes in Type I SCDs involve overwriting existing values in the dimension table, no special design is needed in Analysis Services to support this. Running a Process Update on the dimension will ensure that any changes that have been made in the dimension table are reflected in your Analysis Services dimension. We'll discuss processing in more detail in Chapter 10.

It's at this point we'll see an error if any attributes have changed that should not have changed, that's to say, if any members on attribute hierarchies which have **Rigid** relationship types have changed position in the dimension relative to each other. For example, if on the **Time** dimension, there were **Date** and **Month** attributes that had a **Rigid** attribute relationship defined between them, and the Date 'January 1st 2001' somehow got moved from under the Month 'January 2001' to the Month 'March 2002', we'd expect to get an error because something has clearly gone wrong. It's also possible that a Type I change will result in the data in the dimension not being consistent with the attribute relationships we have defined, and what we thought to be a one-to-many relationship, turns out to be a many-to-many relationship. For example, we might have defined a chain of attribute relationships on a **Customer** dimension going from **Continent** to **Country** to **City**, but then realize that there is an exception to this rule when the cities of Istanbul and Ankara are added: both are in Turkey, but Istanbul could be listed as being in Europe and Ankara in Asia.

You might think that an update to a dimension that invalidates an attribute relationship would raise an error during dimension processing, but it doesn't always. If you run a `Process Full` on a dimension with invalid attribute relationships, and you specifically configure processing error handling to trap duplicate key errors, then processing will fail. However, a `Process Update` will complete successfully in this situation, regardless of how you configure processing error handling, leaving the dimension in a dangerous state where incorrect data could be returned from the cube.

One other thing we'll see is that any aggregations on measure groups this dimension joins to that might have been invalidated by the processing are dropped; they'll need to be rebuilt later on in your processing schedule. These aggregations are called **Flexible** aggregations, and they're aggregations that include at least one attribute that has a **Flexible** relationship somewhere in the chain of attribute relationships between them and the key attribute. We can see whether an aggregation is **Flexible** or **Rigid** in the **Edit Aggregations** dialog of the **BIDS Helper Aggregation Manager**:

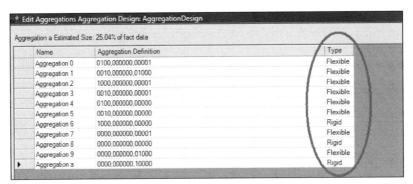

One problem that may result from Type I changes and which may not become apparent immediately, is that previously saved queries and reports will either stop working or not return the data you expect. In MDX, a member is identified by its unique name and this is how it is referenced when you write an MDX query; here are some examples of unique names:

```
[Promotion].[Promotions].[Category].&[Customer]
[Customer].[Customer Geography].[City].&[Alexandria]&[NSW]
[Date].[Calendar Year].&[2001]
```

The format of the unique name will vary depending on the type of hierarchy and various property settings on the dimension, but as we can see from the examples above, the uniqueness of a a unique name usually derives from values in the columns you've used in the `KeyColumns` property of the attribute hierarchy. If a Type I change alters one of these values then that will carry through to a change in the unique names of one or more members on hierarchies in the dimension. If a saved query references the old version of the unique name, one of two things will happen:

- If we have set the `MDXMissingMemberMode` property of the dimension to **Ignore** (and this is what the **Default** option means too), then any queries which refer to the old version of the unique name will simply ignore that member. This would result in rows or columns disappearing from queries or reports with no warning.

- If we have set `MDXMissingMemberMode` to **Error**, then any queries which refer to the old version of the unique name will raise an error when they are run. At best, this will mean you have to manually fix the MDX query so that the old version is replaced with the new version; in some Analysis Services client tools, it will mean you have to delete the entire query or report and recreate it from scratch.

Type II SCDs

Type II SCDs represent a more difficult problem: unlike some other OLAP servers, Analysis Services has no explicit support for different versions of the same dimension, and it's up to us as developers to decide how we should design our dimension to handle such changes.

When a Type II change takes place, a new row is added to a dimension table and this in turn results in the addition of a new member on the key attribute of the Analysis Services dimension. This has some positive implications: if we only allow Type II changes on a dimension, because we are only adding new rows and not updating existing rows, we can do a **Process Add** on our dimension which will be faster than a **Process Update**, and we can set all our attribute relationships to **Rigid** so we do not need to rebuild any aggregations after processing. However, modeling the attributes and attribute relationships on a Type II SCD can require some thought.

Modeling attribute relationships on a Type II SCD

Let's consider a Customer dimension table which features two columns common to many Type II SCDs:

- A surrogate key column, CustomerKey, which is the primary key on the table

- A business key column, CustomerAlternateKey, which identifies a single customer. If several Type II changes take place there may be several rows, each with different surrogate keys, for each customer; each of these rows, though, will have the same value for CustomerAlternateKey

Two attributes should be built on the Analysis Services Customer dimension built from this table:

- One which uses the surrogate key in its `KeyColumns` property, which let's call **Customer SCD** in the following discussion, and

- One which uses the business key in its `KeyColumns` property, which we'll call **Customer**.

Customer SCD will be the key attribute of the dimension and an attribute relationship should be built to reflect the one-to-many relationship between **Customer** and **Customer SCD**. We can then build other attributes on the dimension and configure attribute relationships so that those which will never change have attribute relationships which run through the **Customer** attribute and those which will be subject to Type II changes have attribute relationships which bypass **Customer** and go straight to **Customer SCD**. Here's an example of what a first attempt at modeling these attribute relationships might look like:

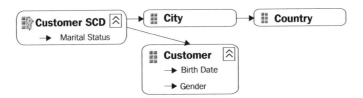

Given that the same customer may appear many times in the **Customer SCD** attribute hierarchy after Type II changes have taken place, and that the end user may be confused by this, it makes sense to hide the **Customer SCD** attribute hierarchy by setting its `AttributeHierarchyVisibleState` to **False**. The user can instead use the **Customer** attribute hierarchy to view individual customers. However, it's also likely that we would want to build a user hierarchy that would allow users to drill from **Country** to **City** and down to **Customer**. With the attribute relationships modeled above, we would have two options, neither of which would be ideal:

- Build the user hierarchy with levels based on the **Country** attribute hierarchy, the **City** attribute hierarchy and the **Customer SCD** attribute hierarchy. This would be a natural user hierarchy so you would get optimal performance, especially important on a dimension like **Customer** which can be very large. But what would happen if a customer got married, and this created a new row in the dimension table? A new member would be created on **Customer SCD**, so when the user drilled down from the **City** level they might see the same **Customer** listed twice, once in their unmarried state and once in their married state; clearly not a good thing.

- Build the user hierarchy with levels based on the **Country** attribute hierarchy, the **City** attribute hierarchy and the **Customer** attribute hierarchy. This would ensure the user only ever saw one instance of a **Customer** per **City**, but it would also be an unnatural user hierarchy and would therefore perform worse.

One solution to this problem is to create an extra attribute hierarchy to represent unique combinations of individual Customers and Cities, with a composite key based on the `CustomerAlternateKey` business key and the key used for the **City** attribute hierarchy. This would allow us to model the attribute relationships as follows:

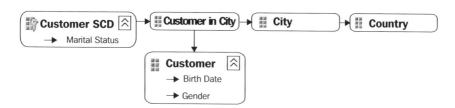

We would then set `AttributeHierarchyVisible` to **False** on this new attribute hierarchy and use it as the bottom level of your user hierarchy. This would guarantee that we only saw one instance of a **Customer** appear under each **City** and since it would be a natural user hierarchy, we would have the best possible performance. The price we would pay for this would be that your dimension processing time would increase because of this new, potentially large attribute; we would have to decide whether this was a price worth paying.

Another benefit of this solution is that the **Customer SCD** attribute hierarchy is never made available for direct querying to the end user. It's still necessary to have it there from a modeling point of view, but the fact it is hidden can be useful: since its key is based on the surrogate key of the dimension table, the unique names of the members on it therefore will incorporate surrogate key values. Although not necessarily the best practice, it is sometimes the case that a data warehouse needs to be completely emptied and reloaded, and if that happens, it's highly likely that a completely new set of surrogate key values will be used in a dimension. If this were to happen it would break existing reports or worse cause them to return unexpected data, and for this reason it's a good idea to avoid exposing surrogate key values through MDX unique names where possible.

Handling member status

Type II SCDs typically also have three columns in their dimension tables to track the status of a row: a column that tells us whether this is the most recent, or current, version of the row, perhaps containing either the values "Current" or "Previous"; and start and end dates that show you the time span for which each row was the current row. It can be useful to include this information in your Analysis Services dimension, although it's by no means always necessary or even a good idea.

Building an attribute from the **current version** column is straightforward: we get an attribute hierarchy with an **All Member** and two members underneath it for the `true` and `false` values. Doing this will, for instance, allows us to write queries and calculations that filter our **Customer SCD** attribute to retrieve only the current versions of each **Customer** so we can answer questions like, "How many of my customers are married?" We may not want to make this attribute visible to our users though because it will also slice measure values so they only show values for the current version of each **Customer**, which probably isn't very helpful.

For the start and end date columns, at this point the only recommendation to make is that rather than storing them as **DateTime** types, it's better to use the same integer surrogate key format we're using for your **Time** dimension surrogate keys. This will give us the option of creating role-playing dimensions based on our Time dimension which can then be joined to your SCD on these columns with a `Referenced` relationship, which again will allow us to filter our **Customer SCD** attribute to only return those members that were current within a specific date range. It will also, if required, provide the platform for building even more sophisticated models for analyzing the changes made to a dimension over time such as those described in the 'Cross Time' and 'Transition Matrix' sections of the white paper *The Many-to-Many Revolution* available at `http://tinyurl.com/m2mrev`

 The `Type` property of an attribute hierarchy can be set to **SCDStatus**, **SCDStartDate** and **SCDEndDate** for these three columns. These properties have no effect on the behavior of Analysis Services and are purely descriptive.

Type III SCDs

A Type III SCD uses two columns to capture the current and either the previous or original states of something – it allows us to store history, but only a limited amount; probably as a result this approach is very rarely used in the real world. In Analysis Services, this translates to two different sets of attributes; for example, in our Customer dimension example, we might have four attributes for **Current City**, **Current Country**, **Previous City** and **Previous Country**, with the attribute relationships modeled as follows:

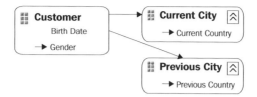

 Using folders

The two sets of attributes we have described for a Type III dimension, 'Current' and 'Previous', are good candidates for being grouped together in folders using the `AttributeHierarchyDisplayFolder` property. Folders can be an important way of improving the usability of dimensions with large numbers of attribute and user hierarchies.

Junk dimensions

As we've already seen, Junk dimensions are built from groups of attributes that don't belong on any other dimension, generally columns from fact tables that represent flags or status indicators. When designing an Analysis Services solution, it can be quite tempting to turn each of these columns into their own dimension, having just one attribute, but from a manageability and usability point of view creating a single Junk dimension is preferable to cluttering up your cube with lots of rarely-used dimensions. Creating a Junk dimension can be important for query performance too. Typically, when creating a Junk dimension, we create a dimension table containing only the combinations of attribute values that actually exist in the fact table—usually a much smaller number of combinations than the theoretical maximum, because there are often dependencies between these attributes and knowing these combinations in advance can greatly improve the performance of MDX queries that display more than one of these attributes crossjoined together.

As with a Type II SCD, when building an Analysis Services dimension from a Junk dimension table we will create a key attribute based on the surrogate key of the dimension, which we can then hide by setting `AttributeHierarchyVisible` to **False**. All other attributes on the dimension can be directly related to this attribute, unless of course we can be 100% certain that attribute relationships can be defined between other attributes. The attribute relationships might look something like this:

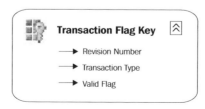

It's sometimes the case that users will request that one or more attributes from a Junk dimension will be split off into a new dimension, and you will need to be careful if you do this because of the risk that existing queries that reference the Junk dimension will break as a result of invalid MDX unique name references.

Ragged hierarchies

Ragged hierarchies are another common design problem to deal with when building an Analysis Services dimension. The hierarchies we've dealt with so far can be easily separated out into distinct levels and can be thought of as pyramid-shaped: all of members on the hierarchy have at least one child, except the members on the lowest level, which have no children at all. Ragged hierarchies, on the other hand, are bush-shaped. The members at any given level may or may not have children. Common examples of ragged hierarchies are those that represent a chart of accounts or the organizational structure of a company.

Parent/child hierarchies

One way of modeling a ragged hierarchy in a data warehouse is with a table with a self-join: every row in the table represents an item somewhere on the hierarchy, and every row has a key column and a foreign key that joins back onto the key column in order to store the key of the parent item. Here's an example taken from the Adventure Works data warehouse:

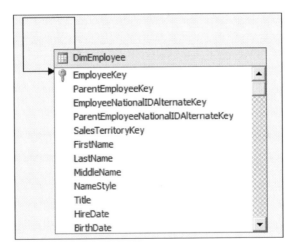

Analysis Services can build a special kind of hierarchy from this type of table called a parent/child hierarchy, and will do so automatically if you run the **New Dimension Wizard** on a table with the appropriate relationship defined in the DSV and build attributes from the key and parent key columns. Once we've done this, we'll have a dimension with two attribute hierarchies:

- The key attribute built from the primary key of the table, which is a flat list of all the members in the table

- The attribute built from the parent key column, which is the parent/child hierarchy and has the same members but organised into a ragged hierarchy. You'll see that the Usage property of this attribute has been set to Parent.

Typically, we will set the `AttributeHierarchyVisible` property of the key attribute to **False** and only let users see the parent/child hierarchy in the dimension.

 We can give the levels on a parent/child hierarchy names by setting the `NamingTemplate` property. This property takes the form of a semi-colon delimited list of names, which are used as the names of levels, starting from the top of the hierarchy: asterisks in the names are replaced with the ordinal of the level. Thankfully, there is a dialog box that allows you to construct these strings easily.

There is, unfortunately, a long list of limitations when it comes to using parent/child hierarchies:

- You can only have one parent/child hierarchy per dimension

- A parent/child hierarchy has to be built from the key attribute of the dimension

- You cannot use a parent/child hierarchy as a level in a user hierarchy

- Dimensions with parent/child hierarchies are slower to process than those without

- Parent/child hierarchies can be very difficult to work with when writing MDX calculations and queries because they do not obey the same rules as regular hierarchies. Scoped assignments, autoexists and any calculation that uses the `Currentmember` function are a particular problem.

- The unique names of parent/child hierarchies include surrogate key values, which as we've already noted, can be a problem if you need to reload the dimension table.

- Use of a parent/child hierarchy in a query can lead to very poor query performance. In general, performance of small parent/child hierarchies of up to a few hundred members is fine but as soon as you have more than a few thousand members on a parent/child hierarchy, the performance can suffer badly.

- Following on from the previous point, you cannot build an aggregation at the granularity of a parent/child attribute hierarchy; you can only build aggregations above the granularity of the hierarchy or ones at the granularity of the key attribute. It is not possible to build aggregations at any of the intermediate levels that appear in a parent/child hierarchy. This makes it more difficult to tune query performance, although it should be noted that it is not the sole cause of the poor query performance of parent/child hierarchies.

We can work around some of these problems (notably: not being able to build multiple parent/child hierarchies on the same dimension; having to build them from the key attribute; and surrogate keys being used in unique names) by creating multiple Analysis Services dimensions from the same physical dimension table. We would create a dimension to hold just the surrogate key and then build separate dimensions for each parent/child hierarchy and use non-surrogate key columns on the dimension table as the key attribute for them; these then would be linked to the main measure group by using a **Referenced** relationship (which we'll talk about in the next chapter) via the new surrogate key dimension. Doing this, however, is likely to have an impact on the processing performance if you materialize the referenced relationships or query performance if you don't materialize the referenced relationships.

> We recommend that you avoid setting the IsAggregatable property of a parent/child hierarchy to **False** whenever you can. If you do, then every query will be forced to the granularity of the key attribute of the dimension with the parent/child hierarchy, even when the query doesn't use the parent/child hierarchy. Setting IsAggregatable to **True** though means that an All Member will be created on the hierarchy and an aggregation can be built at that granularity. For the same reason, we also recommend that you think very carefully before setting the DefaultMember on the parent/child hierarchy.

Avoid using parent/child hierarchies!

For all of the reasons given above, we recommend that you avoid using parent/child hierarchies unless you have absolutely no other choice but to use them. In our experience, the problems caused by using parent/child hierarchies, especially large ones, can be quite serious. In situations where you know there is a fixed maximum number of levels in the hierarchy, you should attempt to flatten out the relational data so that you can build separate attributes for each level. The Analysis Services Parent/Child Dimension Naturalizer utility, available for download at `http://tinyurl.com/pcdimnat` and also incorporated in BIDS Helper, will help you do this. Note that designing a flattened dimension equivalent to a parent/child dimension can be a very time-consuming task, so consider building a true parent/child hierarchy, then using the above tool to naturalize it.

Ragged hierarchies with HideMemberIf

The alternative to using a parent/child hierarchy is to build a regular user hierarchy and then hide certain members in it to make it look ragged by setting the `HideMemberIf` property of a level. `HideMemberIf` has a number of possible settings: hide a member if it has no name, hide a member if it has the same name as its parent, hide a member if it has no name and is the only child, and hide a member if it has the same name as its parent and is the only child. A common situation when you would want to use this functionality is on a geography hierarchy with levels such as **Country**, **State**, **City** and **Customer**; some countries are subdivided into states but some aren't, so it would make no sense to show the **State** level for those countries; some countries are so small that it makes no sense to show either **State** or **City**. With data such as this:

Country	State	City	Customer
UK	Bucks	Amersham	Chris Webb
UK	Bucks	Amersham	Helen Lau
Italy	BI	Biella	Alberto Ferrari
Vatican	Vatican	Vatican	The Pope

We can then set `HideMemberIf` to **OnlyChildWithParentName** on the **State** and **City** levels of a user hierarchy, and so be able to show the user a hierarchy that looked like this:

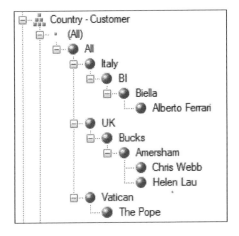

In order to make a ragged hierarchy display correctly in a client tool, we have to ensure that the client tool sets the following connection string property: `MDX Compatibility=2`
Unfortunately, some client tools do not allow you to do this, and will always display the members you wanted to hide in the hierarchy. For instance, Excel 2007 will always set `MDX Compatibility=1` in its connection strings, even if you edit the data source file manually yourself, so it will never show a ragged hierarchy properly.

Since the same column is used as the key and the name of an attribute in many cases, it's better to use the options which hide members when they have the same name as their parent rather than blank names. Blank names could mean empty strings are being used as keys, and this could in turn restrict your ability to build good attribute relationships. For example, if you had two customers in different countries but left both with empty strings for their **State** and **City**, the empty strings would be interpreted as the same distinct member (with an empty string as the name and key) which appeared under both countries. Therefore, you would be wrong to say there were one-to-many relationships between **Country** and **State** and **State** and **City**.

Using `HideMemberIf` on a ragged hierarchy also carries a query performance penalty, although in general, it still performs better than using a parent/child hierarchy.

Summary

In this chapter, we've discussed how to deal with some common problems we might face when designing our Analysis Services dimensions:

- Grouping and banding members and numeric values
- Slowly Changing Dimensions
- Junk Dimensions
- Ragged hierarchies

We've found that we can create new attributes on a dimension to group members and create bandings for numeric values using some simple SQL. This can have a positive impact on the user's experience. We've also found that with a bit of thought, the three different types of SCD can all be modeled satisfactorily. With ragged hierarchies we've learnt that the parent/child hierarchies are very flexible but have several problems, especially with query performance, and should be avoided where possible. We have also seen that using a regular user hierarchy and the `HideMemberIf` property is a better option, although not without its own limitations.

4
Measures and Measure Groups

With our dimensions designed, we can now turn our attention to the cube itself. Taking the basic version of the cube that the 'New Cube' wizard built for us as a starting point, we'll want to add all the dimensions we've built to it, add data from more than one measure group, and make sure that the measures in our cube always aggregate up the way we want them to. In this chapter we'll take a look at the following topics in detail:

- Useful properties to set on measures
- Measure aggregation types and other functionality that affects how measures aggregate
- Using multiple measure groups
- Setting up the relationships between measure groups and dimensions

Measures and aggregation

Measures are the numeric values that our users want to aggregate, slice, dice and otherwise analyze, and as a result, it's important to make sure they behave the way we want them to. One of the fundamental reasons for using Analysis Services is that, unlike a relational database it allows us to build into our cube design business rules about measures: how they should be formatted, how they should aggregate up, how they interact with specific dimensions and so on. It's therefore no surprise that we'll spend a lot of our cube development time thinking about measures.

Useful properties of measures

Apart from the `AggregateFunction` property of a measure, which we'll come to next, there are two other important properties we'll want to set on a measure, once we've created it.

Format String

The Format String property of a measure specifies how the raw value of the measure gets formatted when it's displayed in query results. Almost all client tools will display the formatted value of a measure, and this allows us to ensure consistent formatting of a measure across all applications that display data from our cube.

 A notable exception is Excel 2003 and earlier versions, which can only display raw measure values and not formatted values. Excel 2007 will display properly formatted measure values in most cases, but not all. For instance, it ignores the fourth section of the Format String which controls formatting for nulls. Reporting Services can display formatted values in reports, but doesn't by default; this blog entry describes how you can make it do so: `http://tinyurl.com/gregformatstring`

There are a number of built-in formats that you can choose from, and you can also build your own by using syntax very similar to the one used by Visual BASIC for Applications (VBA) for number formatting. The Books Online topic 'FORMAT_STRING Contents' gives a complete description of the syntax used.

Here are some points to bear in mind when setting the Format String property:

- If you're working with percentage values, using the `%` symbol will display your values multiplied by one hundred and add a percentage sign to the end. Note that only the display value gets multiplied by hundred—the real value of the measure will not be, so although your user might see a value of 98% the actual value of the cell would be 0.98.

- If you have a measure that returns null values in some circumstances and you want your users to see something other than null, don't try to use a MDX calculation to replace the nulls—this will cause severe query performance problems. You can use the fourth section of the Format String property to do this instead—for example, the following:

  `#,#.00;#,#.00;0;\N\A.`

  will display the string **NA** for null values, while keeping the actual cell value as null without affecting performance.

- Be careful while using the **Currency** built-in format: it will format values with the currency symbol for the locale specified in the `Language` property of the cube. This combination of the **Currency** format and the `Language` property is frequently recommended for formatting measures that contain monetary values, but setting this property will also affect the way number formats are displayed: for example, in the UK and the USA, the comma is used as a thousands separator, but in continental Europe it is used as a decimal separator. As a result, if you wanted to display a currency value to a user in a locale that didn't use that currency, then you could end up with confusing results. The value €100,101 would be interpreted as a value just over one hundred Euros to a user in France, but in the UK, it would be interpreted as a value of just over one hundred thousand Euros. You can use the desired currency symbol in a Format String instead, for example '$#,#.00', but this will not have an effect on the thousands and decimal separators used, which will always correspond to the Language setting. You can find an example of how to change the language property using a scoped assignment in the MDX Script here: `http://tinyurl.com/ssascurrency`.

- Similarly, while Analysis Services 2008 supports the translation of captions and member names for users in different locales, unlike in previous versions, it will not translate the number formats used. As a result, if your cube might be used by users in different locales you need to ensure they understand whichever number format the cube is using.

Display folders

Many cubes have a lot of measures on them, and as with dimension hierarchies, it's possible to group measures together into folders to make it easier for your users to find the one they want. Most, but not all, client tools support display folders, so it may be worth checking whether the one you intend to use does.

By default each measure group in a cube will have its own folder containing all of the measures on the measure group; these top level measure group folders cannot be removed and it's not possible to make a measure from one measure group appear in a folder under another measure group. By entering a folder name in a measure's `Display Folder` property, you'll make the measure appear in a folder underneath its measure group with that name; if there isn't already a folder with that name, then one will be created, and folder names are case-sensitive. You can make a measure appear under multiple folders by entering a semi-colon delimited list of names as follows: `Folder One; Folder Two`.

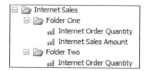

You can also create a folder hierarchy by entering either a forward-slash / or back-slash \ delimited list (the documentation contradicts itself on which is meant to be used—most client tools that support display folders support both) of folder names as follows: `Folder One; Folder Two\Folder Three`.

Calculated measures defined in the MDX Script can also be associated with a measure group, through the `Associated_Measure_Group` property, and with a display folder through the `Display_Folder` property. These properties can be set either in code or in Form View in the **Calculations** tab in the Cube Editor:

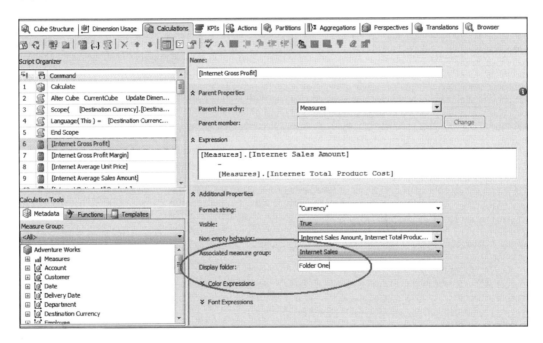

If you don't associate a calculated measure with a measure group, but do put it in a folder, the folder will appear at the same level as the folders created for each measure group.

Built-in measure aggregation types

The most important property of a measure is `AggregateFunction`; it controls how the measure aggregates up through each hierarchy in the cube. When you run an MDX query, you can think of it as being similar to a SQL SELECT statement with a GROUP BY clause—but whereas in SQL you have to specify an aggregate function to control how each column's values get aggregated, in MDX you specify this for each measure when the cube is designed.

Basic aggregation types

Anyone with a passing knowledge of SQL will understand the four basic aggregation types available when setting the `AggregateFunction` property:

- **Sum** is the commonest aggregation type to use, probably the one you'll use for 90% of all the measures. It means that the values for this measure will be summed up.

- **Count** is another commonly used property value and aggregates either by counting the overall number of rows from the fact table that the measure group is built from (when the **Binding Type** property, found on the Measure Source dialog that appears when you click on the **ellipses** button next to the `Source` property of a measure, is set to **Row Binding)**, or by counting non-null values from a specific measure column (when **Binding Type** property is set to **Column Binding**).

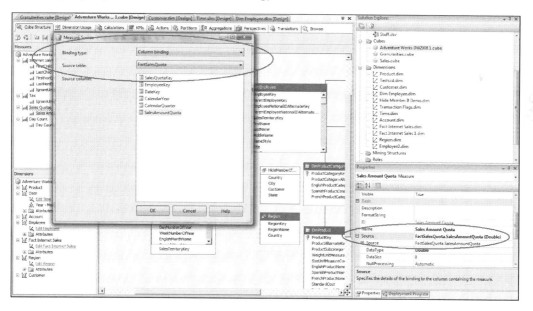

- **Min** and **Max** return the minimum and maximum measure values.

There isn't a built-in Average aggregation type—as we'll soon see, **AverageOfChildren** does not do a simple average—but it's very easy to create a calculated measure that returns an average by dividing a measure with AggregateFunction **Sum** by one with AggregateFunction **Count**, for example:

```
CREATE MEMBER CURRENTCUBE.[Measures].[Average Measure Example] AS
IIF([Measures].[Count Measure]=0, NULL,
[Measures].[Sum Measure]/[Measures].[Count Measure]);
```

Distinct Count

The **DistinctCount** aggregation type counts the number of distinct values in a column in your fact table, similar to a `Count(Distinct)` in SQL. It's generally used in scenarios where you're counting some kind of key, for example, finding the number of unique **Customers** who bought a particular product in a given time period. This is, by its very nature, an expensive operation for Analysis Services and queries that use **DistinctCount** measures can perform worse than those which use additive measures; we'll discuss performance tuning for **DistinctCount** in Chapter 9. It is possible to get distinct count values using MDX calculations but this almost always performs worse; it is also possible to use many-to-many dimensions (discussed in the next chapter) to get the same results and this may perform better in some circumstances; see the section on "Distinct Count" in the "Many to Many Revolution" white paper, available at `http://tinyurl.com/m2mrev`.)

When you create a new distinct count measure, BIDS will create a new measure group to hold it automatically. Each distinct count measure needs to be put into its own measure group for query performance reasons, and although it is possible to override BIDS and create a distinct count measure in an existing measure group with measures that have other aggregation types, we strongly recommend that you do not do this.

None

The **None** aggregation type simply means that no aggregation takes place on the measure at all. Although it might seem that a measure with this aggregation type displays no values at all, that's not true: it only contains values at the lowest possible granularity in the cube, at the intersection of the key attributes of all the dimensions. It's very rarely used, and only makes sense for values such as prices that should never be aggregated.

If you ever find that your cube seems to contain no data even though it has processed successfully, check to see if you have accidentally deleted the `Calculate` statement from the beginning of your MDX Script. Without this statement, no aggregation will take place within the cube and you'll only see data at the intersection of the leaves of every dimension, as if every measure had `AggregateFunction` **None**.

Semi-additive aggregation types

The semi-additive aggregation types are:

- **AverageOfChildren**
- **FirstChild**
- **LastChild**
- **FirstNonEmpty**
- **LastNonEmpty**

They behave the same as measures with aggregation type **Sum** on all dimensions except Time dimensions. In order to get Analysis Services to recognize a Time dimension, you'll need to have set the dimension's `Type` property to **Time** in the Dimension Editor.

> Sometimes you'll have multiple, role-playing Time dimensions in a cube, and if you have semi-additive measures, they'll be semi-additive for just one of these Time dimensions. In this situation, Analysis Services 2008 RTM uses the first Time dimension in the cube that has a relationship with the measure group containing the semi-additive measure. You can control the order of dimensions in the cube by dragging and dropping them in the Dimensions pane in the bottom left-hand corner of the Cube Structure tab of the Cube Editor; the following blog entry describes how to do this in more detail: `http://tinyurl.com/gregsemiadd`. However, this behavior has changed between versions in the past and may change again in the future.

Semi-additive aggregation is extremely useful when you have a fact table that contains snapshot data. For example, if you had a fact table containing information on the number of items in stock in a warehouse, then it would never make sense to aggregate these measures over time: if you had ten widgets in stock on January 1, eleven in stock on January 2, eight on January 3 and so on, the value you would want to display for the whole of January would never be the sum of the number of items in stock on each day in January. The value you do display depends on your organization's business rules.

Let's take a look at what each of the semi-additive measure values actually do:

- **AverageOfChildren** displays the average of all the values at the lowest level of granularity on the Time dimension. So, for example, if **Date** was the lowest level of granularity, when looking at a **Year** value, then Analysis Services would display the average value for all days in the year.
- **FirstChild** displays the value of the first time period at the lowest level of granularity, for example, the first day of the year.

- **LastChild** displays the value of the last time period at the lowest level of granularity, for example, the last day of the year.

- **FirstNonEmpty** displays the value of the first time period at the lowest level of granularity that is not empty, for example the first day of the year that has a value.

- **LastNonEmpty** displays the value of the last time period at the lowest level of granularity that is not empty, for example the last day of the year that has a value. This is the most commonly used semi-additive type; a good example of its use would be where the measure group contains data about stock levels in a warehouse, so when you aggregated along the Time dimension what you'd want to see is the amount of stock you had at the end of the current time period.

The following screenshot of an Excel pivot table illustrates how each of these semi-additive aggregation types works:

Row Labels	FirstChild	FirstNonEmpty	LastChild	LastNonEmpty
2003	99.98	99.98		49.99
July	99.98	99.98		49.99
2003-07-01	99.98	99.98	99.98	99.98
2003-07-02	49.99	49.99	49.99	49.99
2003-07-03				
2003-07-04				
2003-07-05				
2003-07-06				
2003-07-07	149.97	149.97	149.97	149.97
2003-07-08				
2003-07-09				
2003-07-10				
2003-07-11	49.99	49.99	49.99	49.99
2003-07-12				
2003-07-13	99.98	99.98	99.98	99.98
2003-07-14				
2003-07-15	49.99	49.99	49.99	49.99
2003-07-16				
2003-07-17				
2003-07-18				
2003-07-19	49.99	49.99	49.99	49.99
2003-07-20				
2003-07-21				
2003-07-22				
2003-07-23				
2003-07-24	49.99	49.99	49.99	49.99
2003-07-25				
2003-07-26				
2003-07-27				
2003-07-28				
2003-07-29				
2003-07-30				
2003-07-31				
Grand Total	99.98	99.98		49.99

Note that the semi-additive measures only have an effect above the lowest level of granularity on a Time dimension. For dates like July 17th in the screenshot above, where there is no data for the **Sum** measure, the **LastNonEmpty** measure still returns null and not the value of the last non-empty date.

The semi-additive measure aggregation types (and **None**) are only available in Enterprise Edition; it's possible to recreate the same functionality using MDX but query performance will not be quite as good. Here's an example of how you could overwrite the value of a measure with the `AggregateFunction` **Sum** by using an MDX Script assignment to make it behave in the same way as a **LastNonEmpty** measure:

```
SCOPE([Measures].[Sales Amount]);
    THIS = TAIL(
            NONEMPTY(
                {EXISTING [Date].[Date].[Date].MEMBERS}
                * [Measures].[Sales Amount])
            ,1).ITEM(0);
END SCOPE;
```

We may also find that the performance of **LastNonEmpty** is still not good enough, especially on very large cubes. It is not as fast as **LastChild**, so one trick we could try is to calculate the last non empty value for a measure in a new column in your fact table of your ETL. We can then create a new measure from this column, use the **LastChild** measure as its aggregation type, then set its `Visible` property to false and use an MDX Script something like the following to display the new measure's value above the leaf level for the original measure:

```
SCOPE([Measures].[Sales Amount], [Date].[Date].[All]);
    THIS = [Measures].[LastChild];
END SCOPE;
```

This assignment forces each time period to show the value of the last date within that time period. Typically, though, at the tail of your Date dimension you will have dates that have not occurred yet and which cannot contain any data—for example, if today's date is April 16th 2009, you might only have data in the cube up to April 15th, but the Date dimension will probably contain all of the dates up to December 31st 2009. For these future dates you'll either have to ensure your ETL populates the value of the **LastChild** measure up until the end of the current year or use another MDX Script assignment that is similar to the one described at the end of this blog entry: `http://tinyurl.com/gregsemiadd`.

By Account

A **Chart of Accounts** dimension is a feature common to many cubes containing financial data; in many ways it has a lot in common with the measures dimension, because each member on a Chart of Accounts dimension represents a different type of value such as profit and loss or balance sheet values for example. A Chart of Accounts dimension is often implemented with a parent/child hierarchy, and there are often complex business rules that govern how the members on the hierarchy should aggregate up, if they even do at all. Analysis Services provides several features to help you build and manage such a dimension, although it's widely accepted that building financial applications in Analysis Services is not as easy as it should be, or indeed as easy as it is in other OLAP servers.

The **ByAccount** aggregation type (available in Enterprise Edition only) is the first of these features we'll discuss, and it allows us to define different semi-additive behavior for a single measure for different members on the main hierarchy of a Chart of Accounts dimension. The steps to get it working are as follows:

- Create your Chart of Accounts dimension.

- Create another attribute that will be used to flag which members on the main hierarchy will use which semi-additive aggregation type. This should have one member for each type of attribute, where each member represents a different form of semi-additive behavior. Call it something like 'Account Type'.

- Set the following properties:
    - On the dimension itself, set the Type property to **Accounts**.
    - On the main hierarchy, set the Type property to **Account**.
    - On the Account Type attribute, set the Type property to **Account Type**.

- Define how each account type should aggregate. This can be done by right-clicking on the name of the project in the **Solution Explorer** in BIDS and selecting **Edit Database**. In this screen, in the **Account Type Mapping** table, the **Name** column contains the name of the built-in or user-defined account types and the **Alias** column contains a comma-delimited list of member names on the Account Type hierarchy that map to each account type, and **Aggregation Function** allows you to select either **Sum** or one of the semi-additive aggregation types for each account type.

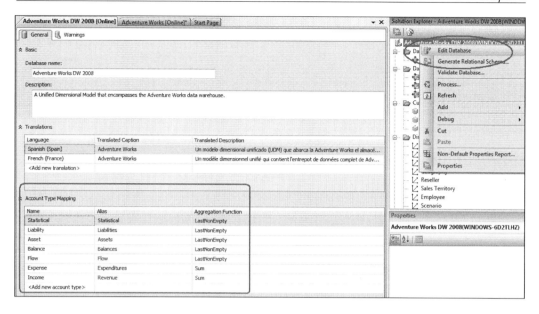

Most of this work can also be done by running the **Define Account Intelligence wizard**. To do this, go to the **Dimension** menu and select '**Add Business Intelligence**' and then select '**Define Account Intelligence**' from the list of available enhancements.

In our experience, the **ByAccount** aggregation type is very rarely used. This is partly because cube developers do not know about it, and partly because most financial applications need to implement more complex logic for aggregation than the built-in semi-additive aggregation types allow. This means that aggregation logic is usually implemented using MDX Script assignments, which give complete flexibility although at the expense of a lot of complexity and do not perform as well as the built-in aggregation types. Probably, the best compromise is to start off by using **ByAccount** and then for the accounts which need more complex aggregation, configure them to use **Sum** in the **Edit Database** screen and then use custom MDX for them.

Dimension calculations

In addition to the `AggregateFunction` property of a measure, there are many other ways of controlling how measures aggregate up. Apart from writing code in the MDX Script, (which we'll talk about in Chapter 6, although a full treatment of this topic is outside the scope of this book), these methods involve different types of dimension calculations.

Unary operators and weights

In a similar way to how you can control semi-additive aggregation with the **ByAccount** aggregation type, you can control how members on a hierarchy (usually parent/child, but not necessarily) aggregate up to their parents by defining unary operators. To do this, you must create a new column in your dimension table to hold the unary operator values and then set the attribute's `UnaryOperatorColumn` property to point to it.

The unary operators supported are:

- **+**, which means that the member's value contributes as a positive value to its parent's total
- **-**, which means that the member's value contributes as a negative value to its parent's total
- *****, which means that the member's value is multiplied with the value of the previous member in the level
- **/**, which means that the member's value is divided by the value of the previous member in the level
- **~** , which means the member's value is ignored when calculating the value of the parent
- Any numeric value, which works the same as + but where the numeric value is multiplied by the member's value first

Let's take a look at a simple example of this working. Once you've defined some unary operators, you can see which members have which operators in the **Browser** tab of the **Dimension Editor**:

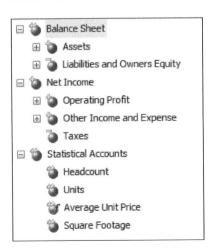

From this, we can see that the **All** member has three children. They are **Balance Sheet**, **Net Income** and **Statistical Accounts**. Since both **Balance Sheet** and **Statistical Accounts** have unary operator ~, **All** member's value is going to be the same as that of **Net Income**. Similarly, we can see that the value of **Net Income** itself will be calculated as follows: + (Operating Profit) + (Other Income and Expense) – (Taxes).

The distributive unary operators, that is + and -, perform much better than calculated members that do the equivalent addition and subtraction in MDX formulas.

Custom Member Formulas

Where unary operators do not give you enough control, you can assign an MDX expression to use to calculate the value for each member on an attribute hierarchy using Custom Member Formulas. To do this, we need to create a new column on our dimension table to hold the MDX expressions and then set the `CustomRollupColumn` property of the attribute to this column.

AccountDescription	AccountType	Operator	CustomMembers	ValueType
Average Unit Price	Balances	~	[Account].[Accounts].[Account Level 04].&[50]/[Account].[Accounts].[Account Level 02].&[97]	Currency
Balance Sheet		~		Currency
Assets	Assets	+		Currency
Current Assets	Assets	+		Currency
Cash	Assets	+		Currency
Receivables	Assets	+		Currency
Trade Receivables	Assets	+		Currency
Other Receivables	Assets	+		Currency
Allowance for Bad Debt	Assets	+		Currency

We can also create another column to hold property values that can be applied to each member on the hierarchy too, which then needs to be assigned in the `CustomRollupPropertiesColumn` property. The contents of this column takes the form of a comma-delimited list of property values, just as you would use at the end of a calculated member definition; for example, if a member had the following expression associated with it in the dimension table:

```
FORMAT_STRING='$#,#.00', BACK_COLOR=RGB(255,0,0)
```

then all values for that measure would have the Format String '$#,#.00' applied to them, and they would be displayed with a red cell background.

Custom Member Formulas offer something very similar to what you can do with MDX Script assignments, so what are the advantages and disadvantages of using them?

- In terms of query performance, Custom Member Formulas and MDX Script assignments are the same.

- As dimension calculations, Custom Member Formulas differ from MDX Script assignments in one important respect: they use the 'Closest Pass Wins' rule rather than the 'Last Pass Wins' rule when a cell's value can be calculated in two different ways from two different calculations. A description of how these rules work is outside the scope of this book (see the book *Microsoft SQL Server Analysis Services 2008 Unleashed (by Gorbach, Berger and Melomed)*, Chapter 13, for this) , but in some respects this means that Custom Member Formulas are easier to work with. You don't have the flexibility you have with MDX Script assignments, but you can always be sure that a member's value will be calculated using the formula you specify and not be accidentally overwritten by another assignment.

- Using Custom Member Formulas means the dimension becomes, in some respects, self-documenting. If the formulas are made visible to the end user somehow, perhaps by creating another attribute with `AttributeHierarchyEnabled`=**False** in the formula column, and the formulas are relatively simple, then users should be able to view and understand them.

- If a dimension with Custom Member Formulas is shared across multiple cubes, then these calculations are automatically applied to all of the cubes. With MDX Script assignments, the code would have to be duplicated across cubes.

- The major drawback to using Custom Member Formulas is that if you need to edit a calculation, you need to edit a value in a relational table. Not only is this inconvenient, it makes debugging calculations much more difficult and it means that your MDX code can be split between two places: the dimension table and the MDX Script.

Non-aggregatable values

In some rare cases, you may encounter non-aggregatable measures, that's to say measures whose aggregated values have to be supplied from the data warehouse and cannot be derived from lower granularity values. It's always worth asking why measures are non-aggregatable: in many cases, it's the result of some kind of pre-aggregation or calculation taking place during the ETL phase. While Analysis Services can handle non-aggregatable measures, it's much better at handling additive data, so if you can build your cube from the additive data, we recommend you do so, even if the data volumes end up being much larger.

However, if you do have to work with non-aggregatable measures, one way of handling them is by using parent/child hierarchies (we'll talk about another approach later on in this chapter). Every non-leaf member on a parent/child hierarchy has an extra, system-generated child called a datamember, and you can control the visibility of these datamembers by setting the MembersWithData property on the parent/child hierarchy. If your fact table contains values for a non-leaf member on a parent/child hierarchy, then these values will in fact be assigned to the member's datamember; by default, the real non-leaf member's values will then be aggregated from its children and its datamember. This can be seen in the following screenshot from Excel:

Row Labels	Sales Amount Quota		
⊟ Sánchez	95714000		
⊟ Welcker	95714000		
⊞ Abbas	1892000		
⊟ Alberts	19234000	←	Non-leaf Member
Alberts	876000	←	DataMember
Pak	10514000		
Valdez	2287000		Child Members
Varkey Chudukatil	5557000		
⊞ Jiang	74588000		

In order to display non-aggregatable values, all you need to do is to use an MDX Script assignment to make each non-leaf member on your parent/child hierarchy display just the value of its datamember, for example:

```
SCOPE([Measures].[Sales Amount Quota]);
    THIS=[Employee].[Employees].CURRENTMEMBER.DATAMEMBER;
END SCOPE;
```

This code would have the following effect on our Excel example:

Row Labels	Sales Amount Quota		
⊟ Sánchez			
⊟ Welcker			
⊟ Alberts	876000	←	Non-leaf member
Alberts	876000	←	Datamember
Pak	10514000		
Valdez	2287000		Child members
Varkey Chudukatil	5557000		

As you can see, the value of the non-leaf member **Alberts** is now no longer the sum of its children and its datamember, but that of its datamember alone.

For more details on working with non-aggregatable values and parent/child hierarchies, see the following paper written by Richard Tkachuk: `http://tinyurl.com/nonaggdata`

Measure groups

All but the simplest data warehouses will contain multiple fact tables, and Analysis Services allows you to build a single cube on top of multiple fact tables through the creation of multiple measure groups. These measure groups can contain different dimensions and be at different granularities, but so long as you model your cube correctly, your users will be able to use measures from each of these measure groups in their queries easily and without worrying about the underlying complexity.

Creating multiple measure groups

To create a new measure group in the **Cube Editor**, go to the **Cube Structure** tab and right-click on the cube name in the **Measures** pane and select 'New Measure Group'. You'll then need to select the fact table to create the measure group from and then the new measure group will be created; any columns that aren't used as foreign key columns in the DSV will automatically be created as measures, and you'll also get an extra measure of aggregation type **Count**. It's a good idea to delete any measures you are not going to use at this stage.

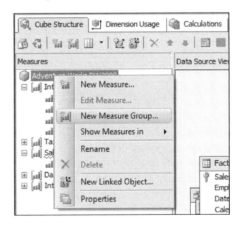

Once you've created a new measure group, BIDS will try to set up relationships between it and any existing dimensions in your cube based on the relationships you've defined in your DSV. Since doing this manually can be time-consuming, this is another great reason for defining relationships in the DSV. You can check the relationships that have been created on the **Dimension Usage** tab of the **Cube Editor**:

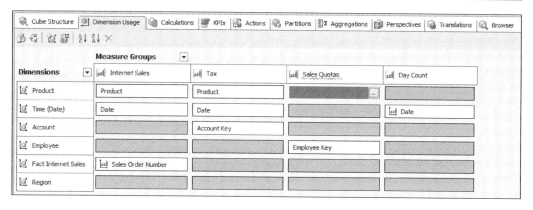

In Analysis Services 2005, it was true in some cases that query performance was better on cubes with fewer measure groups, and that breaking a large cube with many measure groups up into many smaller cubes with only one or two measure groups could result in faster queries. This is no longer the case in Analysis Services 2008. Although there are other reasons why you might want to consider creating separate cubes for each measure group, this is still something of a controversial subject amongst Analysis Services developers. The advantages of a single cube approach are:

- All of your data is in one place. If your users need to display measures from multiple measure groups, or you need to create calculations that span measure groups, everything is already in place.

- You only have one cube to manage security and calculations on; with multiple cubes the same security and calculations might have to be duplicated.

The advantages of the multiple cube approach are:

- If you have a complex cube but have to use Standard Edition, you cannot use Perspectives to hide complexity from your users. In this case, creating multiple cubes might be a more user-friendly approach.

- Depending on your requirements, security might be easier to manage with multiple cubes. It's very easy to grant or deny a role access to a cube; it's much harder to use dimension security to control which measures and dimensions in a multi-measure group cube a role can access.

- If you have complex calculations, especially MDX Script assignments, it's too easy to write a calculation that has an effect on part of the cube you didn't want to alter. With multiple cubes, the chances of this happening are reduced.

Creating measure groups from dimension tables

Measure groups don't always have to be created from fact tables. In many cases, it can be useful to build measure groups from dimension tables too. One common scenario where you might want to do this is when you want to create a measure that counts the number of days in the currently selected time period, so if you had selected a year on your Time dimension's hierarchy, the measure would show the number of days in the year. You could implement this with a calculated measure in MDX, but it would be hard to write code that worked in all possible circumstances, such as when a user multi-selects time periods. In fact, it's a better idea to create a new measure group from your Time dimension table containing a new measure with `AggregateFunction` **Count**, so you're simply counting the number of days as the number of rows in the dimension table. This measure will perform faster and always return the values you expect. This post on Mosha Pasumansky's blog discusses the problem in more detail: `http://tinyurl.com/moshadays`

MDX formulas vs pre-calculating values

If you can somehow model a calculation into the structure of your cube, or perform it in your ETL, you should do so in preference to doing it in MDX only so long as you do not compromise the functionality of your cube. A pure MDX approach will be the most flexible and maintainable since it only involves writing code, and if calculation logic needs to change, then you just need to redeploy your updated MDX Script; doing calculations upstream in the ETL can be much more time-consuming to implement and if you decide to change your calculation logic, then it could involve reloading one or more tables. However, an MDX calculation, even one that is properly tuned, will of course never perform as well as a pre-calculated value or a regular measure. The day count measure, discussed in the previous paragraph, is a perfect example of where a cube-modeling approach trumps MDX. If your aim was to create a measure that showed average daily sales, though, it would make no sense to try to pre-calculate all possible values since that would be far too time-consuming and would result in a non-aggregatable measure. The best solution here would be a hybrid: create real measures for sales and day count, and then create an MDX calculated measure that divided the former by the latter. However, it's always necessary to consider the type of calculation, the volume of data involved and the chances of the calculation algorithm changing in the future before you can make an informed decision on which approach to take.

Handling different dimensionality

When you have different measure groups in a cube, they are almost always going to have different dimensions associated with them; indeed, if you have measure groups that have identical dimensionality, you might consider combining them into a single measure group if it is convenient to do so. As we've already seen, the **Dimension Usage** tab shows us which dimensions have relationships with which measure groups.

When a dimension has a relationship with a measure group it goes without saying that making a selection on that dimension will affect the values that are displayed for measures on that measure group. But what happens to measures when you make a selection on a dimension that has no relationship with a measure group? In fact, you have two options here, controlled by the IgnoreUnrelatedDimensions property of a measure group:

- IgnoreUnrelatedDimensions=**False** displays a null value for all members below the root (the intersection of all of the All Members or default members on every hierarchy) of the dimension, except the Unknown member, or

- IgnoreUnrelatedDimensions=**True** repeats the value displayed at the root of the dimension for every member on every hierarchy of the dimension. This is the default state.

The screenshot below shows what happens for two otherwise identical measures from measure groups which have IgnoreUnrelatedDimensions set to **True** and to **False** when they're displayed next to a dimension they have no relationship with:

Values		
Row Labels ▼	IgnoreUnrelatedDimensions True	IgnoreUnrelatedDimensions False
⊟Sánchez	29358677.22	29358677.22
⊞Bradley	29358677.22	
Bradley	29358677.22	
⊞Duffy	29358677.22	
⊞Hamilton	29358677.22	
⊞Krebs	29358677.22	
⊞Norman	29358677.22	
Norman	29358677.22	
Sánchez	29358677.22	
⊞Trenary	29358677.22	
⊞Welcker	29358677.22	
Unknown	29358677.22	29358677.22

It's usually best to keep `IgnoreUnrelatedDimensions` set to **True** since if the users are querying measures from multiple measure groups, then they don't want some of their selected measures suddenly returning null if they slice by a dimension that has a regular relationship with their other selected measures.

Handling different granularities

Even when measure groups share the same dimensions, they may not share the same granularity. For example, we may hold sales information in one fact table down to the day level, but also hold sales quotas in another fact table at the quarter level. If we created measure groups from both these fact tables, then they would both have regular relationships with our Time dimension but at different granularities.

Normally, when you create a regular relationship between a dimension and a measure group, Analysis Services will join the columns specified in the `KeyColumns` property of the key attribute of the dimension with the appropriate foreign key columns of the fact table (note that during processing, Analysis Services won't usually do the join in SQL, it does it internally). However, when you have a fact table of a higher granularity, you need to change the granularity attribute property of the relationship to choose the attribute from the dimension you do want to join on instead:

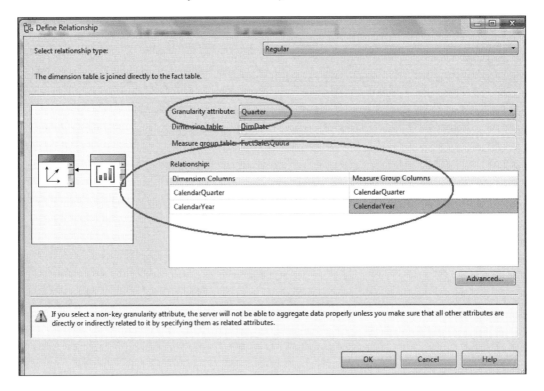

In the previous screenshot, we can see an amber warning triangle telling us that by selecting a non-key attribute, the server may have trouble aggregating measure values. What does this mean exactly? Let's take a look at the attribute relationships defined on our Time dimension again:

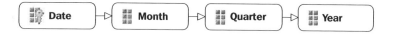

If we're loading data at the Quarter level, what do we expect to see at the Month and Date level? We can only expect to see useful values at the level of the granularity attribute we've chosen, and for only those attributes whose values can be derived from that attribute; this is yet another good reason to make sure your attribute relationships have been optimized. Below the granularity attribute, we've got the same options regarding what gets displayed as we had with dimensions that have no relationship at all with a measure group: either repeated values or null values. The `IgnoreUnrelatedDimensions` property is again used to control this behavior.

Unfortunately, the default **True** setting for `IgnoreUnrelatedDimensions` is usually not the option you want to use in this scenario (users usually prefer to see nulls below the granularity of a measure in our experience) and this may conflict with how we want to set `IgnoreUnrelatedDimensions` to control the behavior of dimensions which have no relationship with a measure group. There are ways of resolving this conflict such as using MDX Script assignments to set cell values to null or by using the `ValidMeasure()` MDX function, but none are particularly elegant.

Non-aggregatable measures: a different approach

We've already seen how we can use parent/child hierarchies to load non-aggregatable measure values into our cube. However, given the problems associated with using parent/child hierarchies and knowing what we now know about measure groups, let's consider a different approach to solving this problem.

A non-aggregatable measure will have, by its very nature, data stored for many different granularities of a dimension. Rather than storing all of these different granularities of values in the same fact table (which is something Ralph Kimball would frown on anyway), we could create multiple fact tables for each granularity of value. Having built measure groups from these fact tables, we would then be able to join our dimension to each of them with a regular relationship but at different granularities.

We'd then be in the position of having multiple measures representing the different granularities of a single, logical measure. What we actually want is a single non-aggregatable measure, and we can get this by using MDX Script assignments to combine the different granularities. Let's say we have a regular (non-parent/child) dimension called **Employee** with three attributes **Manager**, **Team Leader** and **Sales Person**, and a logical non-aggregatable measure called **Sales Quota** appearing in three measure groups as three measures called **Sales Amount Quota_Manager**, **Sales Amount Quota_TeamLead** and **Sales Amount Quota** for each of these three granularities. Here's a screenshot showing what a query against this cube would show at this stage:

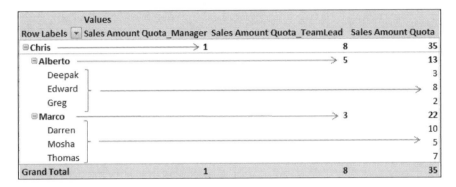

We can combine the three measures into one like this:

```
SCOPE([Measures].[Sales Amount Quota]);
    SCOPE([Employee].[Salesperson].[All]);
        THIS=[Measures].[Sales Amount Quota_TeamLead];
    END SCOPE;
    SCOPE([Employee].[Team Lead].[All]);
        THIS=[Measures].[Sales Amount Quota_Manager];
    END SCOPE;
END SCOPE;
```

This code takes the lowest granularity measure **Sales Amount Quota**, and then overwrites it twice: the first assignment replaces all of the values above the **Sales Person** granularity with the value of the measure containing **Sales Amount Quota** for **Team Leaders**; the second assignment then replaces all of the values above the **Team Leader** granularity with the value of the measure containing **Sales Quotas** for **Managers**. Once we've set `Visible`=**False** for the **Sales Amount Quota_TeamLead** and **Sales Amount Quota_Manager** measures, we're left with just the **Sales Amount Quota** measure visible, thus displaying the non-aggregatable values that we wanted. The user would then see this:

Row Labels ▼	Sales Amount Quota
⊟ **Chris**	1
⊟ **Alberto**	5
Deepak	3
Edward	8
Greg	2
⊟ **Marco**	3
Darren	10
Mosha	5
Thomas	7
Grand Total	1

Using linked dimensions and measure groups

Creating linked dimensions and measure groups allows you to share the same dimensions and measure groups across separate Analysis Services databases, and the same measure group across multiple cubes. To do this, all you need to do is to run the 'New Linked Object' wizard from the Cube Editor, either by clicking on the button in the toolbar on the Cube Structure or Dimension Usage tabs, or by selecting it from the right-click menu in the Measures pane of the Cube Structure tab.

Doing this has the advantage of reducing the amount of processing and maintenance needed: instead of having many identical dimensions and measure groups to maintain and keep synchronized, all of which need processing separately, you can have a single object which only needs to be changed and processed once. At least that's the theory—in practice, linked objects are not as widely used as they could be because there are a number of limitations in their use:

- Linked objects represent a static snapshot of the metadata of the source object, and any changes to the source object are not passed through to the linked object. So for example, if you create a linked dimension and then add an attribute to the source dimension, you then have to delete and recreate the linked dimension—there's no option to refresh a linked object.

- You can also import the calculations defined in the MDX Script of the source cube using the wizard. However, you can only import the entire script and this may include references to objects present in the source cube that aren't in the target cube, and which may need to be deleted to prevent errors. The calculations that remain will also need to be updated manually when those in the source cube are changed, and if there are a lot, this can add an unwelcome maintenance overhead.

- A linked measure group can only be used with dimensions from the same database as the source measure group. This isn't a problem when you're sharing measure groups between cubes in the same database, but could be if you wanted to share measure groups across databases.

- As you would expect, when you query a linked measure group, your query is redirected to the source measure group. If the source measure group is on a different server, this may introduce some latency and hurt query performance. Analysis Services does try to mitigate this by doing some caching on the linked measure group's database, though. By default, it will cache data on a per-query basis, but if you change the `RefreshPolicy` property from **ByQuery** to **ByInterval** you can specify a time limit for data to be held in cache.

Linked objects can be useful when cube development is split between multiple development teams, or when you need to create multiple cubes containing some shared data, but, in general, we recommend against using them widely because of these limitations.

Role-playing dimensions

It's also possible to add the same dimension to a cube more than once, and give each instance a different relationship to the same measure group. For example, in our Sales fact table, we might have several different foreign key columns that join to our Time dimension table: one which holds the date an order was placed on, one which holds the date it was shipped from the warehouse, and one which holds the date the order should arrive with the customer. In Analysis Services, we can create a single physical Time dimension in our database, which is referred to as a **database dimension**, and then add it three times to the cube to create three 'cube dimensions', renaming each cube dimension to something like Order Date, Ship Date and Due Date. These three cube dimensions are referred to as role-playing dimensions: the same dimension is playing three different roles in the same cube.

Role playing dimensions are a very useful feature. They reduce maintenance overheads because you only need to edit one dimension, and unlike linked dimensions, any changes made to the underlying database dimension are propagated to all of the cube dimensions that are based on it. They also reduce processing time because you only need to process the database dimension once. However, there is one frustrating limitation with role-playing dimensions and that is that while you can override certain properties of the database dimension on a per-cube dimension basis, you can't change the name of any of the attributes or hierarchies of a cube dimension. So if you have a user hierarchy called 'Calendar' on your database dimension, all of your cube dimensions will also have a user hierarchy called 'Calendar', and your users might find it difficult to tell which hierarchy is which in certain client tools (Excel 2003 is particularly bad in this respect) or in reports. Unfortunately, we have seen numerous cases where this problem alone meant role-playing dimensions couldn't be used.

Dimension/measure group relationships

So far we've seen dimensions either having no relationship with a measure group or having a regular relationship, but that's not the whole story: there are many different types of relationships that a dimension can have with a measure group. Here's the complete list:

- No relationship
- Regular
- Fact
- Referenced
- Many-to-Many
- Data Mining

We'll discuss many-to-many relationships in the next chapter because they are an important topic on their own, but before that let's talk briefly about the relationship types we've not seen so far.

Fact relationships

Fact or degenerate dimensions are, as we saw in Chapter 1, dimensions that are built directly from columns in a fact table, not from a separate dimension table. From an Analysis Services dimension point of view, they are no different from any other kind of dimension, except that there is a special fact relationship type that a dimension can have with a measure group. There are in fact very few differences between a fact relationship and a regular relationship, and they are:

- A fact relationship will result in marginally more efficient SQL being generated when the fact dimension is used in ROLAP drillthrough, a subject we'll discuss in much more detail in the next chapter.

- Fact relationships are visible to client tools in the cube's metadata, so client tools may choose to display fact dimensions differently.

- A fact relationship can only be defined on dimensions and measure groups that are based on the same table in the DSV.

- A measure group can only have a fact relationship with one database dimension. It can have more than one fact relationship, but all of them have to be with cube dimensions based on the same database dimension.

It still makes sense though to define relationships as fact relationships when you can. Apart from the reasons given above, the functionality might change in future versions of Analysis Services and fact relationship types might be further optimized in some way.

Referenced relationships

A referenced relationship is where a dimension joins to a measure group through another dimension. For example, you might have a Customer dimension that includes geographic attributes up to and including a customer's country; also, your organization might divide the world up into international regions such as North America, Europe, Middle East and Africa (EMEA), Latin America (LATAM) and Asia-Pacific and so on for financial reporting, and you might build a dimension for this too. If your sales fact table only contained a foreign key for the Customer dimension, but you wanted to analyze sales by international region, you would be able to create a referenced relationship from the Region dimension through the Customer dimension to the Sales measure group.

When setting up a referenced relationship in the **Define Relationship** dialog in the **Dimension Usage** tab, you're asked to first choose the dimension that you wish to join through and then which attribute on the reference dimension joins to which attribute on the intermediate dimension:

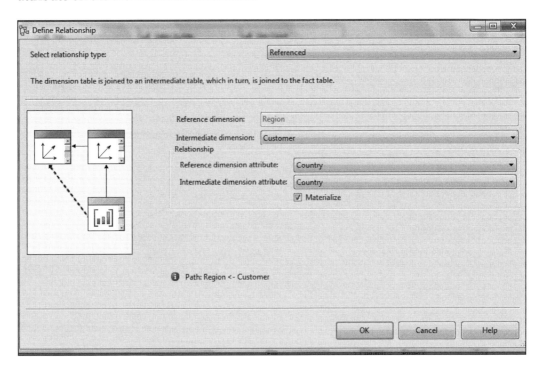

When the join is made between the attributes you've chosen on the reference dimension, once again it's the values in the columns that are defined in the `KeyColumns` property of each attribute that you're in fact joining on.

The **Materialize** checkbox is automatically checked, and this ensures maximum query performance by resolving the join between the dimensions at processing time—which, as mentioned in Chapter 1, can lead to a significant decrease in processing performance. Unchecking this box means that no penalty is paid at processing time but query performance may be worse.

The question you may well be asking yourself at this stage is: why bother to use referenced relationships at all? It is in fact a good question to ask, because, in general, it's better to include all of the attributes you need in a single Analysis Services dimension built from multiple tables rather than use a referenced relationship. The single dimension approach will perform better and is more user-friendly: for example, you can't define user hierarchies that span a reference dimension and its intermediate dimension.

That said, there are situations where referenced relationships are useful because it's simply not feasible to add all of the attributes you need to a dimension. You might have a Customer dimension, for instance, that has a number of attributes representing dates—the date of a customer's first purchase, the date of a customer's tenth purchase, the date of a customer's last purchase and so on. If you had created these attributes with keys that matched the surrogate keys of your Time dimension, you could create multiple, referenced (but not materialized) role-playing Time dimensions joined to each of these attributes that would give you the ability to analyze each of these dates. You certainly wouldn't want to duplicate all of the attributes from your Time dimension for each of these dates in your Customer dimension. Another good use for referenced relationships is when you want to create multiple parent/child hierarchies from the same dimension table, as discussed in Chapter 3.

Data mining relationships

The data mining functionality of Analysis Services is outside the scope of this book, so we won't spend much time on the data mining relationship type. Suffice to say that when you create an Analysis Services mining structure from data sourced from a cube, you have the option of using that mining structure as the source for a special type of dimension, called a data mining dimension. The wizard will also create a new cube containing linked copies of all of the dimensions and measure groups in the source cube, plus the new data mining dimension, which then has a data mining relationships with the measure groups.

Summary

In this chapter, we've looked more closely at the problems we're likely to face when designing real-world cubes. We saw how to configure measures to aggregate in the way we wanted, how to create new measure groups and handle the problems of different dimensionality and granularity, and we've started to look at the different types of relationships that are possible between dimensions and measure groups. In the next chapter we'll continue with that theme and explore drillthrough (which is related to the topic of fact relationships) and many-to-many relationships.

5
Adding Transactional Data such as Invoice Line and Sales Reason

In this chapter we will analyze how to add detailed information about each transaction in a fact table, such as invoice document and line number. We'll compare the use of MOLAP and ROLAP dimensions for this purpose, and we will use the drillthrough feature to expose this data to the end user. We will also explain the reason why this approach is better than exposing a large dimension directly to the end user.

In the second part of this chapter we will add to the sales cube a dimension that describes the reasons for a sale. Since each sale can have multiple reasons associated with it, we will make use of the many-to-many dimensions relationship feature of Analysis Services, discussing its properties and possible performance issues. We will also take a brief look at possible modeling patterns available using many-to-many dimensions relationships.

Details about transactional data

The goal of a multidimensional cube is to analyze aggregated data across several dimensions. However, when there is some interesting data, the user might be interested in drilling down to a lower level of detail. For example, when it comes to sales analysis, it could be interesting to look at the individual invoices that caused a particular high volume of sales in a single month. This is a very common request for end users to make – in fact, the question is not if the users will need this, but when.

One approach to solve this issue is to add a regular dimension to the cube which has the same granularity as the fact table – as we saw in Chapter 2, this is referred to as a **Fact dimension**. Using columns on the fact table like invoice number, invoice line number, notes and so on, we can link each fact sale with a dimension member, calling the dimension itself something like "Document". At this point, the end users will have a dimension that can be used with other one. If they filter by a particular month in their client tool and put the Invoice Number attribute of the Document dimension on rows, the resulting query will display the list of invoices of that particular month. However, this is not a good idea.

The most important reason to avoid making a fact dimension navigable to end users is performance. Adding a large dimension to the cube (and a dimension with a granularity near to the fact table like Document will be always large) increases the multidimensional space that can be queried. The Analysis Services engine might spend a lot of time filtering the visible members of the Document dimension, and this could be critical when the query involves calculated members or other MDX calculations. The performance of this type of scenario has been improved in Analysis Services 2008 if compared to 2005. However, even if the query were lightning fast, there is still an issue for the client tool: before making a query, many client tools get all cube and dimension metadata to populate their navigation controls. A Document dimension might have millions of members on a single attribute, with no possible hierarchies to group them. Getting this metadata will slow down the client tools even before the user is able to query the cube. Some client tools are able to handle large dimensions quite well, but the original problem is always the same: why should we expose a dimension when we really don't need to navigate it?

If we consider the original requirement carefully, there is a similarity between the need to get information at the transaction level and the need to get descriptive properties of an attribute member of a dimension. When we see a member on the Customer hierarchy, we might want to see the customer's phone number, their picture, or their address on a map, but this information will never be used as the filter in a query. For this reason we should set the `AttributeHierarchyEnabled` property of all these descriptive attributes to false: this means they are only visible as properties of a Customer member. The need to see transaction details is somewhat similar, with the difference that the information is related to each single row of the fact table. Analysis Services offers the Drillthrough feature, which should satisfy this kind of need. However, this functionality is not perfect in its actual implementation. There are limitations in its use and you'll often encounter performance issues using it. In the next section, we will describe how to use drillthrough in the most effective way.

Drillthrough

In conceptual terms, the drillthrough feature of Analysis Services allows you to retrieve data at the fact table granularity for any multidimensional tuple. From a practical point of view, when users look at a pivot table result, they can request the list of fact table rows that are aggregated into any specific cell in the result set. For example, the next figure shows the sales of a particular month divided by product categories and regions.

With Excel 2007, when you double click on a cell (for instance the sales of Accessories in Europe, which value is 1,140.65) a DRILLTHROUGH query is sent to Analysis Services and the result is shown in a new worksheet, returning the list of fact table rows that correspond to that cell, as shown in the next screenshot.

The drillthrough operation differs from a generic drill-down because it is intended to retrieve a set of rows from the relational source data that have been aggregated into a single cell, while drill-down typically operates on pre-defined hierarchies of data. While drill-down navigates in a multidimensional space returning a "cellset" (a sort of array with usually two or three dimensions), the drillthrough goes directly to the lowest granularity of data.

In terms of MDX language, there is a specific keyword for this purpose: DRILLTHROUGH. It precedes an MDX SELECT statement that has to return only one cell, which is the one to be expanded with the drillthrough operation.

What is happening behind the scenes? From an MDX point of view, the DRILLTHROUGH query can be built by the client using any attributes from any of the dimensions in the cube. From a functional point of view, the choice of the columns to display can be customized defining Drillthrough Actions on the cube. Next, we will start describing how to define drillthrough actions and how to customize them. Later, we will describe the DRILLTHROUGH operation in detail and how to model the cube and its dimensions to better leverage this feature.

Actions

Before we start, let's take a brief look at what we can do with Actions. Actions are pieces of metadata that are passed to the client to customize the user interface, offering the possibility to perform specific operations in a context-related way. For example, with an action you tell a client tool that when a user clicks on the name of a City in a Geography dimension it should open up a web browser with a given URL, generated by Analysis Services, to display a map of that particular city. An action defines a target (the part of the cube on which it can be activated), a condition (an MDX expression that must result true to make the action usable) and a set of parameters that define what action is required.

There are three types of actions:

- **Generic Action**: is a general purpose action with a specific action type, which can be:
  - URL
  - Rowset
  - DataSet
  - Proprietary
  - Statement

- **Reporting Action**: generates a link to a report stored in an instance of SQL Server Reporting Services, and pass parameters to that report that are generated using context-sensitive MDX expressions
- **Drillthrough Action**: executes a DRILLTHROUGH query using the cell on which the action has been called as a reference for the drillthrough

URL and Reporting actions are very commonly used to link external reporting systems to cubes, and allow you not to have to worry too much about what client will be used to navigate the cube.

Drillthrough actions are used to bring data back into the client tool, instead of for linking to an external resource. For example, when calling a drillthrough action in Excel 2007, a DRILLTHROUGH query is executed and a new worksheet is created to display what it returns to the end user. Note that Excel 2003 does not directly support drillthrough operations.

It is not our goal to cover action types other than drillthrough; for more information on them, please refer to Books Online.

Drillthrough actions

The definition of a drillthrough action on a cube is simply a set of metadata that is passed to the client. This metadata defines a set of columns that will be used by the client to build the DRILLTHROUGH statement that will be sent back to the server. There is no direct DRILLTHROUGH statement generation made in this metadata, except for the default drillthrough setting that we will cover later in this section. In the following figure we can see the **Actions** panel displaying the settings for a new Drillthrough Action. We will refer to the action field names in the following part of this section.

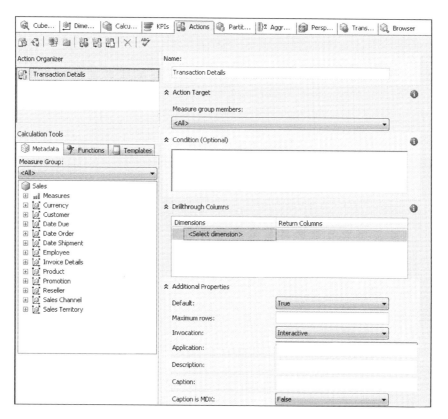

The **Action Target** defines the measure group on which the action can be used. If we define <**All**>, then every measure group will have this drillthrough action available, otherwise we can limit the action to all the measures of a single measure group in the cube. The **Condition** property defines an optional MDX expression that is evaluated on a cell to evaluate whether the action can be used on that cell or not (for example, we might limit the measures on which the drillthrough operates inside a specific measure group). It is not common to use this property for a drillthrough action, while it could be helpful to limit the display of URL or Reporting actions in cases where there is data available for the selected cell.

The Drillthrough Columns property is the most important one. We can specify one or more dimensions belonging to the cube and for each one we can specify one or more attributes that will be used as columns in the result. We can choose only attributes that have the `AttributeHierarchyEnabled` property set to true.

We will not go into the details of the properties in the **Additional Properties** section, except for the **Default** property. We should set the **Default** property to **True** for only one Drillthrough Action per measure group. This defines the default action for that measure group.

Excel 2007 allows you to execute a default drillthrough action by double-clicking a cell in a pivot table. This operation will execute the default Drillthrough Action for the measure group to which the selected measure belongs. However, even if there are no Drillthrough Actions defined, Excel 2007 will generate a drillthrough operation by asking for all the measures of the relevant measure group, plus the key attribute for each related dimension. We can disable all drillthrough operations on the server through role security. We can define whether a specific Drillthrough Action is enabled or not for a particular user by using the Condition property (there is an example at `http://tinyurl.com/actioncondition`). However, disabling all Drillthrough Actions for a user in this way does not prevent them from sending a DRILLTHROUGH statement to the server.

If we have more than one default Drillthrough Action defined for a measure group, only the first one will be used as the default. Thus, it makes sense to define a default drillthrough action for the <All> measure groups option at the end of the **Measure Group Members** dropdown list, which will be used as the default drillthrough action if one has not been defined for a particular measure group.

After we have defined new actions or updated existing ones, we can deploy the new version of our cube without needing to reprocess it. Actions operate only on cube metadata and do not have any effect on cube data.

Drillthrough Columns order

The user interface of the **Actions** pane has some limitations: for instance, we cannot modify the order of the Drillthrough Columns—they will always be displayed in the same order as the dimensions are shown in the list. Moreover, we do not have control over the order of the columns displayed for each dimension: they are always shown in the same order as the attributes they relate to are defined. The combination of these limitations can be very annoying. It is common to have drillthrough actions that return many columns and we might want to control the order that these columns are displayed, just to improve readability when the user get the results of the drillthrough.

The good news is that these limitations only exist in the user interface of the Actions pane. In our Visual Studio project, the cube is defined as an XML file with the `.cube` extension. We can open it by right-clicking the cube in the **Solution Explorer** and then choosing the **View Code** menu item. This file can be modified to get the desired order for **Drillthrough Columns**, but this manual modification will be lost if we will further modify the action using the Action pane.

For example, consider the **Drillthrough Columns** setting shown in the following figure. It will return drillthrough columns in the order: **Sales Amount**, **Tax Amount**, **Product**, **Category**, and finally **List Price**.

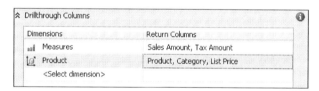

This is the XML produced by the settings above – we can easily find the Actions definitions by looking for the `<Actions>` tag in a cube file.

```
<Actions>
<Action xsi:type="DrillThroughAction">
  <ID>Drillthrough Action</ID>
  <Name>Sales Details</Name>
  <TargetType>Cells</TargetType>
  <Target>MeasureGroupMeasures("Sales")</Target>
  <Type>DrillThrough</Type>
  <Default>true</Default>
  <Columns>
    <Column xsi:type="MeasureBinding">
      <MeasureID>Sales Amount</MeasureID>
    </Column>
    <Column xsi:type="MeasureBinding">
```

```
        <MeasureID>Tax Amount</MeasureID>
      </Column>
      <Column xsi:type="CubeAttributeBinding">
        <CubeID>Adv DM 1</CubeID>
        <CubeDimensionID>Product</CubeDimensionID>
        <AttributeID>Products</AttributeID>
        <Type>All</Type>
      </Column>
      <Column xsi:type="CubeAttributeBinding">
        <CubeID>Adv DM 1</CubeID>
        <CubeDimensionID>Product</CubeDimensionID>
        <AttributeID>Category</AttributeID>
        <Type>All</Type>
      </Column>
      <Column xsi:type="CubeAttributeBinding">
        <CubeID>Adv DM 1</CubeID>
        <CubeDimensionID>Product</CubeDimensionID>
        <AttributeID>List Price</AttributeID>
        <Type>All</Type>
      </Column>
    </Columns>
  </Action>
</Actions>
```

As we can see, the XML definition does not have constraints that force the columns of the same dimension to stay grouped together. In fact, we can move the columns in any order. For example, the following XML shows us how to arrange the columns definition to get the order Sales Amount, Product, List Price, Tax Amount, and Category.

```
<Actions>
<Action xsi:type="DrillThroughAction">
  <ID>Drillthrough Action</ID>
  <Name>Sales Details</Name>
  <TargetType>Cells</TargetType>
  <Target>MeasureGroupMeasures("Sales")</Target>
  <Type>DrillThrough</Type>
  <Default>true</Default>
  <Columns>
    <Column xsi:type="MeasureBinding">
      <MeasureID>Sales Amount</MeasureID>
    </Column>
    <Column xsi:type="CubeAttributeBinding">
      <CubeID>Adv DM 1</CubeID>
      <CubeDimensionID>Product</CubeDimensionID>
```

```
      <AttributeID>Products</AttributeID>
      <Type>All</Type>
    </Column>
    <Column xsi:type="CubeAttributeBinding">
      <CubeID>Adv DM 1</CubeID>
      <CubeDimensionID>Product</CubeDimensionID>
      <AttributeID>List Price</AttributeID>
      <Type>All</Type>
    </Column>
    <Column xsi:type="MeasureBinding">
      <MeasureID>Tax Amount</MeasureID>
    </Column>
    <Column xsi:type="CubeAttributeBinding">
      <CubeID>Adv DM 1</CubeID>
      <CubeDimensionID>Product</CubeDimensionID>
      <AttributeID>Category</AttributeID>
      <Type>All</Type>
    </Column>
    </Columns>
  </Action>
  </Actions>
```

At this point, if we close the XML file and return to the **Actions** pane, we will see the updated **Drillthrough Columns** list as shown in the following figure:

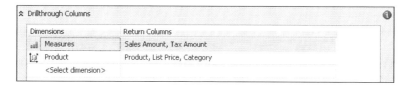

The only visible change is that the **Category** column has been switched with **List Price** in the **Product** dimension. However, the output columns returned by this drillthrough action will be in the order we specified when we manually altered the XML file, with columns from different dimensions appearing wherever we want them to. We have to be careful about making further modifications in the **Drillthrough Columns** list. If we don't make any further modifications to the columns of the dimensions we manually altered in the XML file, we should be able to keep the order we defined manually. Otherwise, we have to repeat the manual modification of the XML file to get the desired column order.

Drillthrough and calculated members

We have seen that the drillthrough feature can apparently operate on any cell of the cube. In particular, we define drillthrough by choosing the measure group on which the drillthrough action will be active. However, the drillthrough operation works only on "real" measures. If we have defined calculated measures, drillthrough will not operate on these cells. Moreover, drillthrough does not operate on any cell that references any calculated member on any dimension, not just measures.

The rationale behind this is very simple. A calculated member may not have a direct relationship with a set of rows in the fact table. In reality, that relationship could be described for many calculated members, but Analysis Services does not offer a way to define this relationship. For this reason, drillthrough is not supported on calculated members.

There are two possible workarounds. The first is to create real members instead of calculated members on a dimension, and use assignments to overwrite their value in the MDX Script. For example, take a look at the **DateTool** dimension described in Chapter 6: drillthrough is enabled on any non-calculated member that belongs to a dimension, even if that dimension is not related to any measure group! However, if the calculation in the MDX Script refers to values from somewhere else in the cube, drillthrough does not reflect this and always returns the same result, ignoring the possibility that it might not have any connection at all to the value displayed in the cell.

For example, the DateTool dimension may include a member to calculate the Year-to-Date sum of any measure. Therefore, looking at the result for March 2009 we could expect that drillthrough would return the set of fact table rows from January 1st to March 31st. However, in reality we will only receive data from March 1st to March 31st if we look at the March member; similarly, if we go down to the Day level and drillthrough on March 31st, we will get only the transactions of that day. In both cases, we might prefer that drillthrough operations would follow the calculation logic as well as the physical coordinates, but it is not possible to customize the way Analysis Services determines which rows should be returned.

The second workaround is to create an Action of type Rowset, defining as target type all the cells and using the Condition expression to ensure it is only enabled for the calculated measures we want to use it on. This type of action can have an MDX DRILLTHROUGH statement which returns the data we want and we have full control over the rows and columns returned by this action. Clients like Excel 2007 support Rowset actions and display their results in the same way they do those of drillthrough actions, because we always get a Rowset as a result. However, in this case the MDX query for the drillthrough is not built by the client but by the server and there are some other differences in behavior. For example, the maximum rows returned by a drillthrough cannot be controlled by the client if we are using a Rowset action. More information about this workaround is available on Mosha Pasumansky's blog in this post: `http://tinyurl.com/drillcalc`.

> As an alternative to drillthrough, it's also possible to implement an Action that returns a Rowset and specify your own SQL for the query that it runs. To do this, however, you need to create an Analysis Services stored procedure in .NET and call it from the Action expression. More information on how to do this can be found here: `http://tinyurl.com/ssas-sql`

Drillthrough modeling

We started this chapter with a precise requirement. We wanted to add detailed information about each transaction, such as invoice document and line number, to our cube. The drillthrough feature we introduced is what we will use to display this data. However, there are several ways to model this data in the cube so that it can be queried using the drillthrough feature.

We have seen that drillthrough can show both measures and related dimension attributes. Thus, we have two possible ways to model our data—in a dimension or in measures. The most common approach is to define a separate dimension with transaction details. This dimension would have a fact dimension relationship with the related measure group. The other option is to store this data in measures defined in a separate measure group, with their `AggregateFunction` property set to `None` (although this is only possible in Enterprise edition). This option is limited to numeric attributes, but document and line numbers might be numeric values that could leverage this option, which we will call Drillthrough on Alternate Fact Table.

Drillthrough using a transaction details dimension

The Sales fact table has two fields, `SalesOrderNumber` and `SalesOrderLineNumber`, which we want to display in drillthrough queries. We need to create a dimension that will have these two attributes. To keep our model using surrogate keys in the key attribute of a dimension, we will use the surrogate key of the Sales fact table (`ID_FactSales`) as the key of this dimension. All the degenerate dimension attributes will be attributes of this dimension. In other words, we are creating a dimension which will have the same granularity as the fact table.

> If our degenerate attributes have a cardinality that results in the dimension's granularity being much higher than the fact table, then creating a separate dimension table in the relational model, and a regular Analysis Services dimension, would be a better idea.

Considering that the surrogate key of the fact table will not have any meaning to our users we will not expose it directly to them, but we will use it in the KeyColumns property of the **key** attribute. In the following figure, we can see the resulting Invoice Details dimension. The Line Number attribute has the KeyColumns property set to ID_FactSales and the NameColumn property set to SalesOrderLineNumber. The Order Number attribute has the KeyColumns property set to SalesOrderNumber.

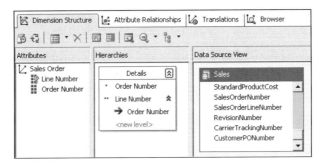

We might wonder why we didn't want to waste an attribute on the **Surrogate key** column on the fact table. The reason is that this dimension will be a very large one. Its number of members will be the same as the number of rows in the fact table. Using MOLAP storage for the dimension (which is the default of the dimension's StorageMode property) a SELECT DISTINCT is sent to the relational source for each attribute of the dimension.

Setting the dimension ProcessingGroup property to ByTable may be not a good idea here. This setting reduces the number of SQL queries generated during dimension processing to just one, with Analysis Services finding the distinct dimension members itself. However, for a very large dimension such as this it would mean Analysis Services doing a lot of work that could exhaust its memory resources and cause dimension processing to fail.

The next step is to build the relationship between this dimension and the fact table. We can use two relationship types: **Fact** and **Regular**. If we choose the Regular relationship type, we have to identify Line Number as the granularity attribute, and use ID_FactSales for both **Dimension Columns** and **Measure Group Columns** in the **Define Relationship** dialog box. Choosing the Fact relationship type does not require that any further properties be set. Both relationship types are equivalent in this case. We might prefer the Fact relationship type just because, when looking at the **Dimension Usage** tab, it immediately reminds us that we are using the fact table as a dimension.

At this point, it is clear that having a large dimension for transaction details might be time and resource consuming. The dimension process operation will take a very long time (similar if not slower than the measure group process!) and it is hard to optimize in an incremental update since there is no way to partition a dimension. If we have a few million rows in our fact table, this solution will probably work well enough. But if we have tens, hundreds or even thousands of millions of rows in our fact table then processing time is likely be too long to be affordable. At this point we need to consider some alternatives that can improve processing time.

Drillthrough with ROLAP dimensions

The simplest change we can make to our dimension is on its `StorageMode` property. It is set to MOLAP by default, which means that all dimension data is read during dimension processing and is stored in Analysis Services' own native compressed, indexed and optimized format; at query time Analysis Services only uses this copy of the data. Usually, this will give us the fastest query response times we can hope to have.

As an alternative, we can try to change the `StorageMode` property of the **Sales Order** dimension to ROLAP. At this point, we'll see different behavior for both dimension processing and drillthrough queries. Processing a ROLAP dimension does not require any SQL queries to be generated to fetch data; it simply empties the Analysis Services cache. When it comes to querying, we'll see different behavior depending on the relationship type used between the measure group and the ROLAP dimension.

In all cases, a drillthrough query on a ROLAP dimension will produce a complex SQL statement that will join the fact table with all the dimensions included in the cube, filtering data with the same criteria specified in the drillthrough query in MDX. This is, unfortunately, necessary to ensure that Analysis Services returns correct results. However, this is extremely expensive. We could try to index and optimize the relational tables, but it will be hard to avoid complete scans of the fact table for all possible queries. Only extremely clever partitioning of the fact table could give acceptable results. As a result, think carefully before using ROLAP dimension in large cubes for drillthrough operations, because query response times might be very long and will consume a lot of resources on the relational source database.

 Our personal opinion is that we recommend you do not use drillthrough with ROLAP measure groups and/or dimensions and large volume of data. It's really not worth the pain! Look for some kind of workaround, like Reporting Services reports linked to the cube with Reporting Actions.

Moreover, if we decide to use ROLAP dimensions anyway, pay attention to the relationship type used with the measure group. In this situation, it is much better to use the Fact relationship type. This is because, if we use a regular relationship type, before the time consuming query we just talked about, a SELECT DISTINCT over the whole fact table (without filters) will be executed just to populate the possible dimension values in memory. It would be the same as the SELECT statement executed to process a dimension with ProcessingGroup set to ByTable, and it could fail if there is too much data to process.

Drillthrough on Alternate Fact Table

As we said before, there is another option for storing the information to be queried using drillthrough, but it can be used only on numeric attributes. We can add measures to the cube, making them not visible in the cube metadata and so not visible to the end users We can also add these measures in a separate measure group so they can have a different storage mode.

These special measures cannot be aggregated and for this reason they should have their AggregateFunction property set to None (which is available only in the Enterprise edition). This approach might seem strange, but it is common to separate measures built on degenerate dimension attributes from cube measures because they have a different meaning and the main measure group is faster if it does not contain useless measures (smaller is always faster).

If we need to implement drillthrough on a single ID which can be stored in a 32 bit integer, putting it in an invisible measure in the measure group and including it in the **Drillthrough Columns** will always be the fastest and cheapest way to do it. If, on the other hand, there are several fields, all numeric, that we want to see in **Drillthrough Columns** and that are not already measures in the cube, we might opt for a separate measure group. We could use a separate fact table too, but if one hasn't been created it is better to create another view that will be used as the basis for the secondary measure group that will only contain measures used for drillthrough operations. This secondary measure group will not need to have any aggregations designed for it.

It is possible to create two measure groups from the same fact table in the cube editor, but it isn't obvious how to do it. First of all you have to add a new distinct count measure to an existing measure group. Every time you do this, a new measure group is created and immediately afterwards we can change the AggregateFunction of the new measure from DistinctCount to None. Adding other measures requires some manual modification of the XML file containing the cube definition. Having a separate fact table, even if only through a view, is much simpler to handle.

Processing a MOLAP measure group does not require sending a SELECT DISTINCT query to the relational source in the way that a dimension does—a simple SELECT query is used instead. Therefore, if we are going to use MOLAP storage, the alternate fact table technique processes faster than the dimension approach, and can also leverage partitioning, if needed. Also, this new measure group can be processed incrementally or on a per-partition basis like any other measure group.

If we want to use the Alternate Fact Table approach, we might also consider shortening processing time and lowering used disk space by changing the StorageMode of the measure group to ROLAP. However, this is not a good idea for reasons similar to those that discourage the use of ROLAP dimensions for drillthrough purposes. While processing time for a ROLAP measure group is practically nothing, at query time Analysis Services generates a SQL query that is similar to the one generated for drillthrough on a ROLAP dimension. This query will have several **JOIN** conditions and it often produces a full scan of the fact table. Therefore, with large cubes choosing ROLAP storage for measure groups can be dangerous; choosing MOLAP for measure groups created expressly for drillthrough operations is usually a better idea.

To make the measures we added in this way visible to drillthrough operations, we have to be careful. The drillthrough operation must be usable from the main measure group, but the Drillthrough Columns list will contain only measures from the new measure group. We can specify measures from measure groups different to the one specified in the Action Target with no problems; the only constraint is that all the measures in a Drillthrough Action must belong to the same measure group.

Drillthrough recap

In the following table we can see all the combinations of drillthrough techniques, storage modes and dimension relationships and their impact on cube processing and queries. It is a shame that ROLAP storage always has very slow performance if you keep the data in the relational database.

Technique	Storage	Dimension Relationship	Impact on Processing	Impact on Querying
Transaction Detail Dimension	MOLAP	Regular	Execute a SQL `SELECT DISTINCT` on drillthrough attributes	Fast query
		Fact		Fast query
	ROLAP	Regular	No operations in cube process	Complex SQL query to get the drillthrough result. It also executes a `SELECT DISTINCT` on drillthrough attributes.
		Fact	No operations in cube process	Complex SQL query to get the drillthrough result.
Alternative Measure Group (only for numeric attribute)	MOLAP	N/A	Executes SQL `SELECT`s on the fact table, without using any `SELECT DISTINCT` before.	Fast query
	ROLAP	N/A	No operations in cube process	Complete scan in the fact table. Dangerous with large fact tables.

Many-to-many dimension relationships

In the dimensional model, the fact table has a many-to-one relationship with each dimension. However, sometimes this kind of modeling cannot represent the real world: for example, a product might belong to several categories. One way of solving this problem might be to choose a "primary" category for each product, to allow the use of a classical star schema. But, doing this, we lose possibly important information.

Analysis Services 2005 introduced the ability to handle many-to-many relationships between dimensions. This feature brings to the OLAP world the approach of modeling many-to-many relationships using bridge tables or factless fact tables that we saw in Chapter 2.

Implementing a many-to-many dimension relationship

Our example scenario for implementing a many-to-many relationship is based on **Sales Reason**. In **Adventure Works**, each internet sale has a list of reasons for the transaction. This list is the result of the customer being asked a multiple choice question. Therefore, each transaction can have zero, one or more sales reasons linked to it. To represent this in the relational model we have a regular dimension, **SalesReasons**, that has all the possible reasons for a sale, and a bridge table that makes the connection between a regular dimension (in this case the Sales Order degenerate dimension we created in the drillthrough section) and the dimension with the many-to-many relationship. The bridge table has a row for each existing combination of order and sales reason, in this way defining the many-to-many relationship that exists between **Sales Reasons** and **Sales Orders**.

Usually, a bridge table links two regular dimensions and is represented in the relational model like the following figure.

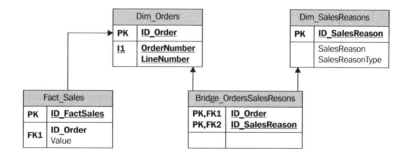

However, in this case we do not have the relational table corresponding to the dimension that links the two measure groups. The following figure describes the situation we are modeling in our scenario. The dimension is created from the **OrderNumber** and **LineNumber** fields in the fact table, forming a degenerate dimension. For this reason we cannot graphically represent the relationship between the bridge table and the degenerate dimension.

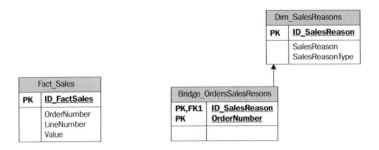

We can model this relationship directly in our **Analysis Services** cube without needing to materialize the degenerate dimension into a physical table. We already have the **SalesReason** dimension defined in our cube and we only need to add a measure group corresponding to the bridge table **BridgeOrdersSalesReasons** defined in the **Sales** schema of our data mart. First of all, we make this table visible through a view, named **BridgeOrdersSalesReasons** in the **CubeSales** schema. Then, we add this table to the **Data Source View** of our project, adding a relationship between its ID_SalesReason field and the corresponding primary key of the **SalesReasons** table, as in the following figure.

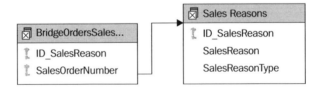

At this point, we create a new measure group named **Bridge Sales Reasons**, containing a single, hidden measure named **Bridge Sales Reasons Count** that will count the number of rows of the **BridgeOrdersSalesReasons** table; this measure might never be used in queries, but every measure group has to contain at least one measure. This will be our intermediate measure group in the many-to-many dimension relationship. In the **Dimension Usage** tab we add the Sales Reason dimension, which will have a regular relationship with the Bridge Sales Reasons measure group. What is less intuitive is how to create the relationship between the Sales Order dimension and the new measure group.

The Sales Order dimension is a degenerate dimension and its content is stored in the fact table. Moreover, the granularity of the bridge table is the order number, while the granularity of the Sales Order dimension is the order line number. However, we can define a regular relationship with a non-key granularity attribute, like the **Order Number** using the **SalesOrderNumber** column as we can see in the next figure.

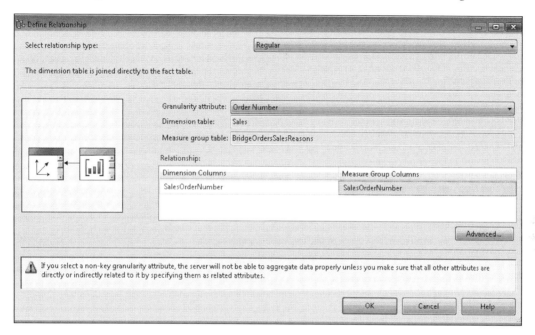

As we saw in Chapter 4, when we define a dimension relationship using a non-key granularity attribute there is a warning about possible issues when aggregating data. However, using this technique with bridge tables for many-to-many relationships shouldn't have any side effects because the bridge table doesn't contain visible measures – so the user will never query this measure group directly – and Analysis Services will only use data at the granularity of the fact table to resolve the many-to-many relationship.

Finally, we have to define the relationship between the **Sales Reason** dimension and the Sales measure group. To do that, we use a **Many-to-Many** relationship type in the **Define Relationship** dialog box as shown in the next figure. The intermediate measure group must be the **Bridge Sales Reasons** we have just defined. Note that we cannot use a measure group as an intermediate one in this dialog box if it does not have a regular relationship with one of the other dimensions of the primary measure group where we are defining the many-to-many dimension relationship.

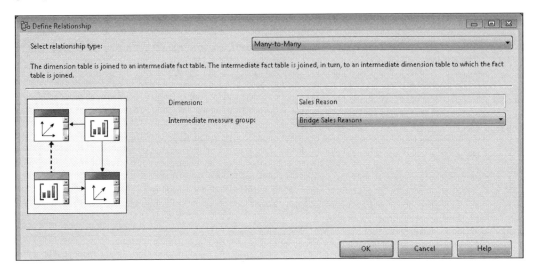

After these changes, we will have the following configuration in the **Dimension Usage** tab.

Now we can process the cube and navigate it. In the following figure we can see a pivot table showing the **Order Quantity** measure filtered by sales made in Central U.S. through the Internet **Sales Channel**. We are filtering on sales made over the Internet because **Sales Reasons** are gathered only for this kind of sale. The filter for Central U.S. is only to get a small enough subset of data to make the calculation easy to explain.

Sales Channel	Internet				
Sales Territory	Central				
Order Quantity	Column Labels				
Row Labels	⊞ Bikes		⊞ Clothing	⊞ Accessories	Grand Total
On Promotion	1		1	2	4
Other			1	2	3
Price	1		3	14	18
Review	1				1
Television Advertisement			1		1
Grand Total	**2**		**4**	**14**	**20**

The total number of bikes sold is 2. However, we have 3 different reasons shown in this column. It means that at least one bike sale has more than one related reason. The same is true for the other product categories. We can see that the total in each column does not correspond to the sum of the rows above. However, the total for each row corresponds to the sum of the preceding columns. This is because the **Sales Reason** dimension that is displayed on rows has a many-to-many relationship with the measure we are analyzing, while the **Product Categories** that is displayed on columns has a regular relationship and can be aggregated in the traditional way.

The aggregation of measures on a many-to-many relationship is a sort of "distinct sum". In other words, when summing values each item has to be summed only once. If a bike has been sold because it was "On Promotion", we don't have to sum its value twice if it has been sold also because of its "Price". This kind of behavior requires that calculations on measures over a dimension having a many-to-many dimension relationship need to be done at query time and cannot be calculated in advance and stored in the fact table. However, these calculations can still leverage the cache of Analysis Services.

Advanced modelling with many-to-many relationships

Many-to-many dimension relationships can be leveraged to present data in ways that are not feasible with a traditional star schema. This opens a brand new world of opportunities that transcends the limits of traditional OLAP and enables advanced data analysis by using pivot tables without writing queries.

One common scenario where many-to-many relationships can be used is a survey consisting of questions that have predefined answers with both simple and multiple choices. The typical star schema model (one fact table with answers joined with a questions/answers dimension and a case dimension) is fully queryable using SQL. However, while it is very simple to compare different answers to the same question, it could be very difficult to relate answers to more than one question. For example, if we have a question asking the respondent which sports they played (multiple choices) and another one asking what job they did, we would probably like to know what relationships exists between those two attributes. The normal way to solve it is to have two different attributes (or dimensions) that users can combine on rows and columns of a pivot table. Unfortunately, having an attribute for each question is not very flexible; more important, we have to change our star schema to accommodate having a single row into the fact table for each case. This makes it very difficult to handle any multiple choices question.

Instead, we can change our perspective and leverage many-to-many relationships. We can build a finite number (as many as we want) of question/answer dimensions, using role-playing dimensions to duplicate an original dimension and providing to the user a number of "filter" dimensions that can be nested in a pivot table or can be used to filter data that, for each case, satisfy defined conditions for different questions.

Another scenario is the one where a snapshot fact table contains the state of data over time, recording "snapshots" of that state. If, for example, we register the credit rating of a customer each month, an OLAP cube is pretty good at returning the number of customers for each rating rank in each month. However, it is usually much harder to analyze the flow of changes. For example, if we had 30 customers rated AAA and 20 rated AAB in January, then we see that we have 20 customer rated AAA and 35 rated AAB in June, what does it mean? It could be that we had 10 customers previously-rated AAA that have been downgraded to AAB and we acquired 5 new customer AAB. But it could also be that we had lost 5 AAA customers and 2 AAB customers, we retained 5 AAA downgraded to AAB and got 12 new customer rated AAB. Looking at the total numbers, any hypothesis could be true, but in reality the data can be examined to give the real numbers. By using a many-to-many relationship, it is possible to create a multidimensional model having a "start period" and an "end period" date and a rating dimension. Using a pivot table the user can create a transition matrix that correlates each possible rating at the start period with each possible rating at the end period.

Further description of this kind of advanced modeling technique is beyond the goal of this book. These scenarios and many others are described in detail in a paper named "The many-to-many revolution", which is downloadable from `http://tinyurl.com/m2mrev`.

Performance issues

The particular calculations made at runtime to resolve queries involving many-to-many dimension relationships can be quite expensive and result in performance issues. To understand why this is, we need to understand how queries involving many-to-many dimensions are resolved. Taking the example query we've been looking at using **Sales Reason**, when the query is run Analysis Services first takes the set of sales reasons selected, then scans the intermediate measure group to find all of the individual sales orders from the **Sales Order** dimension associated with each sales reason, and then queries the main measure group to aggregate the requested measures for all of these sales orders. If there are a large number of sales orders associated with each sales reason, this could take a lot of time to do, and because the query on the main measure group is resolved at the sales order granularity, this severely restricts the ability of Analysis Services to use aggregations to improve performance.

The critical issue is the size (that is the number of rows) in the intermediate measure group. If it is small, it could be possible to build some aggregations on the main measure group at the level of the granularity attributes of the dimensions that make the join with the intermediate measure group. In these cases, aggregations can improve the execution time of the queries. However, if the intermediate measure group has millions of rows, aggregations will not improve execution time much.

In general, to optimize cubes with many-to-many dimension relationships it is necessary to reduce the number of rows in the intermediate measure groups somehow – this can be achieved by "compressing" the data so that frequently occurring patterns of relationships are represented by a single row in the intermediate measure group instead of multiple rows. After that, we can try to minimize the number of rows scanned for each query, for example by partitioning the intermediate measure group using one of the dimensions that has a regular relationship with the intermediate measure group as well as the "primary" measure group. In the case of transition matrix, the date dimension should be related to both measure groups as a regular dimension, and partitioning the intermediate measure group by members of the Date dimension will reduce the number of rows scanned at query time.

The optimization of many-to-many dimension relationships, including the 'compression' technique mentioned above, is covered in a white paper named *Analysis Services Many-to-Many Dimensions: Query Performance Optimization Techniques* downloadable here: `http://tinyurl.com/m2moptimize`.

Finally, in some scenarios where there is a large dimension linking the intermediate measure group and the main measure group, the users do not actually need to be able to query it directly – it is just used to resolve the many-to-many relationship and its `Visible` property is set to false. If this is the case we can avoid the processing overhead associated with such a large dimension by breaking it up into multiple smaller dimensions, and at the same time improve performance of many-to-many queries too. This technique is described in detail here: `http://tinyurl.com/breaklargedims`.

Summary

In this chapter we have seen how to use the drillthrough feature, discussing in detail several options available to model and optimize Drillthrough Actions. We have seen the differences between using MOLAP and ROLAP dimensions to enable drillthrough on transaction details. We have also discussed how to include a many-to-many dimension relationship in our model, highlighting that this single feature enables much more complex modeling techniques, giving some examples of the possible scenarios and providing links to external resources about modeling and optimization for this feature.

6
Adding Calculations to the Cube

This chapter explains how to enhance the analytical capabilities of our cube with MDX calculations. Calculations, especially calculated members, are very common in cubes as they are a very easy and convenient way to generate new and useful business metrics from the data you have imported.

This chapter does not cover basic MDX concepts, although we will provide several examples of MDX usage. For a complete reference of the MDX language or for a thorough tutorial you should refer to other books such as *MDX Solutions*, *Fast Track to MDX*, or *Microsoft SQL Server 2008 MDX Step by Step*.

Reading this chapter you will learn about:

- The different kinds of calculated members
- Several ready-to-use examples of calculated members
- The difference between using calculated measures and calculation dimensions
- Defining and using named sets

Different kinds of calculated members

There are three kinds of calculated member:

- **Query-scoped calculated members** are calculated members defined in the WITH clause of an MDX query. They are specific to the query and cannot be referenced outside it. They are very useful to developers for testing, debugging, and "ad hoc" reporting, but as defining a calculated member requires knowledge of MDX it is not something a normal end-user will be able to do.

- **Session-scoped calculated members** are calculated members that exist in the context of the session that is created when a user connects to a cube. These calculated members are available for use in all queries executed in a particular session until either the session is closed or the calculated members are dropped. Session calculations are a convenient means for a client tool to simplify the queries it generates but, apart from that, they are rarely used. They are created by the client tool executing a CREATE MEMBER. statement.
- **Globally-scoped calculated members** are calculated members defined in the MDX Script of the cube using CREATE MEMBER statements. They are available for use in queries to all users and can be used in exactly the same way as physical members are, and are the most common kind of calculated member.

At a first glance we might think that the only difference between these three ways to define a calculated member is how long they are available and to whom. However, as we'll see in Chapter 9, the scope of a calculated member determines how long the values it returns can be cached for, and this in turn can have a significant impact on query performance.

At this stage, though, all we need to understand is that globally-scoped calculated members are best from a performance point of view. Remember also that by defining a calculated member on the cube we are removing the need for other developers (for example Reporting Services report authors) to define these calculations in their own queries. If too many calculations end up being defined in queries rather than on the cube it can lead to duplication of effort, confusion when different calculations are given the same name in different queries, and maintenance problems when fixing a bug in a calculation involves tracking down multiple instances of the same calculation. For all of these reasons we recommend you should always try to create calculated members on the cube, and only use session-scoped or query-scoped calculations when you have no other choice.

Common calculations

We are now going to show some very common types of calculated member. As stated before, the goal here is not to spend a lot of time explaining how the MDX code actually works, but to show some examples of calculations that can be copied and adapted easily for almost any cube.

Simple calculations

The simplest kind of calculated members are those that perform basic arithmetic on other measures. For example, we might have two real measures in the cube that represent our sales and our costs; to calculate our profit we just need to subtract costs from sales.

To add a calculation like this to the cube all we need to do is open the **Cube Editor** in BI Development Studio, go to the **Calculations** tab, and once we're there we have a choice of two ways to create a calculated measure. By default the Calculations tab opens in Form View, and to create a calculated member here we simply need to click on the **New Calculated Member** button and fill in all of the properties as required; behind the scenes BIDS will generate an MDX CREATE MEMBER statement for us that will create the calculated member.

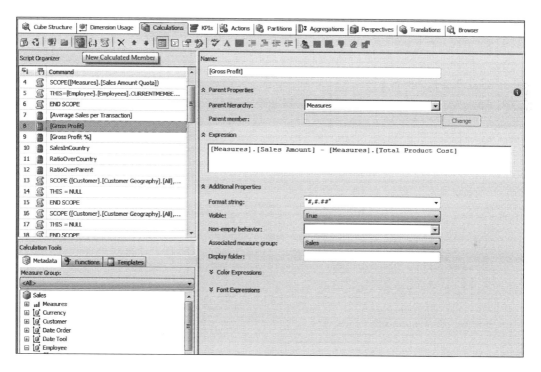

If we click on the **Script View** button on the toolbar, we're able to see what the MDX generated actually looks like and we can also write our own code there if need be:

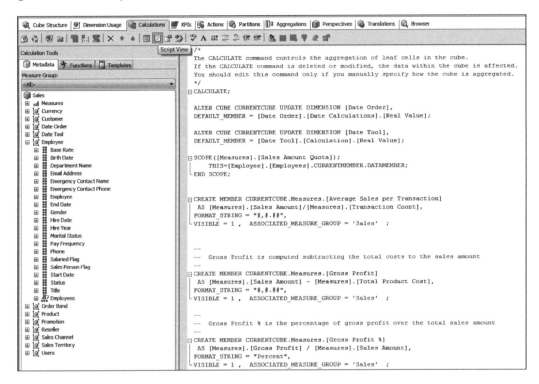

Here's an example of what the `CREATE MEMBER` statement for a Profit calculated measure looks like:

```
CREATE MEMBER CURRENTCUBE.Measures.[Gross Profit]
  AS [Measures].[Sales Amount] - [Measures].[Total Product Cost],
FORMAT_STRING = "#,#.##",
VISIBLE = 1;
```

This statement creates a new member on the Measures dimension. As you can see, the expression used to do the calculation is very simple:

```
[Measures].[Sales Amount] - [Measures].[Total Product Cost]
```

One point to note here is that we refer to each real measure in the expression using its Unique Name: for example, the Sales Amount measure's unique name is `[Measures].[Sales Amount]`. A unique name is exactly what you'd expect, a way of uniquely identifying a member among all the members on all the hierarchies in the cube. You can write MDX without using unique names, just using member names instead:

```
[Sales Amount] - [Total Product Cost]
```

However, we strongly recommend you always use unique names even if it means your code ends up being much more verbose. This is because there may be situations where Analysis Services takes a long time to resolve a name to a unique name; and there is also the possibility that two members on different hierarchies will have the same name, in which case you won't know which one Analysis Services is going to use.

Referencing cell values

A slightly more complex requirement that is often encountered is to be able to reference not just another measure's value, but the value of another measure in combination with other members on other hierarchies. For example, you might want to create a calculated measure that always displays the sales for a particular country. Here's how you can do this:

```
CREATE MEMBER CURRENTCUBE.Measures.[USA Sales Amount]
  AS
([Measures].[Sales Amount], [Customer].[Country].&[United States]),
FORMAT_STRING = "#,#.##",
VISIBLE = 1 ;
```

The expression we've used here in our calculated measure definition consists of a single tuple. In MDX a tuple is a way of referencing the value of any cell in the cube; the definition of a tuple consists of a comma-delimited list of unique names of members from different hierarchies in the cube, surrounded by round brackets. In the example above our tuple fixes the value of the calculated measure to that of the Sales Amount measure and the Customer Country United States.

The behavior of this new calculation can be easily seen when we browse the cube by Customer Country:

	Values	
Row Labels	USA Sales Amount	Sales Amount
Australia	9,389,789.51	9,061,000.58
Canada	9,389,789.51	1,977,844.86
France	9,389,789.51	2,644,017.71
Germany	9,389,789.51	2,894,312.34
N/A	9,389,789.51	80,460,838.06
United Kingdom	9,389,789.51	3,391,712.21
United States	9,389,789.51	9,389,789.51
Grand Total	9,389,789.51	109,819,515.28

As you can see, while the Sales Amount measure always shows the sales for the country displayed on rows, the new calculated measure always shows sales for the USA. This is always the case, no matter what other hierarchies are used in the query, or where the measure itself is used:

Row Labels	USA Sales Amount (CY 2001)	Sales Amount (CY 2001)	USA Sales Amount (CY 2002)	Sales Amount (CY 2002)	Total USA Sales Amount	Total Sales Amount
Australia	975,456.8	1,225,145.28	2,211,661.71	2,161,723.67	3,187,118.52	3,386,868.95
Canada	975,456.8	128,938.46	2,211,661.71	625,589.57	3,187,118.52	754,528.02
France	975,456.8	169,137.78	2,211,661.71	497,614.71	3,187,118.52	666,752.50
Germany	975,456.8	215,298.73	2,211,661.71	526,173.72	3,187,118.52	741,472.45
N/A	975,456.8	8,065,435.31	2,211,661.71	24,144,429.65	3,187,118.52	32,209,864.96
United Kingdom	975,456.8	273,000.07	2,211,661.71	579,353.77	3,187,118.52	852,353.84
United States	975,456.8	975,456.80	2,211,661.71	2,211,661.71	3,187,118.52	3,187,118.52
Grand Total	**975,456.8**	**11,052,412.43**	**2,211,661.71**	**30,746,546.81**	**3,187,118.52**	**41,798,959.24**

The calculated measure always shows the value of sales for the USA, even when we have broken sales down by Year. If we wanted to fix the value of the calculated measure by one more hierarchy, perhaps to show sales for male customers in the USA, we would just add another member to the list in the tuple as follows:

```
([Measures].[Sales Amount], [Customer].[Country].&[United States],
[Customer].[Gender].&[Male])
```

Aggregating members

A tuple cannot, however, contain two members from the same hierarchy. If we need to do something like show the sum of sales in the UK and USA, we need to use the Aggregate function on a set containing those two members:

```
CREATE MEMBER
CURRENTCUBE.[Customer].[Customer Geography].[All].[UK and USA] AS
AGGREGATE(
{[Customer].[Customer Geography].[Country].&[United Kingdom],
 [Customer].[Customer Geography].[Country].&[United States]});
```

The statement above creates a new member on the Customer Geography hierarchy of the Customer dimension called "UK and USA", and uses the AGGREGATE function to return their combined value.

Row Labels	Sales Amount
⊞ United Kingdom	3,391,712.21
⊞ United States	9,389,789.51
⊞ UK and USA	12,781,501.72
Grand Total	**12,781,501.72**

Year-to-dates

Year-to-date calculations calculate the aggregation of values from the 1st of January up to the current date. In order to create a year-to-date calculation we need to use the YTD function, which takes a single date member as a parameter and returns the set of members on the same hierarchy as that member starting from the first day of the year up to and including the selected member. So, for example, if we passed the member 23rd July into the YTD function we'd get a set containing all of the dates from 1st January to 23rd July; it also works at higher levels, so if we passed in the member Quarter 3, we'd get a set containing Quarter 1, Quarter 2, and Quarter 3.

In order for the YTD function to work properly you need to have a dimension whose Type property is set to **Time**, an attribute hierarchy in that dimension whose Type property is set to **Years**, and a user hierarchy including that attribute hierarchy (see the section *Configuring a Time Dimension* in Chapter 3 for more details on the Type property). This is because the way the function works is to take the member you pass into it, find its ancestor at the Year level, find the first member of that year on the same level as the original member we passed in, and then return the set of all members between the first member in the year and the member we passed in.

Passing a static member reference into the YTD function is not going to be very useful—what we want is to make it dynamic and return the correct year-to-date set for all of the dates we use in our queries. To do this, we can use the CurrentMember function on our date hierarchy, and use it to pass a reference to the current date member from the context of our query into our calculated member.

Finally, the YTD function only returns a set object, and what we need to do is to return the sum of that set for a given measures. As a result our first attempt at writing the calculated member, building on what we saw in the previous section, might be something like this:

```
CREATE MEMBER CURRENTCUBE.Measures.[Sales Amount YTD] AS
    SUM (
        YTD ([Date Order].[Calendar].CurrentMember),
        Measures.[Sales Amount]);
```

This computes the Sales Amount YTD member as the sum of the sales amount from the first date in the year up to and including the currently selected member in the date order calendar hierarchy.

The formula is correct in this case but, in order to make it work properly for any measure, we should use the following:

```
CREATE MEMBER CURRENTCUBE.Measures.[Sales Amount YTD] AS
    AGGREGATE (
        YTD ([Date Order].[Calendar].CurrentMember),
        Measures.[Sales Amount]);
```

Here we replaced the MDX SUM function with AGGREGATE. The result, for Sales Amount, is the same. However, if we need to use this formula on a measure that does not have its AggegationFunction property set to **Sum**, AGGREGATE will aggregate values differently for each different AggregationFunction whereas SUM will always provide the sum. For example consider a measure that has its AggregationFunction property set to **DistinctCount**: if we had 5 distinct customers on 1st January, 3 distinct customers on 2nd January and 4 distinct customers on 3rd January, the total number of distinct customers from the 1st to the 3rd January would not be 5+3+4=12 because some customers might have bought from us on more than one day. Using AGGREGATE in this case will give us the correct number of distinct customers in the year-to-date.

Ratios over a hierarchy

Another very common pattern of calculated member is the ratio. A good example of this is when we want to compute the ratio of a measure (for example sales amount) on a member of a hierarchy against its parent.

Let us take, for example, the Customer Geography hierarchy in the Customer dimension. We might want to compute two different kinds of ratios:

- Ratio over Country: We take the ratio of the selected member against the whole of the country. This gives a percentage that shows how much a State or City's sales contribute to the sales of the whole country.

- Ratio over Parent: We take the ratio of the selected member against its parent in the hierarchy rather than the whole country. So for example, we would see the percentage contribution of a City to the Region it was in, if City was the level immediately underneath Region in the hierarchy.

The difference between the two ratios is evident in the following picture:

Row Labels	Values Sales Amount	RatioOverCountry	RatioOverParent
⊞ Australia	9,061,000.58	100.00%	8.25%
⊞ Canada	1,977,844.86	100.00%	1.80%
⊟ France	2,644,017.71	100.00%	2.41%
⊞ Charente-Maritime	34,441.73	1.30%	1.30%
⊞ Essonne	279,297.18	10.56%	10.56%
⊞ Garonne (Haute)	54,641.72	2.07%	2.07%
⊞ Hauts de Seine	263,416.19	9.96%	9.96%
⊞ Loir et Cher	21,473.74	0.81%	0.81%
⊞ Loiret	91,562.91	3.46%	3.46%
⊞ Moselle	94,046.23	3.56%	3.56%
⊞ Nord	391,400.20	14.80%	14.80%
⊞ Pas de Calais	11,342.92	0.43%	0.43%
⊟ Seine (Paris)	539,725.80	20.41%	20.41%
⊟ Paris	539,725.80	20.41%	100.00%
⊞ 75002	49,791.54	1.88%	9.23%
⊞ 75003	65,034.63	2.46%	12.05%
⊞ 75005	30,923.95	1.17%	5.73%
⊞ 75006	30,695.25	1.16%	5.69%

We can easily see that the RatioOverCountry of the ZIP code 75002 in Paris is 1.88% while the RatioOverParent is 9.23%. The difference is in the denominator in the formula: in the RatioOverCountry the denominator is the total of France while in the RatioOverParent the denominator is the total of Paris.

The RatioOverCountry measure is slightly easier to define because the denominator is clearly defined as the Country defined by the selection. The MDX code is pretty simple:

```
CREATE MEMBER CURRENTCUBE.Measures.RatioOverCountry AS
    ([Measures].[Sales Amount]) /
    (
        [Measures].[Sales Amount],
        Ancestor (
            [Customer].[Customer Geography].CurrentMember,
            [Customer].[Customer Geography].Country
        )
    ),
FORMAT_STRING = "Percent";
```

As the numerator we put the sales amount; in the denominator we override the `Geography` hierarchy with the ancestor of the `CurrentMember` at the level of `Country`. So, if this measure is evaluated for ZIP code 75002 of Paris, the following will happen: `[Customer].[Customer Geography].CurrentMember` evaluates to 75002 and its ancestor, at country level, evaluates to "France". The ratio between those two values for the Sales Amount measure is the percentage required.

We use the format string "Percent" that transforms decimal numbers into percentages (0.1234 is 12.34%, 1 is 100%, 2.5 is 250%).

The second version of the ratio is similar, and simply changes the denominator from the fixed ancestor at the `Country` level to a relative one. The denominator is relative to the `CurrentMember`: it is its parent. The formula is:

```
CREATE MEMBER CURRENTCUBE.Measures.RatioOverParent AS
    (Measures.[Sales Amount])
    /
    (
        Measures.[Sales Amount],
        Customer.[Customer Geography].CurrentMember.Parent
    ),
FORMAT_STRING = "Percent";
```

The numerator is the same measure, the denominator changes each time the `CurrentMember` changes and it is expressed as the parent of the `CurrentMember`. The `Parent` function returns the immediate ancestor of a member in its hierarchy. So, when the `CurrentMember` evaluates to ZIP code 75002, its parent will be Paris. When the `CurrentMember` is Paris, its parent will be `Seine (Paris)` and so on.

If we query the cube with these two formulas, we will get this result:

Row Labels	Values Sales Amount	RatioOverCountry	RatioOverParent
⊞ Australia	9,061,000.58	100.00%	8.25%
⊞ Canada	1,977,844.86	100.00%	1.80%
⊞ France	2,644,017.71	100.00%	2.41%
⊞ Germany	2,894,312.34	100.00%	2.64%
⊞ N/A	80,460,838.06	100.00%	73.27%
⊞ United Kingdom	3,391,712.21	100.00%	3.09%
⊞ United States	9,389,789.51	100.00%	8.55%
Grand Total	**109,819,515.28**	**#NUM!**	**#NUM!**

We can easily check that the value is correctly computed but, at the **Grand Total** level, we get two errors. The reason for this is straightforward: the Customer Geography hierarchy is at the All level and so the denominator in the formula has no value because:

- There is no ancestor of the CurrentMember at the country level, as it is already at the top level, so this causes the error in RatioOverCountry.

- There is no parent at the top level in the hierarchy, so this causes the error in RatioOverParent.

Since we know that the ratio has no meaning at all at the top level, we can use a SCOPE statement to overwrite the value at the top level with NULL.

```
SCOPE ([Customer].[Customer Geography].[All], Measures.
RatioOverParent);
    THIS = NULL;
END SCOPE;

SCOPE ([Customer].[Customer Geography].[All], Measures.
RatioOverCountry);
    THIS = NULL;
END SCOPE;
```

The two SCOPE statement will provide a better user experience, clearing values that should not be computed, due to functional limitations on their meaning:

Row Labels	Values Sales Amount	RatioOverCountry	RatioOverParent
⊞Australia	9,061,000.58	100.00%	8.25%
⊞Canada	1,977,844.86	100.00%	1.80%
⊞France	2,644,017.71	100.00%	2.41%
⊞Germany	2,894,312.34	100.00%	2.64%
⊞N/A	80,460,838.06	100.00%	73.27%
⊞United Kingdom	3,391,712.21	100.00%	3.09%
⊞United States	9,389,789.51	100.00%	8.55%
Grand Total	**109,819,515.28**		

There is still a problem that should be addressed: what if the denominator evaluates to zero in some cases? The evaluation of any number divided by zero will show a value of infinity — which will look like an error to an end user — and this is not a situation we would like to happen. For this reason, it is always a good practice to check for a zero denominator just before performing the division.

The function we're going to use to make this check is IIF. It takes three parameters and, if the first evaluates to True, then it returns the value of the second parameter, otherwise it returns the third one. We can now rephrase the ratio as:

```
CREATE MEMBER CURRENTCUBE.Measures.RatioOverCountry AS
    IIF (
        (
            [Measures].[Sales Amount],
            Ancestor (
                [Customer].[Customer Geography].CurrentMember,
                [Customer].[Customer Geography].Country
            )
        ) = 0,
        NULL,
        ([Measures].[Sales Amount]) /
        (
            [Measures].[Sales Amount],
            Ancestor (
                [Customer].[Customer Geography].CurrentMember,
                [Customer].[Customer Geography].Country
            )
        )
    ),
    FORMAT_STRING = "Percent";
```

You might be wondering: what happens if we try to divide by NULL instead of zero? In fact the same thing happens in both cases, but the code above traps division by NULL as well as division by zero because in MDX the expression 0=NULL evaluates to true. This behavior can come as a bit of a shock, especially to those people with a background in SQL, but in fact in MDX it causes no practical problems and is actually quite helpful.

Even if this formula is correct, it still has two problems:

- It is not very easy to understand because of the repetition of the formula to get the sales at the country level, first in the division-by-zero check and second in the ratio calculation itself.

- The value of the sales at the country level will not be cached and so it will lead to a double computation of the same value. Analysis Services can only cache the value of an entire calculation, but can't cache the results of expressions used inside a calculation.

Luckily, one simple correction to the formula solves both problems, leading to a much clearer and optimized expression. We define a hidden member `SalesInCountry` that returns the sales in the current country and then substitute it for the expression returning sales at country level in the original calculation:

```
CREATE MEMBER CURRENTCUBE.Measures.SalesInCountry AS
    (
        [Measures].[Sales Amount],
        Ancestor (
            [Customer].[Customer Geography].CurrentMember,
            [Customer].[Customer Geography].Country
        )
    ),
VISIBLE = 0;

CREATE MEMBER CURRENTCUBE.Measures.RatioOverCountry AS
    IIF (
        Measures.SalesInCountry = 0,
        NULL,
        ([Measures].[Sales Amount]) / Measures.SalesInCountry
    ),
FORMAT_STRING = "Percent";
```

The new intermediate measure has the property `VISIBLE` set to 0, which means that the user will not see it. Nevertheless, we can use it to make the next formula clearer and to let the formula engine cache its results in order to speed up computation.

Previous period growths

A previous period growth calculation is defined as the growth, either in percentage or absolute value, from the previous time period to the current time period. It is very useful when used with a time hierarchy to display the growth of the current month, quarter or year over the previous month, quarter or year.

The key to solving this particular problem is the `PrevMember` function, which returns the member immediately before any given member on a hierarchy. For example, if we used `PrevMember` with the Calendar Year 2003, it would return the Calendar Year 2002. As a first step, let's create a calculated member that returns Sales for the previous period to the current period, again using the `Currentmember` function to get a relative reference to the current time period:

```
CREATE MEMBER CURRENTCUBE.Measures.PreviousPeriodSales AS
    (Measures.[Sales Amount],
    [Date Order].[Calendar].CurrentMember.PrevMember),
FORMAT_STRING = "#,#.00";
```

Here we take the `Currentmember` on the `Calendar` hierarchy, and then use `PrevMember` to get the member before it. In order to get the sales for that time period we've created a tuple, which is simply a comma-delimited list of members from different hierarchies in the cube enclosed in round brackets. You can think of a tuple as a co-ordinate to a particular cell within the cube; when we use a tuple in a calculation it will always return the value from the cell it references.

	Values	
Row Labels	Sales Amount	PreviousPeriodSales
⊟ CY 2001	11,331,808.96	
⊟ H1 CY 2001	3,007,316.75	
⊞ Q2 CY 2001	3,007,316.75	
⊟ H2 CY 2001	8,324,492.22	3,007,316.75
⊟ Q3 CY 2001	8,324,492.22	3,007,316.75
⊞ September 2001	1,639,840.11	2,044,600.00
⊞ October 2001	1,358,050.47	1,639,840.11
⊞ November 2001	2,868,129.20	1,358,050.47
⊞ December 2001	2,458,472.43	2,868,129.20
⊟ CY 2002	30,674,773.18	11,331,808.96
⊟ H1 CY 2002	19,069,963.91	
⊟ Q1 CY 2002	7,407,476.72	8,324,492.22
⊟ January 2002	1,309,863.25	2,458,472.43
January 1, 2002	725,046.42	22,168.72
January 2, 2002	14,313.08	725,046.42
January 3, 2002	28,041.32	14,313.08

Having calculated the previous member sales, it is now very easy to compute the growth percentage, taking care to handle, as before, division by zero.

```
CREATE MEMBER CURRENTCUBE.Measures.PreviousPeriodGrowth AS
    IIF (Measures.PreviousPeriodSales = 0,
        NULL,
        (Measures.[Sales Amount] - Measures.PreviousPeriodSales)
        / Measures.PreviousPeriodSales),
    FORMAT_STRING = "#,#.00%";
```

This produces the following output:

Row Labels	Sales Amount	PreviousPeriodSales	PreviousPeriodGrowth
CY 2001	11,331,808.96		
H1 CY 2001	3,007,316.75		
Q2 CY 2001	3,007,316.75		
H2 CY 2001	8,324,492.22	3,007,316.75	176.81%
Q3 CY 2001	8,324,492.22	3,007,316.75	176.81%
September 2001	1,639,840.11	2,044,600.00	-19.80%
October 2001	1,358,050.47	1,639,840.11	-17.18%
November 2001	2,868,129.20	1,358,050.47	111.19%
December 2001	2,458,472.43	2,868,129.20	-14.28%
CY 2002	30,674,773.18	11,331,808.96	170.70%
H1 CY 2002	19,069,963.91		
Q1 CY 2002	7,407,476.72	8,324,492.22	-11.02%
January 2002	1,309,863.25	2,458,472.43	-46.72%
February 2002	2,451,605.62	1,309,863.25	87.17%
March 2002	2,099,415.62	2,451,605.62	-14.37%
April 2002	1,546,592.23	2,099,415.62	-26.33%
Q2 CY 2002	11,662,487.19	7,407,476.72	57.44%

Same period previous year

In a similar way to the previous period calculation, we might want to check the sales of the current month against the same month in the previous year. The function to use here is `ParallelPeriod` which takes as parameters a level, the number of periods to go back and a member. It takes the ancestor of the member at the specified level, goes back the number of periods specified at that level, and then finds the child of the member at the same level as the original member, in the same relative position as the original member was. Here's an example of how it can be used in a calculated measure:

```
CREATE MEMBER CURRENTCUBE.Measures.SamePeriodPreviousYearSales AS
    (Measures.[Sales Amount],
    ParallelPeriod (
        [Date Order].[Calendar].[Calendar Year],
        1,
        [Date Order].[Calendar].CurrentMember)),
FORMAT_STRING = "#,#.00";
```

Here we pass to `ParallelPeriod` the `Year` level, the fact we want to go back 1 period, and as a starting point the current member of the Date Order dimension's Calendar hierarchy; the result is that `ParallelPeriod` returns the same period as the current member on Calendar but in the previous year.

Having calculated the sales in the same period in the previous year, it is straightforward to calculate the percentage growth. Note that here we are handling two different situations where we want to return a NULL value instead of a number: when there were no sales in the previous period (when it would otherwise show a useless 100%) and when there were no sales in the current period (when it would otherwise show a useless – 100%).

```
CREATE MEMBER CURRENTCUBE.Measures.SamePeriodPreviousYearGrowth AS
    IIF (
        Measures.SamePeriodPreviousYearSales = 0,
        NULL,
        IIF (
            Measures.[Sales Amount] = 0,
            NULL,
            (Measures.[Sales Amount] -
            Measures.SamePeriodPreviousYearSales) /
            Measures.SamePeriodPreviousYearSales)),
FORMAT_STRING = "Percent";
```

The final result of this formula is shown here:

Row Labels	Values Sales Amount	SamePeriodPreviousYearSales	SamePeriodPreviousYearGrowth
⊞ CY 2001	11,331,808.96		
⊞ CY 2002	30,674,773.18	11,331,808.96	170.70%
⊟ H1 CY 2002	19,069,963.91	3,007,316.75	534.12%
⊞ Q1 CY 2002	7,407,476.72		
⊟ Q2 CY 2002	11,662,487.19	3,007,316.75	287.80%
⊞ May 2002	2,942,672.91		
⊞ June 2002	1,678,567.42		
⊞ July 2002	2,894,054.68	962,716.74	200.61%
⊞ August 2002	4,147,192.18	2,044,600.00	102.84%
⊟ H2 CY 2002	11,604,809.27	8,324,492.22	39.41%
⊞ Q3 CY 2002	11,604,809.27	8,324,492.22	39.41%
⊞ CY 2003	41,997,636.44	30,674,773.18	36.91%
⊟ H1 CY 2003	23,652,105.10	19,069,963.91	24.03%
⊟ Q1 CY 2003	9,051,551.50	7,407,476.72	22.19%
⊞ January 2003	1,756,407.01	1,309,863.25	34.09%
⊞ February 2003	2,873,936.93	2,451,605.62	17.23%
⊞ March 2003	2,049,529.87	2,099,415.62	-2.38%
⊞ April 2003	2,371,677.70	1,546,592.23	53.35%
⊞ Q2 CY 2003	14,600,553.60	11,662,487.19	25.19%
⊟ H2 CY 2003	18,345,531.34	11,604,809.27	58.09%
⊞ CY 2004	25,815,296.70	41,997,636.44	-38.53%
⊞ CY 2005		25,815,296.70	
Grand Total	109,819,515.28		

Moving averages

Moving averages are another very common and useful kind of calculation. While the calculations we've just seen compare the current period against a fixed point in the past, moving averages are useful in determining the trend over a time range, for example showing the average sales of the last 12 months relative to the current month.

Depending on our requirements we'll want to use different time ranges to calculate the average. This is because moving averages are generally used to show long-term trends by reducing seasonal, or random, variations in the data. For example, if we are looking at the sales of ice cream then sales in summer will be much greater than in winter, so we would want to look at an average over 12 months to account for seasonal variations. On the other hand if we were looking at sales of something like bread where there was much less of a seasonal component, a 3 month moving average might be more useful.

The formula we show below for a moving average uses a function similar to the YTD function used before to compute Year-to-Date values, but more flexible: LastPeriods. We can think of YTD as returning a time range that always starts at January 1st, while moving averages use dynamic range that starts at a given number of periods before the current member. LastPeriods returns a range of time periods of a given size, ending with a given member.

In some situations the number of items in the moving window might be less than we specified. At the start of our time dimension, or before sales for a particular product have been recorded, the number of periods in our range will be smaller because if we use a six month window we might not have data for a whole six months. It is important to decide what to show in these cases. In our example we will show empty values since, having fewer months, we consider the average not meaningful.

Let us start with a basic version of the calculation that will work at the month level:

```
CREATE MEMBER CURRENTCUBE.Measures.AvgSixMonths AS
    IIF (
      Count (
        NonEmpty (
          LastPeriods (6, [Date Order].[Calendar].CurrentMember),
          Measures.[Sales Amount]
        )
      ) <> 6,
      NULL,
      Avg (
        LastPeriods (6 ,[Date Order].[Calendar].CurrentMember),
        Measures.[Sales Amount]
      )
    ),
    FORMAT_STRING = "#,#.00" ;
```

The first part of the calculation makes use of two functions, NonEmpty and LastPeriods, to check if the required six months are available to have a meaningful average.

- NonEmpty takes two sets and removes the tuples from the first set that are empty when evaluated across the tuples in the second set. As our second parameter is a measure, we get only the tuples in the first set where the measure evaluates to a non NULL value.

- LastPeriods returns, as we've seen, the previous n members from its second parameter.

So, the calculation takes the set of the last six months, then removes the ones where there are no sales and checks if the number of items left in the set is still six. If not, then the set contains months without sales and the average will be meaningless, so it returns a null. The last part of the formula computes the average over the same set computed before using the AVG function for Sales Amount.

This version of the calculation works fine for months, but at other levels of the Calendar hierarchy it doesn't—it's a six time period moving average, not a six month moving average. We might decide we want to use completely different logic at the Date or Quarter level; we might even decide that we don't want to display a value at anything other than the Month level. How can we achieve this?

We have two options: use scoped assignments, or add some more conditional logic in the calculation itself. In Analysis Services 2005 scoped assignments were the best choice for performance reasons but in Analysis Services 2008 the two approaches are more or less equivalent in this respect; and since adding conditional logic in the calculation itself is much easier to implement we'll take that approach instead. What we need is another test that will tell us if the CurrentMember on Calendar is at the Month level or not. We can use the Level function to return the level of the CurrentMember; we then need to use the IS operator to compare what the Level function returns with the Month level as follows:

```
CREATE
MEMBER CURRENTCUBE.Measures.AvgSixMonths AS
IIF (
    (NOT [Date Order].[Calendar].CurrentMember.Level IS [Date Order].
    [Calendar].[Month])
    OR
    Count (
        NonEmpty (
            LastPeriods (6,[Date Order].[Calendar].CurrentMember),
            Measures.[Sales Amount]
        )
```

```
    ) <> 6,
    NULL,
    Avg (
            LastPeriods (6,[Date Order].[Calendar].CurrentMember),
            Measures.[Sales Amount]
    )
),
FORMAT_STRING = "#,#.00" ;
```

For more detail on implementing more complex moving averages, such as weighted moving averages, take a look at the following post on Mosha Pasumansky's blog: http://tinyurl.com/moshaavg.

Ranks

Often we'll want to create calculated measures that display rank values, for example the rank of a product based on its sales. Analysis Services has a function for exactly this purpose: the Rank function, which returns the rank of a member inside a set. It's important to realise that the Rank function does not sort the set it uses so we'll have to do that ourselves using the Order function as well.

Here's an example calculated measure that displays the rank of the current member on the Products hierarchy within all of the members on the same level, based on the Sales Amount measure:

```
CREATE MEMBER CURRENTCUBE.Measures.ProductRank AS
    IIF (
            Measures.[Sales Amount] = 0,
            NULL,
            Rank (
                    Product.Products.CurrentMember,
                    Order (
                            Product.Products.CurrentMember.Level.MEMBERS,
                            Measures.[Sales Amount],
                            BDESC
                    )
            )
    );
```

Once again, we test to see if the Sales Amount measure is zero or empty; if it is, then there's no point displaying a rank. Then we take the set of all members on the same level of the Products hierarchy as the current member, order that set by Sales Amount in descending order, and return the rank of the CurrentMember inside that set.

Then, we can use the calculated member in reports like this:

Product Category	Accessories			

	Column Labels			
	2003			
	July		August	
Row Labels	Sales Amount	Product Rank	Sales Amount	Product Rank
All-Purpose Bike Stand	636	68	3339	45
Bike Wash - Dissolver	159	88	532.65	99
Fender Set - Mountain	1099	57	3362.94	44
Hitch Rack - 4-Bike	1080	58	3000	47
HL Mountain Tire	945	61	3745	41
HL Road Tire	912.8	62	2640.6	50
Hydration Pack - 70 oz.	1044.81	60	2804.49	49
LL Mountain Tire	74.97	95	1849.26	58
LL Road Tire	365.33	80	1762.18	59
ML Mountain Tire	209.93	83	2579.14	51
ML Road Tire	474.81	76	1724.31	61
Mountain Bottle Cage	529.47	74	1398.6	79
Mountain Tire Tube	129.74	91	1272.45	82
Patch Kit/8 Patches	112.21	93	593.11	95
Road Bottle Cage	683.24	65	925.97	86
Road Tire Tube	159.6	87	746.13	91
Sport-100 Helmet, Black	1469.58	54	5143.53	38
Sport-100 Helmet, Blue	1854.47	48	5143.53	39
Sport-100 Helmet, Red	1644.53	52	5598.4	37
Touring Tire	289.9	81	1884.35	57
Touring Tire Tube	39.92	97	489.02	100
Water Bottle - 30 oz.	553.89	70	1521.95	71

You can see that the rank of a product changes over time. As the calculated measure is evaluated in the context of the query, with the ordering of the set taking place for each cell, it will calculate the rank correctly no matter what is used on the rows, columns, or slicer of the query. As a result, rank calculations can perform quite poorly and should be used with caution. In situations where you have control over the MDX queries that are being used, for example when writing Reporting Services reports, you may be able to optimize the performance of rank calculations by ordering the set just once in a named set, and then referencing the named set from the calculated measure. The following query shows how to do this:

```
WITH
    SET OrderedProducts AS
        Order (
            [Product].[Product].[Product].MEMBERS,
            [Measures].[Sales Amount],
            BDesc
```

```
                )
        MEMBER MEASURES.[Product Rank] AS
                IIF (
                        [Measures].[Sales Amount] = 0,
                        NULL,
                        Rank (
                                [Product].[Product].CurrentMember,
                                OrderedProducts
                        )
                )
SELECT
        {
                [Measures].[Sales Amount],
                [Measures].[Product Rank]
        }
        ON 0,
        NON EMPTY
                [Product].[Product].[ Product].MEMBERS
        ON 1
FROM [Adventure Works]
```

As always, Mosha Pasumansky's blog is a goldmine of information on the topic of ranking in MDX and the following blog entry goes into a lot of detail on it: http://tinyurl.com/mosharank.

Formatting calculated measures

Format strings allow us to apply formatting to the raw numeric values stored in our measures, as we saw in Chapter 4. They work for calculated measures in exactly the same way as they work for real measures; in some cases a calculated measure will inherit its format string from a real measure used in its definition, but it's always safer to set the FORMAT_STRING property of a calculated measure explicitly.

However, one important point does need to be made here: don't confuse the actual value of a measure with its formatted value. It is very common to see calculated members like this:

```
CREATE MEMBER CURRENTCUBE.Measures.PreviousPeriodGrowth AS
    IIF (Measures.PreviousPeriodSales = 0,
        'N/A',
        (Measures.[Sales Amount] - Measures.PreviousPeriodSales)
        / Measures.PreviousPeriodSales),
FORMAT_STRING = "#,#.00%";
```

What is wrong with this calculation? At least four things:

- We are defining one of the return values for the measure as a string, and Analysis Services is not designed to work well with strings—for example it cannot cache them.

- If we use the measure's value in another calculation, it is much easier to check for NULL values then for the N/A string. The N/A representation might also change over time due to customer requests.

- Returning a string from this calculation will result in it performing sub-optimally; on the other hand returning a NULL will allow Analysis Services to evaluate the calculation much more efficiently.

- Most client tools try to filter out empty rows and columns from the data they return by using NON EMPTY in their queries. However, the calculation above never returns an empty or NULL value; as a result users might find that their queries return an unexpectedly large number of cells containing N/A.

Always work on the basis that the value of a measure should be handled by the main formula, while the human representation of the value should be handled by the FORMAT_STRING property. A much better way to define the calculated member above is:

```
CREATE MEMBER CURRENTCUBE.Measures.PreviousPeriodGrowth AS
    IIF (Measures.PreviousPeriodSales = 0,
        NULL,
        (Measures.[Sales Amount] - Measures.PreviousPeriodSales)
        / Measures.PreviousPeriodSales),
FORMAT_STRING = "#,#.00%;-#,#.00%;;\N\/\A";
```

The formula here returns a NULL when appropriate, and the format string then formats the NULL as the string N/A (although as we noted in the previous chapter, this won't work in Excel 2007). The users sees the same thing as before but this second approach does not suffer from the four problems listed above.

Calculation dimensions

All the calculations we have described so far have been calculated measures—they have resulted in a new member appearing on the Measures dimension to display the result of our calculation. Once created, these calculated measures can be used just like any other measure and even used in the definition of other calculated measures.

In some circumstances, however, calculated measures can be rather inflexible. One example of this is time series calculations. If we want to let our users see, for example, the year-to-date sum of the Sales Amount measure, we can use the technique explained earlier and create a Sales Amount YTD measure. It will be soon clear though that users will want to see the year-to-date sum not only for the Sales Amount measure but on many others. We can define a new calculated measure for each real measure where the YTD function might be useful but, doing so, we will soon add too many measures to our cube, making it harder for the user to find the measure they need and making maintenance of the MDX very time-consuming. We need a more powerful approach.

The technique we're going to describe here is that of creating a 'Calculation Dimension' (also known as 'Time Utility Dimensions' or 'Shell Dimensions'); while it may be conceptually difficult, it's an effective way of solving the problems we've just outlined and has been used successfully in the Analysis Services community for many years. It involves creating a new dimension, or a new hierarchy on an existing dimension, in our cube specifically for the purpose of holding calculations—and because our calculations are no longer on the Measures dimension, when we select one of them in a query it will be applied to all of the measures in the cube. This means, for example, we could define our year-to-date calculation just once and it would work for all measures.

Trying to describe how this technique works in purely theoretical terms is very difficult, so let's look at some practical examples of how it can be implemented.

Implementing a simple calculation dimension

Here is what we need to do to create a simple calculation dimension, using the approach of creating a new hierarchy on our existing Date dimension:

- Add a new attribute hierarchy to the Date dimension. We will call it `Date Calculations`.

- Ensure that hierarchy only has one member on it, called `Real Value` and set it as the default member. The new hierarchy should also have its `IsAggregatable` property set to `False`, so there is no All Member. Since the `Real Value` member is the only real member on the hierarchy, at this point it will always be selected either implicitly or explicitly for every query we run and will have no impact on what data gets returned. We have not expanded the virtual space of the cube at all at this point.

- Add a new calculated member to the Date Calculations hierarchy called Year To Date.

- Define the Year To Date member so that it calculates the year-to-date value of the current measure for the Real Value member on the Date Calculations hierarchy. By referencing the Real Value member in our calculation, we're simply referencing back to every value for every measure and every other hierarchy in the cube — this is how our new calculation will work for all the measures in the cube.

The first step is easily accomplished by adding a new named calculation to the Date view in the Data Source View. The SQL expression in the named calculation will return the name of the only member on the Date Calculations hierarchy, in our case the string: Real Value. We will then need to use the new column to create a new attribute called Date Calculations in our Date dimension.

The last two steps are the most important ones. We define the new calculated member and we use a scoped assignment to perform the actual calculation:

```
CREATE MEMBER CURRENTCUBE.[Date Order].[Date Calculations].[All].[Year
To Date] AS NULL;

SCOPE ([Date Order].[Date].MEMBERS,
[Date Order].[Calendar Semester].[Calendar Semester].MEMBERS , [Date
Order].[Date Calculations].[Year To Date]);
    THIS = AGGREGATE (
        (YTD ([Date Order].[Calendar].CurrentMember) *
        [Date Order].[Date Calculations].[Real Value]),
        Measures.CurrentMember
          );
END SCOPE;
```

The CREATE MEMBER statement is straightforward: it creates the calculated member and gives it a default value of Null. The SCOPE is the part that does the magic: from everything from the Date level up to the Calendar Semester level, when the Year To Date member is selected in the Date Calculations hierarchy, it aggregates the set returned by YTD by the Real Value member and the current Measure.

| Date Order.Calendar Year | CY 2003 | | | |

Row Labels	Sales Amount Real Value	Year To Date	Gross Profit Real Value	Year To Date
January 2003	1,756,407.01	1,756,407.01	233,884.66	233,884.66
February 2003	2,873,936.93	4,630,343.93	281,949.29	515,833.94
March 2003	2,049,529.87	6,679,873.80	270,302.2	786,136.15
April 2003	2,371,677.70	9,051,551.50	295,559.41	1,081,695.56
May 2003	3,443,525.24	12,495,076.75	353,878.89	1,435,574.45
June 2003	2,542,671.93	15,037,748.68	335,459.25	1,771,033.7
July 2003	3,552,964.81	18,590,713.50	180,512.16	1,951,545.86
August 2003	5,061,391.60	23,652,105.10	102,966.31	2,054,512.17
September 2003	5,059,473.22	28,711,578.32	143,251.94	2,197,764.12
October 2003	3,362,565.46	32,074,143.78	445,886.17	2,643,650.28
November 2003	4,680,484.53	36,754,628.31	519,093.19	3,162,743.47
December 2003	5,243,008.13	41,997,636.44	742,897.5	3,905,640.98
Grand Total	41,997,636.44	41,997,636.44	3,905,640.98	3,905,640.98

We can see from the screenshot that the **Year To Date** calculation works with both **Sales Amount** and **Gross Profit**, even though we did not write any specific code for the two measures. Moreover, the picture shows why the `Real Value` member is needed: it is the reference back to the original physical space of the cube, while Year To Date is the new virtual plane in the multidimensional space that holds the results of our calculation.

Calculation dimension pitfalls and problems

Now we understand roughly how calculation dimensions work, we need to look at the specifics of how they can be implemented and point out certain problems that we might encounter with them. There are several different methods for implementing calculation dimensions and there are pros and cons to each of them that we need to understand.

One approach we do not recommend is using the "Time Intelligence Wizard" that is built into BI Development Studio. This functionality can be used to build a calculation dimension automatically for us; it can be found by running the **Add Business Intelligence** wizard (found under the Cube menu) and choosing the **Define Time Intelligence** option. The wizard uses, essentially, the same technique as the one we described in the previous section—and as we'll see, there are several problems with this approach that seriously limit its usefulness. We'll now explain what these problems are.

Attribute overwrite

The first issue with the approach that the Time Intelligence Wizard takes is that it creates a new hierarchy on an existing dimension to hold calculations, and this can lead to some unexpected behavior. Once again, though, before trying to understand the theory let's take a look at what actually happens in practice.

Consider the following, very simple query:

```
SELECT
    NON EMPTY {
        ([Date Order].[Date Calculations].[Real Value]),
        ([Date Order].[Date Calculations].[Previous Period])
    } ON 0,

    [Date Order].[Calendar].[Date].&[20010712] ON 1
FROM
    Sales
WHERE
    Measures.[Sales Amount]
```

The query returns the real member from the hierarchy that the Time Intelligence Wizard creates, Current Date Order, and the Previous Period calculated member, for the Sales Amount measure and July, 12 2001:

	Current Date Order	**Previous Period**
July 12, 2001	14,134.80	14,313.08

However, if we rewrite the query using a calculated member, as in:

```
WITH
    MEMBER Measures.SalesPreviousPeriod AS
        ([Measures].[Sales Amount],
         [Date Order].[Date Calculations].[Previous Period])
SELECT
    {
        Measures.[Sales Amount],
        SalesPreviousPeriod
    } ON 0,
    NON EMPTY
        [Date Order].[Calendar].[Date].&[20010712]
    ON 1
FROM
    Sales
```

The result seems to be incorrect:

	Current Date Order	SalesPreviousPeriod
July 12, 2001	14,134.80	NULL

As we can see, the value of `SalesPreviousPeriod` is `Null`. This isn't a bug and although it's hard to understand there is a logical explanation for why this happens; it's certainly not what you or your users would expect to happen, though, and is likely to cause some complaints. This behavior is a result of the way attribute relationships within a dimension interact with each other; this is referred to "attribute overwrite" and you can read a full discussion of it here: `http://tinyurl.com/attoverwrite`. There's a discussion of how attribute overwrite causes this particular problem in the following blog entry: `http://tinyurl.com/chrisattoverwrite`.

 The easiest way to avoid this problem is to **never implement a calculation dimension as a new hierarchy on an existing dimension**.

Calculation dimensions should be implemented as new, standalone dimensions, and should not have any relationship with any other dimension.

Limitations of calculated members

As we have seen, a calculation dimension does not need not to have a relationship with any fact table. Since all of the values on it will be calculated, there is no need to have any physical records to hold its data. As a result we might think that all of the calculations on a calculation dimension can be implemented using calculated members, and indeed this is what the Time Intelligence wizard does.

Nevertheless, even if they are indistinguishable from real members to the end user, calculated members suffer some limitations in Analysis Services 2008 and we need to be well aware of them before trying to build a calculation dimension:

- Drillthrough does not work with calculated members. Even if they can be used to make up a set of coordinates to a cell in the cube, just like real members, Analysis Services will refuse to initiate a drillthrough action on a cell covered by a calculated member. Of course, even when we can do a drillthrough we still have the problem of getting it to return the results we'd expect, but that's a problem we'll deal with later.

- There are severe limitations in the security model for calculated members. These limitations will be described in chapter 9 but, basically, although you can use dimension security to restrict access to a real member on a hierarchy, you cannot do the same for a calculated member.

- Some clients handle calculated members in a different way compared to real members. Even if this is a client tool limitation, we need to be aware of it because our users will always interact with a cube through a client tool and will not care whether the limitation is on the client or the server. The most commonly-used client tool that suffers from this problem is Excel 2007, which does not display calculated members on non-measures dimensions by default and which in some circumstances forces you to select all or none of the calculated members on a hierarchy, rather than just the ones you need (see http://tinyurl.com/marcoexcel2007 for more details).

Therefore, from the point of view of usability and flexibility, calculated members are second class citizens. We need to create a proper, physical structure as the basis for our calculation dimension—we need to create real members, not calculated members.

What we are not going to do is pre-calculate all of the values for our calculated members and store them in fact table. What we will do is to fool Analysis Services, creating a real member, while under the hood we will overwrite the value of that real member with the result of an MDX calculation.

Calculation dimension best practices

Now that we are confident with both the basic concept of a calculation dimension and how it should be built, let's now go through the process of building one in more detail, following the best practices we've mentioned.

The first step is to create a new, physical dimension, with real members for each of the calculations we're going to need. We don't actually need to create a table in our data warehouse for this purpose, we can do this with a view something like this:

```
CREATE VIEW DateTool AS
    SELECT ID_Calc = 1, Calc = 'Real Value'
    UNION ALL
    SELECT ID_Calc = 2, Calc = 'Year To Date'
    UNION ALL
    SELECT ID_Calc = 3, Calc = 'Previous Period'
```

This view contains three rows, one for each member we need.

Next, we need to add this view to our DSV and create a dimension based on it. The dimension must have one hierarchy and this hierarchy must have its `IsAggregatable` property set to `False`: it makes no sense to have an All Member on it because the members on it should never be aggregated. The `DefaultMember` property of this hierarchy should then be set to the `Real Value` member. Giving this dimension a name can be quite difficult as it should be something that helps the users understand what it does—here we've called it "Date Tool" but other possibilities could be "Time Calculations" or "Date Comparisons".

After it has been processed the single hierarchy should look like this:

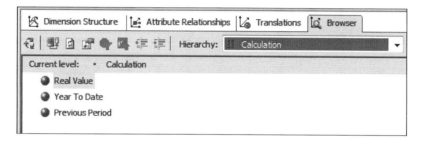

We now need to add it to the cube. What relationship should it have to the measure groups in the cube? In fact it needs no relationship to any measure group at all to work:

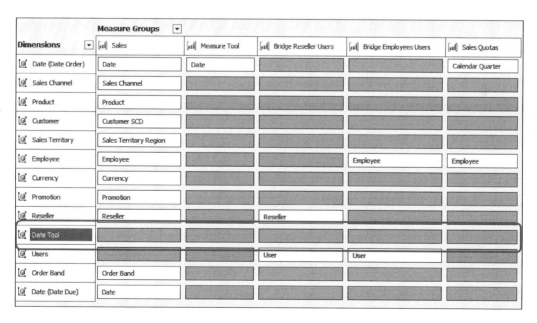

At this point, if we query the cube using this new dimension, we'll see something like what's shown in the following screenshot:

Sales Amount	Column Labels			
Row Labels	Real Value	Year To Date	Previous Period	Grand Total
⊟ CY 2001	1,309,047.20	1,309,047.20	1,309,047.20	1,309,047.20
⊟ H1 CY 2001	432,191.19	432,191.19	432,191.19	432,191.19
⊟ Q2 CY 2001	432,191.19	432,191.19	432,191.19	432,191.19
⊞ July 2001	209,652.90	209,652.90	209,652.90	209,652.90
⊞ August 2001	222,538.29	222,538.29	222,538.29	222,538.29
⊞ H2 CY 2001	876,856.00	876,856.00	876,856.00	876,856.00
⊞ CY 2002	2,154,284.88	2,154,284.88	2,154,284.88	2,154,284.88
⊞ CY 2003	3,033,784.21	3,033,784.21	3,033,784.21	3,033,784.21
⊞ CY 2004	2,563,884.29	2,563,884.29	2,563,884.29	2,563,884.29
Grand Total	9,061,000.58	9,061,000.58	9,061,000.58	9,061,000.58

The same value will be returned for each member on the hierarchy as there is no relationship between the dimension and any measure group.

Our next task is to overwrite the value returned by each member so that they return the calculations we want. We can do this using a simple SCOPE statement in the MDX Script of the cube:

```
SCOPE ([Date Tool].[Calculation].[Year To Date]);
    THIS = AGGREGATE (
            YTD ([Date Order].[Calendar].CurrentMember)
            ,[Date Tool].[Calculation].[Real Value]);
END SCOPE;
```

If we now query the cube, with this calculation in place, we will get the result we want for the Year To Date member of the Date Tool dimension:

Sales Amount	Column Labels			
Row Labels	Real Value	Year To Date	Previous Period	Grand Total
⊟ CY 2001	1,309,047.20	1,309,047.20	1,309,047.20	1,309,047.20
⊟ H1 CY 2001	432,191.19	432,191.19	432,191.19	432,191.19
⊟ Q2 CY 2001	432,191.19	432,191.19	432,191.19	432,191.19
⊞ July 2001	209,652.90	209,652.90	209,652.90	209,652.90
⊞ August 2001	222,538.29	432,191.19	222,538.29	222,538.29
⊞ H2 CY 2001	876,856.00	1,309,047.20	876,856.00	876,856.00
⊞ CY 2002	2,154,284.88	2,154,284.88	2,154,284.88	2,154,284.88
⊞ CY 2003	3,033,784.21	3,033,784.21	3,033,784.21	3,033,784.21
⊞ CY 2004	2,563,884.29	2,563,884.29	2,563,884.29	2,563,884.29
Grand Total	9,061,000.58		9,061,000.58	9,061,000.58

A more complete, worked example of a Calculation Dimension, including many more calculations, is available here: `http://tinyurl.com/datetool`. In some cases, it can even be useful to have more than one calculation dimension in the same cube so that the calculations can interact with each other—for example applying the same period previous year growth calculation to a year-to-date. This is discussed in the following blog entry: `http://tinyurl.com/multicalcdims`

Named sets

Another very interesting topic, slightly related to calculated members, is that of named sets. A named set is, simply, a set of members or tuples to which we assign a name. We define named sets to make it easier for users to build their queries, and also to help us as developers to write more readable code.

Regular named sets

Let's take a look at an example of how named sets can be used. Our user might want to build an Excel report that shows detailed information about the sales of the current month, the sales of the previous month, and the total sales of the last three years. Without a named set, at each start of the month the user would need to update the dates selected in the report in order to display the most recent month with data. In order to avoid having to do this, we can define a named set containing exactly the date range the user wants to see in the report that will never need manual updating. Here's how to do this.

First of all, since the Date Order dimension contains dates in the future that do not contain any sales, we first need to define the set of months where there are sales. This is easy to do using the `NonEmpty` function:

```
CREATE HIDDEN SET ExistingSalePeriods AS
    NonEmpty (
            [Date Order].[Calendar].[Month].Members,
        Measures.[Sales Amount]
    );
```

We define the set as HIDDEN because we do not want to make it visible to the user; we are only going to use it as an intermediate step towards constructing the set we want.

Next, since we are interested in the latest month where there are sales, we can simply define a new set that contains the last item in the `ExistingSalePeriods`:

```
CREATE SET LastSaleMonth AS
    Tail (ExistingSalePeriods, 1);
```

This set, even if it is another step towards our ultimate goal, might be useful for the user to see so we have left it visible. Our final set will contain members at the Year level, so we need to define a new set containing the latest year containing sales:

```
CREATE SET LastSaleYear AS
    Ancestor (
        LastSaleMonth.Item (0),
        [Date Order].[Calendar].[Calendar Year]
    );
```

The last step is to create our final set:

```
CREATE SET LastSaleAnalysisPeriod AS
    {
        LastSaleYear.Item (0).Lag(2) :
        LastSaleYear.Item (0),
        LastSaleMonth.Item (0).PrevMember,
        LastSaleMonth.Item (0)
    };
```

Now that the set has been created, the user will be able to select the set in their client tool and use it in their report very easily:

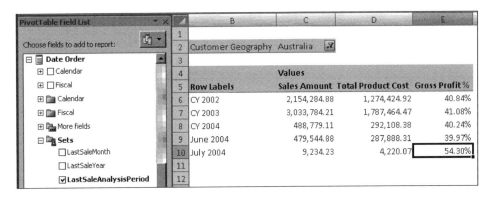

Named sets are evaluated and created every time the cube is processed, so as a result whenever a new month with sales appears in the data, the set will reflect this and the report will automatically show the required time periods when it is refreshed.

Dynamic named sets

As we've just seen, named sets are, by default, static — their contents will always stay the same until the next time the cube is processed. This is useful in some situations, for example when you're trying to improve query performance, but in others it can be quite frustrating. Imagine, for example, we wanted to define a set containing our 10 best-selling products. We can easily build it using the `TopCount` function:

```
CREATE SET Best10Products AS
    TopCount (
            Product.Product.Product.Members,
            10,
            Measures.[Sales Amount]
    );
```

Since this set is evaluated once, before any queries are run, it will contain the top-selling products for all time, for all customers and so on. In other words, when the set is evaluated it knows nothing about any queries we might want to use it in. However, this set isn't much use for reporting: it's highly likely that there will be a different top-ten set of products for each month and each country, and if we wanted to build a report to show the top ten products on rows with month and country on the slicer we'd not be able to use a static named set. For example, the two following queries show the same list of products on rows – and in neither case do they show the top products for the years selected:

```
SELECT Measures.[Sales Amount] ON COLUMNS,
    Best10Products ON ROWS
FROM
    Sales
WHERE
  ([Date Order].[Calendar].[Calendar Year].&[2001])

SELECT Measures.[Sales Amount] ON COLUMNS,
    Best10Products ON ROWS
FROM
    Sales
WHERE
  ([Date Order].[Calendar].[Calendar Year].&[2004])
```

To handle this problem, Analysis Services 2008 introduced DYNAMIC sets. Dynamic sets are evaluated once per query, in the context of the Where clause of that query. In order to make a static set dynamic, all we have to do is add the DYNAMIC keyword just before the SET definition, as in:

```
CREATE DYNAMIC SET Best10ProductsDynamic AS
    TopCount (
            Product.Product.Product.Members,
            10,
            Measures.[Sales Amount]
    );
```

Now, if we run this query:

```
SELECT Measures.[Sales Amount] ON COLUMNS,
    Best10ProductsDynamic ON ROWS
FROM
    Sales
WHERE
  ([Date Order].[Calendar].[Calendar Year].&[2001])

SELECT Measures.[Sales Amount] ON COLUMNS,
    Best10ProductsDynamic ON ROWS
FROM
    Sales
WHERE
  ([Date Order].[Calendar].[Calendar Year].&[2004])
```

We get the correct set of top ten products for each year.

However, dynamic sets are still quite limited in their uses because they are not completely aware of the context of the query they're being used in. For example, if a user tried to put several years on the rows axis of a query they would not be able to use a dynamic set to show the top ten products for each year. Also, the way some client tools generate MDX (once again, Excel 2007 is the main offender here) means that dynamic sets will not work correctly with them. As a result they should be used with care and users must be made aware of what they can and can't be used for.

Summary

In this chapter we have seen many ways to enhance our cube by adding calculations to it. Let us briefly recall them:

- Calculated Measures create new measures whose value is calculated using MDX expressions. The new measures will be available as if they are real measures.

- Calculation dimensions allow us to apply a single calculation to all of the measures in our cube, avoiding the need to create multiple calculated measures.

- Named sets allow us to pre-define static or semi-static sets of members that in turn make building reports easier for our users.

In the next chapter we'll move on to look at a much more complex, but nonetheless common type of calculation: currency conversion.

7
Adding Currency Conversion

In this chapter we will discuss how we can implement currency conversion in an Analysis Services solution. As we will see, it is not always a good idea to perform this currency conversion in the cube itself, it could be better to implement it in the ETL phase—it all depends on our requirements and analysis needs. We will provide some examples of different choices that are available in different circumstances.

BI Development Studio provides a wizard to implement currency conversion in the cube, automatically generating the necessary objects and MDX scripts. We will describe how to use this wizard in the most effective way. Then, we will see how to implement currency conversion using the `MeasureExpression` property of a measure, a feature that is faster but that is also only available in the Enterprise Edition of Analysis Services.

Introduction to currency conversion

The need for currency conversion occurs when measure values have to be reported in a currency that is different from the one used to collect the data originally. It might seem as though this can be solved using a simple calculation; however, your assumptions might be wrong. Consider the following approach to currency conversion:

- Collect currency exchange rates on a daily basis
- Use daily exchange rates to convert each transaction into the desired currency

Why could this pattern be wrong? It might be correct in some cases, but it might be wrong for a variety of reasons. For example, the date used to link the exchange rate value to a transaction might be not the right one, because the date of payment is not recorded in the transaction itself. In another example, if the payment has been made to a foreign currency bank account, the conversion to a different currency should be made using a fixed exchange rate instead of a daily changing exchange rate.

Therefore, before making any decisions on how to implement currency conversion, it is necessary to have very good and detailed business specifications. When they are not available, sit down with a business user who has the necessary knowledge of the data and work through the issues with him.

 More often than not, decisions about currency conversion are not technical issues but business decisions.

After we defined the requirements for currency conversion, we probably might find that they resemble one of the following three scenarios:

- Data is collected in a single currency and we need to display the results using multiple currencies. For example, a company has a list price defined using Euros and they want to show a product catalog on the Web using different currencies.

- Data is collected in several different currencies and we always need to display the results using just one currency. For example, different subsidiaries of a company operate in different countries using different currencies, but all data must be converted into a reference currency for reporting at the company's headquarters.

- Data is collected in several different currencies and we need to display the results using multiple currencies. For example, an international corporation wants to publish balance sheets of its various subsidiaries on its intranet, and allow users to select the currency to be used to show the data.

We will describe these scenarios in more detail and then we will provide guidance on the use of currency conversion related features in Analysis Services.

Data collected in a single currency

If our source data is already stored in a single currency, we probably don't have very much work to do. If the original transactions were made using different currencies, probably the conversion to a single reference currency is done at the transaction level, otherwise it happens somewhere during the ETL phase. If the original transactions were made using a single currency, then conversion is not necessary at all.

In both cases, the only reason we'll need to convert values from one currency to another is for reporting purposes, because we don't have information about the original currency of the transaction any more (if indeed it was different from the one used to store the transaction amount in our fact table). This kind of conversion can happen at the highest level of aggregation, using the same exchange rate regardless of the date of the transactions. However, one common requirement is to perform the conversion using the exchange rate that was correct on the date of each transaction. We suggest double-checking this kind of requirement if you have it, as if all the transactions have been stored using the same currency, it is probably the currency that was used when the transaction was originally made. From a business point of view, forcing the use of a different exchange rate for each day does not respect reality, because no currency conversion took place when the transactions were loaded into the `fact` table. The story is different if the original transactions were made using different currencies and they were converted to a single currency before loading the `fact` table. In that case we should also store the original currency of the transaction, and also the original amount itself and/or the exchange rate that was used.

Thus, in the situation where we have data collected in a single currency, there are two possible subcases:

- Transactions were originally made in the same currency, and there are no signs of currency conversion having taken place for any transactions, so:
    - It should be possible to convert an aggregated amount by a fixed exchange rate
    - There should be no relationship between the fact table containing the transaction data and a historical exchange rate table

- Transactions were made in different currencies, and currency conversion took place during the transaction or in the ETL phase:
    - Each transaction could have the exchange rate used recorded with the transaction itself, or
    - There could be a relationship between the fact table containing the transaction data and a historical exchange rate table

Data collected in a multiple currencies

Our source data might have transactions stored in their original currency. When this happens, the transaction amount is not aggregatable across different currencies, because we cannot add Euros to Dollars without converting them to a reference currency first. This normalization requires currency conversion using an exchange rate that could be different for each transaction, or at the very least for each day if we can apply the same exchange rate to all the transactions that took place on the same day.

We'll assume that, in this case, for each transaction we have the currency used and the amount expressed in that currency stored in the `fact` table, but that we don't have a measure value in a single reference currency, otherwise we'd be in the situation described in the previous section (data collected in a single currency).

Again, we have two possible subcases:

- Data collected in multiple currencies has to be displayed in a reference currency chosen by the end user at query time:

    ○ Conversion to the reference currency must take place at query time; if we don't do this we will have to convert the source data into all the possible reference currencies in advance, during ETL.

- Data collected in multiple currencies can only ever be displayed in a single reference currency:

    ○ In this case, we could perform the conversion at query time or during the ETL phase.

Where to perform currency conversion

In the next section, we will see how to use the "Add Business Intelligence Wizard" in BI Development Studio to implement currency conversion. This wizard can be useful when we decide to implement currency conversion inside the Analysis Services cube itself. However, this is not always the best choice, as we are going to explain in this section.

Generally speaking, it's always better to perform any currency conversion during the ETL phase. However, this is usually only feasible when data will only ever be displayed in one reference currency—in other words, when the end user is not able to modify the currency to be used to display aggregated data. This does not mean we do not need to have a currency dimension in our cube, because it could be useful to know the original currency of the transactions. It only means that aggregated data will always be displayed in the same currency, regardless of any selection made on any dimension.

For example, end users could see how many transactions were originally made in Euros and how many in US dollars. However, the aggregated values of transactions originally made in those currencies are always shown in US dollars, perhaps because the company's headquarters are in New York.

Doing the currency conversion in the ETL phase does not remove the need for an analysis of what the right exchange rate to apply is. For some businesses, the date of the payment is more relevant than the date of the transaction. In other cases, a monthly average of exchange rates would be more accurate because the real currency conversion is not made transaction by transaction, but takes place separately in bulk conversion operations. Henceforth, we will assume that an analysis of the right exchange rate to apply has already been done, for whatever scenario we are going to face.

Thus, there are at least three cases where we suggest implementing currency conversion directly in an Analysis Services cube. The first is when the requirement is to display aggregated data in several different currencies to the end user, regardless of the original currency that the transaction was made in. If the requirement is to display values in a small number of currencies, for example just Euros or US Dollars, the conversion can be handled in the ETL phase, but if end user potentially wants to see values converted to every currency in the world, then it is not going to be feasible to do the conversion in the ETL. The second case is when the user wants to modify the exchange rate values stored in the cube using writeback, which means we cannot know what the rates we need to use are going to be at ETL time.

The third case is when we are not able to implement conversion in the ETL phase. In reality, this third case is more a workaround than a good pattern. For example, we might not have access to the ETL code, or there might be time constraints on ETL development, or we simply might not have any ETL at all, for example if the cube was built directly on an OLTP database (definitely not something we suggest doing!). For these reasons, we will describe how to implement all of the scenarios we described in Analysis Services, but we will focus mainly on the case where the end user wants to display aggregated data and choose the reference currency at query time.

The existence of a feature does not mean that you should use it. Before performing currency conversion inside Analysis Services, check if your requirements can be met by implementing conversion during your ETL phase instead.

The Add Business Intelligence Wizard

The "Add Business Intelligence Wizard" can be used to implement currency conversion in a cube; you can find it under the **Cube** menu by clicking the menu option **Add Business Intelligence** and then, on the second step of the resulting wizard, selecting the **Define Currency Conversion** option. This wizard leverages Analysis Services features that are available in both Standard and Enterprise editions, such as MDX Script calculations. We can achieve the same result without using the wizard, or we can modify the objects and code produced by the wizard so they do what we want.

Concepts and prerequisites

Before using the wizard, we have to model our cube so that we have:

- A Currency dimension:
  - The Type property of the dimension must be set to Currency
  - The Type property of one attribute for the dimension must be set to CurrencyName
  - The IsAggregatable property must be set to False for the key attribute

- A Time dimension:
  - The Type property of the dimension must be set to Time.
  - The Type properties of dimension attributes must be set appropriately. For example, for an attribute representing a date it must be set to Date.

- An Exchange Rate measure group containing:
  - A regular dimension relationship with the Time dimension
  - A regular dimension relationship with the Currency dimension
  - The Type property of the measure group is set to ExchangeRate (this is optional, but it is a best practice)

- One or more other measure groups containing measures to be converted and which have:
  - A regular dimension relationship with the Time dimension
  - If the measures are stored in multiple currencies, a regular dimension relationship with the Currency dimension

Many of the objects above are equivalent to objects that are created by the wizard, such as a `Currency` and `Time` dimension, or an Exchange Rate measure group. There are also other important concepts to learn before using the wizard.

The Exchange Rate measure group contains the exchange rates for converting many different currencies to a single reference currency that we will call the **Pivot Currency**. For example, consider the following table.

Date	Currency	Rate
2009-02-06	EUR	1.2871
2009-02-05	EUR	1.2835
2009-02-06	CHF	0.8550
2009-02-05	CHF	0.8578

The `Rate` column here contains the exchange rate between the currency in the **Currency** column and the US dollar (USD). In this case, the Pivot Currency is USD. Note that the Pivot Currency is not an attribute of the table above and the use of USD is implicit.

The measures that have to be converted using the Currency wizard store their values in a **Local Currency**. The local currency can be identified directly (for example, when the `Currency` dimension is directly related to the measure group) or indirectly (for example, when it is defined as an attribute of another dimension with a regular relationship to the measure group, such as the Country of a Customer). When data is collected in just one currency, the Local Currency will always be the same. In this case, making the Local Currency the same as the Pivot Currency is a good idea, just to make the conversion process more linear and easier to debug.

Finally, we will refer to the currency that users want to display data in as the **Reporting Currency**. It will be a member that the end user selects from the `Reporting Currency` Dimension, a dimension which will be created by the wizard and which will contain all the possible values for the Reporting Currency. This dimension will be based on a named query defined in the Data Source View, which in turn queries the main table of the `Currency` dimension.

How to use the Add Business Intelligence wizard

We will demonstrate the use of the wizard in three main scenarios. As we will see, the key decision you have to make in using the wizard comes on the third step, the **Select Conversion Type** page. Some of what the wizard generates is the same regardless of which option you choose and we will discuss these parts in the first scenario, and then we will comment only on what is different for the remaining scenarios.

Data collected in a single currency with reporting in multiple currencies

The first scenario we consider is probably the most common, where we have data collected using a single currency, and the same currency is used as the Pivot Currency. We will use a simple model to show the steps of the wizard. This model has a transaction fact table with two dimensions (`Product` and `Date`) and a currency exchange rate fact table with two dimensions (`Date` and `Currency`), as seen in the following screenshot. The Pivot Currency in the Rate measure group and the Local Currency in the transaction measure group are US dollars.

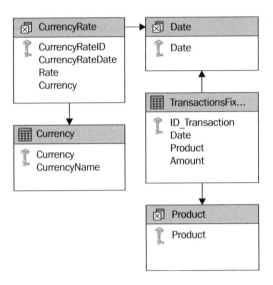

After having selected the **Add Business Intelligence** on the Cube menu in the Cube Editor in BI Development Studio, and having chosen **Define Currency Conversion** on the list of available enhancements, the first step of the wizard is **Set Currency Conversion Options**, which we can see in the following picture.

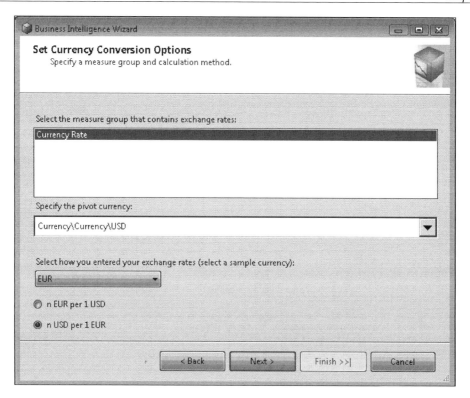

The list of measure groups containing exchange rates will display all measure groups in the cube that are related to a `Currency` dimension. Remember that it is best practice to set the `Type` property of the exchange rates measure group to `ExchangeRate`; however, this is not mandatory for the wizard to work. The choice of the Pivot Currency must be consistent with the data we have in the Exchange Rate measure group. In the example shown, we use USD as the Pivot Currency. Finally, we have to specify if the exchange rate we have is from the Conversion Currency to the Pivot Currency or vice versa. In our previous example, the rate represents how many US dollars are equal to one Euro. The only purpose of the combo box for selecting a sample currency is to show the right currency names in the examples next to the two radio buttons below it.

The next step of the wizard is the **Select Members** page. Here, we can select the measures that will be converted using the exchange rates defined in the previous step. Instead of converting the value of one or more measures, we could select members from an Account hierarchy—useful if only some members on your Account hierarchy contain currency values. This option is disabled in the following picture, because there are no Account hierarchies defined in the cube we're using here.

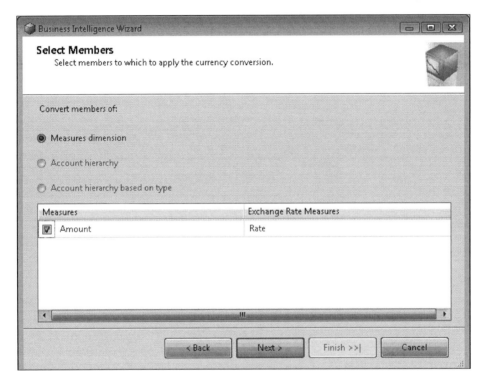

The following step is the **Select Conversion Type** page, which is the most important step for the scenario we are describing now. In this case we have to choose the **One-to-many** option, because in the `fact` table we have measures collected using a single currency and we just want to be able to display the aggregated data using the Reporting Currency of our choice.

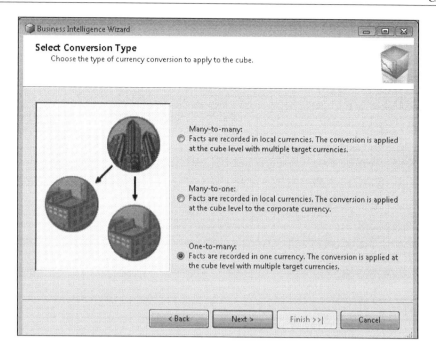

In the next step, the **Specify Reporting Currencies** page, we can filter the list of currencies that can be used as Reporting Currencies. The result of this choice determines the list of currencies included in the WHERE condition of the Named Query that is created in the Data Source View for the Reporting Currency dimension.

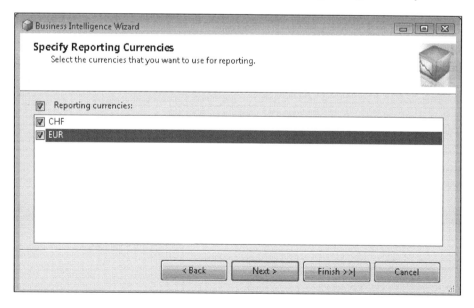

The last step of the wizard, the **Completing the Wizard** page, simply summarizes the changes to the cube that the wizard is going to make. Note that cancelling the wizard at this point will not apply any of the changes to the cube. One other important thing to point out is that if we run the wizard twice on the same cube, the second time it will show only the differences made to the cube on this second run, which will typically affect only the MDX Script.

 The section of the MDX Script generated by the wizard is completely replaced if the wizard is executed again. Bear this in mind before modifying any of the MDX code enclosed by the commented out `<Currency Conversion>` tag in the Script.

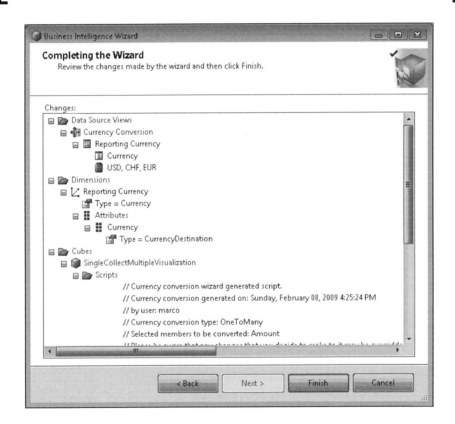

After having clicked Finish, we can see that the wizard has created a **Reporting Currency** dimension, which has been added to the cube, and which has no relationship with any measure group as we can see in the following picture:

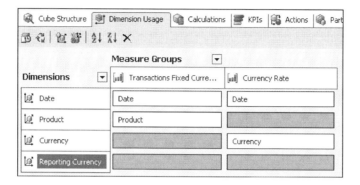

It might seem strange that now we have two Currency dimensions. However, there is a good reason for this: it's the way it supports the requirement to be able to allow only some currencies to be used for reporting purposes.

> If we don't need the filter on available currencies provided by the Reporting Currency dimension, we could simplify the structure of the cube by using the original Currency dimension instead (although this would also require some modifications to the MDX Script generated by the wizard).

To make the Reporting Currency dimension work, the wizard adds a section of MDX code to the Script similar to what's shown below:

```
// All currency conversion formulas are calculated for the
// non pivot currency and at leaf of the time dimension
SCOPE ( { Measures.[Amount] } );
    SCOPE( Leaves([Date]) ,
                     Except(
        [Reporting Currency].[Currency].[Currency].Members,
        [Reporting Currency].[Currency].[Currency].[USD]));

        SCOPE( { Measures.[Amount] } );
            THIS = [Reporting Currency].[Currency].[USD] /
                (Measures.[Rate], LinkMember(
                    [Reporting Currency].[Currency].CurrentMember,
                    [Currency].[Currency])) ;
        END SCOPE;
    END SCOPE; // Leaves of time and non pivot currency
END SCOPE; // Measures
```

This script is interesting as it shows off some of the capabilities of MDX. The nested SCOPE statements define the area within the multidimensional space of the cube that the assignment affects. In the first and third SCOPEs, the space is restricted to the Amount measure. The second SCOPE is the most important one because it defines the granularity of the assignment we are going to do. The LEAVES function returns the most detailed level of the Date hierarchy (which is an attribute hierarchy in our sample cube) that corresponds to the day level. The remaining part of the SCOPE excludes the Pivot Currency from this calculation. Thus, the assignment will change the value of the Amount measure only at the day level. If we will query any part of the cube above the day level (for example, a month or a year), the calculations will take place at the day level and the result will be aggregated up to the level we're querying at. The important concept here is that a scoped assignment at a low level of granularity on a real measure leads to the results of the calculations being aggregated up using the natural aggregation behavior of the measure (which is SUM in our case).

The assignment inside the SCOPE statements converts the Pivot Currency value (which is in USD) into the selected currency in the Reporting Currency dimension. The LinkMember function transfers the selection made on Reporting Currency dimension to the Currency dimension. Since this is the case, the user might not ever need to select anything directly on the Currency dimension, so it could be made invisible to them to avoid confusion.

In the following picture, we can see the result of a query which has the Reporting Currency dimension on rows and two dates on columns. The original data contained sales of 210.00 USD for both the selected days. The conversion to the other two currencies has been made using the daily exchange rate applicable for each day. Thus, values above the day granularity cannot be precalculated using cube aggregations, because MDX script will always aggregate the daily calculated data at runtime.

Amount	Column Labels ▼		
Row Labels ▼	2009-02-05	2009-02-06	Grand Total
CHF	244.81	245.61	490.43
EUR	163.62	163.16	326.77
USD	210.00	210.00	420.00

Data collected in multiple currencies with reporting in a single currency

The second scenario we're going to look at is not so common. In fact, if we have transactions stored in different currencies and we want to report in a single fixed currency, it would make sense to implement the currency conversion for each transaction during the ETL phase. However, there could be reasons why this is not possible. For example, we might receive exchange rate data very late and we don't want to delay data processing, or to have to reprocess that data once the exchange rates are available. Another reason could be that users want to use Analysis Services writeback to change exchange rates in an interactive way, and watch the impact of these changes on the aggregated transactional data in the cube. Whatever the reason, we can use the wizard to implement this kind of currency conversion in Analysis Services.

The data model we will use in this section is shown in the following screenshot. It is similar to the previous model, but this time the transaction fact table also has a link to the Currency dimension. In this example, the Pivot Currency in the Rate measure group is still US dollars, but the Local Currency in the transaction measure group will vary for each transaction and is recorded using the Currency dimension.

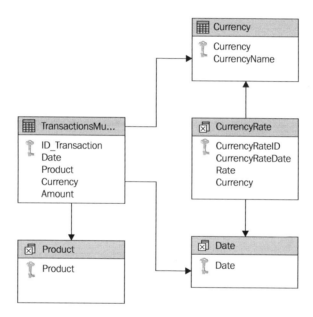

The same selections should be made on the wizard as in previous scenario, until we reach the **Select Conversion Type** page. Here we have to choose the **Many-to-one:** option, because the Local Currency is specific to each transaction and we want to report on our data using a single, fixed currency. The destination currency will be the one chosen as Pivot Currency.

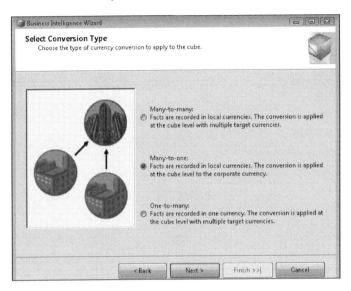

At this point, the wizard shows a new page, **Define Local Currency Reference**, where we tell the wizard how to determine the Local Currency used in each transaction. In the examples we are using, we have to select the Currency attribute of the Currency dimension.

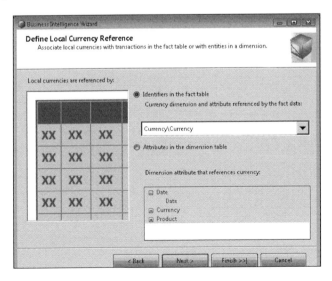

Alternatively, it is possible to use an attribute of another dimension to store the Local Currency. This would be the case, for example, if the currency to use was stored in an attribute related to a `Country` attribute on the `Customer` dimension.

> It is very unlikely you'll have a source data mart where measures are stored in a Local Currency but where you don't know what that currency is. This is only likely to happen in prototypes of cubes based on raw data imported from several sources without any ETL in the middle.

The wizard then finishes and displays the **Completing the Wizard** summary page. At this point we have a new `Reporting Currency` dimension, which has its `IsAggregatable` property set to `false`, and contains only two members: one is USD, which we have used as the Pivot Currency, and the other is the constant `Local`. The default member for this dimension is USD, but the user can always choose to see the original value of the measure in its Local Currency by choosing the `Local` member on the `Reporting Currency` dimension.

> If the data type of the field used to store the currency name in the `Currency` attribute on the `Currency` dimension is less than five characters long, then the wizard creates a `Reporting Currency` dimension with an attribute that is too short to hold the string `Local`. To avoid a truncation error during dimension processing, use a field at least five characters long to store the currency name in the relational table on which the `Currency` dimension is based. Alternatively, we can modify the Named Query that the wizard generates in the Data Source View for the `Reporting Currency` dimension, for example using a cast in the SQL statement.

This is the MDX created by the wizard.

```
SCOPE ( { Measures.[Amount] } );
    SCOPE( Leaves([Date]) ,
            [Reporting Currency].[USD],
            Leaves([Currency]));
        SCOPE( { Measures.[Amount] } );
            THIS = [Reporting Currency].[Local]
                 * Measures.[Rate];
        END SCOPE;
    END SCOPE;
END SCOPE; // Measures
```

The code here is similar to the MDX generated in the previous scenario. In this case, we have a single Reporting Currency (USD) and the conversion formula is applied to all the Local Currencies through a scoped assignment on `LEAVES([Currency])`.

The resulting cube will have two currency dimensions: the original dimension is used for the Local Currency and the dimension added by the wizard is used for the Reporting Currency. When nothing is selected on these dimensions the end user will see USD used as the Reporting Currency; the following screenshot shows both the original values of the Local Currencies and the converted USD values.

Amount	Local Currency ▼		
Reporting Currency ▼	**EUR**	**USD**	**Grand Total**
Local	210.00	320.00	530.00
USD	270.26	320.00	590.26

One important thing to point out is that to get the results we just showed, we need to define an exchange rate for converting USD values to USD. This is a requirement of the MDX code generated by the wizard; if we don't do this, we'll see an empty cell for the USD/USD cell in the previous report and this will affect the Grand Total too. This is not smart behavior on the part of the wizard-generated code, because after all there should be no need to convert a currency into itself. As a result, we need an exchange rate table like this:

Date	Currency	Rate
2009-02-06	USD	1.0000
2009-02-05	USD	1.0000
2009-02-06	EUR	1.2871
2009-02-05	EUR	1.2835
2009-02-06	CHF	0.8550
2009-02-05	CHF	0.8578

Data stored in multiple currencies with reporting in multiple currencies

The third and last scenario is the most complex one. Here, we have transactions stored in different currencies, but this time we want to report in any currency chosen by the end user. Even in this case, some currency conversion could take place during the ETL phase to normalize data to the Pivot Currency, but we might need to do the conversion in Analysis Services for the same reasons we discussed in the previous scenario.

The data model that we're going to use is the same as in the previous scenario. We'll also make the same selections in the wizard until the **Select Conversion Type** page, where we have to choose the **Many-to-many** option. The next step will be the **Define Local Currency Reference** page, and after that will be the **Specify Reporting Currencies** step, just the same as in the first scenario.

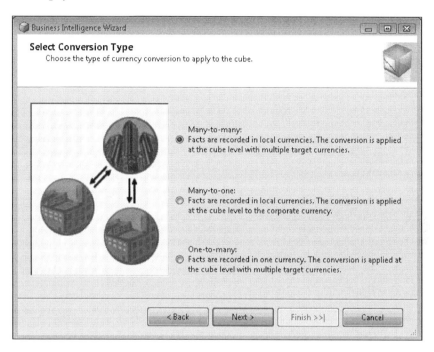

The MDX generated is a combination of that seen in both the previous scenarios:

```
SCOPE ( { Measures.[Amount] } );
    SCOPE( Leaves([Date]) ,
            [Reporting Currency].[USD],
            Leaves([Currency]));
        SCOPE( { Measures.[Amount] } );
            THIS = [Reporting Currency].[Local]
                    * Measures.[Rate];
        END SCOPE;
END SCOPE; // Leaves of time and non pivot currency
SCOPE( Leaves([Date]) ,
                    Except(
        [Reporting Currency].[Currency].[Currency].Members,
        { [Reporting Currency].[Currency].[Currency].[USD],
          [Reporting Currency].[Currency].[Currency].[Local] }));
        SCOPE( { Measures.[Amount] } );
```

```
                  THIS = [Reporting Currency].[Currency].[USD] /
                    (Measures.[Rate], LinkMember(
                       [Reporting Currency].[Currency].CurrentMember,
                       [Currency].[Currency])) ;
              END SCOPE;
          END SCOPE; // Leaves of time and non pivot currency
      END SCOPE; // Measures
```

The first assignment converts the Local Currency into the Pivot Currency, USD, as in the previous scenario. The second assignment converts the Pivot Currency we just calculated into the Reporting Currency. This second statement has a slightly different SCOPE to the one we saw in the first scenario, because it has to exclude both the USD and Local members from the Local Currency dimension (which is simply named Currency).

After having run the wizard, we can combine any Local Currency with any Reporting Currency, as in the following screenshot:

Amount	Local Currency ▾		
Reporting Currency ▾	EUR	USD	Grand Total
CHF	316.04	374.19	690.23
EUR	210.00	248.66	458.66
Local	210.00	320.00	530.00
USD	270.26	320.00	590.26

Notice that, once again, a special Local member has been added to the Reporting Currency dimension. And once again, an exchange rate with the value 1 for the currency used as Pivot Currency has to be present in the Exchange Rate measure group.

Measure expressions

We have now seen how to implement currency conversion using the Add Business Intelligence wizard in BI Developer Studio. The wizard implements currency conversion using techniques, such as MDX Script calculations, that are available in both the Standard and Enterprise editions of Analysis Services. However, there is an alternative way to implement currency conversion without the need for calculations in the MDX Script. We can use the MeasureExpression property of a measure instead, combined with a many-to-many dimension relationship in the cube.

The data model that we'll use to demonstrate this technique is very similar to the data model we used in the first scenario for the wizard. The only change is the definition of a many-to-many dimension relationship between the Currency dimension and the measure group containing the transaction data.

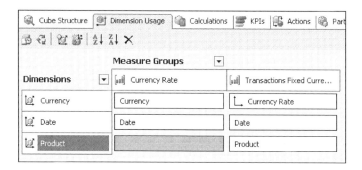

The Currency dimension will, here, work in the same way as the Reporting Currency dimension does in the solution generated by the wizard. The MeasureExpression property contains an MDX expression that returns the value of the measure. This expression will be evaluated at the lowest common granularity of the two measure groups before aggregation takes place. Functionally, it is not much different to the MDX Script calculations generated by the currency conversion wizard. However, from the point of view of query performance, it is potentially faster.

The MDX expression used in a MeasureExpression property must be in the form M1 op M2, where the operator op can be only * or /. M1 and M2 must be measures from different measure groups, with the condition that these measure groups share at least one common dimension. In our example, we have two dimensions that are used by both measure groups: one is Date, the other is Currency (which has a many-to-many relationship). We can use the following expression in the MeasureExpression property of the Amount measure:

```
Amount / Rate
```

The MeasureExpression is not recursive: when the MDX expression refers to Amount in the division, it will use the raw value of the Amount measure before any MDX script calculations have taken place. The Rate measure in the expression contains the exchange rate value stored in the Exchange Rate measure group. The calculation will take place at the Date and Currency granularity and the result will then be summed up to higher levels of granularity.

The MeasureExpression expression is evaluated before the calculations in the MDX Script are evaluated. Thus, if you perform a calculation in the MDX Script on a measure which has its MeasureExpression property set, the value of that measure will have already been changed as a result of the calculation of the measure expression.

At query time the results we get are identical to the ones we obtained in the first example in this chapter, as we can see in the following screenshot:

Amount	Date		
Currency ▾	2009-02-05	2009-02-06	Grand Total
CHF	244.81	245.61	490.43
EUR	163.62	163.16	326.77
USD	210.00	210.00	420.00
Grand Total	66.85	66.83	133.69

At this point we still need to have a row containing a rate of 1 for US Dollars for each day in the Date dimension. Thus, USD values are still converted to USD using the MeasureExpression property, even if it is not really necessary. However, in this case we can optimize the conversion using the DirectSlice property of the many-to-many dimension relationship that relates the Currency dimension to our Transactions measure group.

DirectSlice property

The DirectSlice property of a many-to-many dimension relationship can be set to contain an MDX tuple. When that tuple is selected in a query the MeasureExpression property will be ignored and the raw measure value will be returned instead. In other words, for certain parts of the cube we want the original value of the measure instead of the calculated value returned by the expression in the MeasureExpression property. For example, we can skip the MeasureExpression calculation when the Reporting Currency is the same as the Pivot Currency, which is USD in our example. This has two consequences:

- First, there is no need to put rows in the Exchange Rate fact table containing the rate 1 for US Dollars for each day.

- Second, when the user requests the USD Currency and looks at data that is stored as US Dollars in the fact table, the query response will be faster because there is no need to resolve the many-to-many relationship or perform any currency conversion.

Please note that we cannot use MDX functions to build dynamic expressions in the DirectSlice property, we can only write an explicit tuple such as ([Currency].[Currency].&[USD]).

At the time of writing, on Service Pack 1 of Analysis Services 2008, there is a important bug concerning the DirectSlice property. Please check http://tinyurl.com/BugDirectSlice to find out more about this bug and see whether it has been fixed or not. If it has not been fixed, using the DirectSlice property could mean your queries return inconsistent results.

Writeback

As we mentioned above, when working with exchange rates our users may need to do "what-if" analysis to see what the impact of different exchange rates would be on the company's profitability. We can let our users do this by "write-enabling" a measure group: on the **Partitions** tab of the **Cube** Editor, right-click on any partition within the measure group and select **Writeback Settings** to display the **Enable Writeback** dialog.

 You cannot enable writeback on a measure group if it contains a measure whose AggregateFunction property is set to anything other than **Sum**.

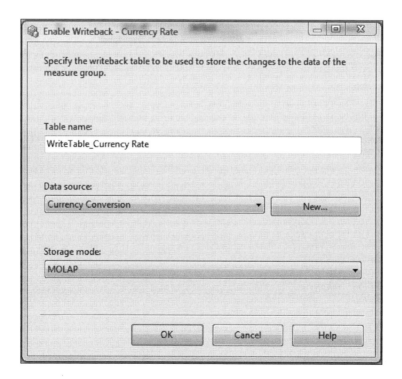

When you click **OK**, Analysis Services will create a new writeback partition in your measure group and also a new `fact` table in your relational data source. The `fact` table does not hold the values that users write back to the cube; instead it holds delta values so that the sum of the original values in the measure group plus the deltas adds up to the last value written back to a cell.

Writeback can lead to poor query performance on larger measure groups, although in the case of an exchange rate measure group this is not likely. There are two pain points:

- When a user commits an updated cell value back to the cube, this value must be allocated down to the granularity of the writeback fact table. If the cell you're writing back to is at a much higher granularity than the `fact` table, this can take a very long time.

- When a user queries a cube with writeback enabled, the writeback partition has to be queried along with the original partitions. Using **MOLAP** storage mode for your writeback partition, which is the default, reduces this performance penalty and we recommend you always do this rather than use **ROLAP** storage. However, using **MOLAP** storage means committing updated cell values will take slightly longer because Analysis Services now has to process the writeback partition as well.

 If you intend to use writeback, first check whether your chosen client tool supports it. Some, for example Excel 2007, do not.

Summary

In this chapter we have seen how to implement currency conversion in several different ways. In many cases currency conversion can take place in the ETL phase and where this is possible it is the best option to take. However, there are some situations that require that currency conversion be implemented in Analysis Services.

We have seen how to use the "Define Currency Conversion" option in the "Add Business Intelligence" wizard. This wizard generates the necessary objects and MDX Script calculations to implement currency conversion in both the Standard and Enterprise editions of Analysis Services. For better query performance, we have also discussed how to implement currency conversion using the `MeasureExpression` property instead, which is available only in Enterprise edition.

Query Performance Tuning

8

One of the main reasons for building Analysis Services cubes as part of a BI solution is because it should mean you get better query performance than if you were querying your relational database directly. While it's certainly the case that Analysis Services is very fast it would be naive to think that all of our queries, however complex, will return in seconds without any tuning being necessary. This chapter will describe the steps you'll need to go through in order to ensure your cube is as responsive as possible, covering the following topics:

- Partitioning measure groups
- Building aggregations
- Tuning MDX calculations and queries
- Using caching to your advantage
- Scale-out options

 This chapter should be read in conjunction with the very detailed white paper, *The Analysis Services 2008 Performance Guide*, which can be downloaded from `http://tinyurl.com/ssas2008perfguide`

How Analysis Services processes queries

Before we start to discuss how to improve query performance, we need to understand what happens inside Analysis Services when a query is run. The two major parts of the Analysis Services engine are:

- **The Formula Engine** processes MDX queries, works out what data is needed to answer them, requests that data from the Storage Engine, and then performs all calculations needed for the query.
- **The Storage Engine** handles all reading and writing of data; it fetches the data that the Formula Engine requests when a query is run and aggregates it to the required granularity.

When you run an MDX query, then, that query goes first to the Formula Engine where it is parsed; the Formula Engine then requests all of the raw data needed to answer the query from the Storage Engine, performs any calculations on that data that are necessary, and then returns the results in a cellset back to the user. There are numerous opportunities for performance tuning at all stages of this process, as we'll see.

Performance tuning methodology

When doing performance tuning there are certain steps you should follow to allow you to measure the effect of any changes you make to your cube, its calculations or the query you're running:

- Wherever possible, test your queries in an environment that is identical to your production environment. Otherwise ensure that the size of the cube and the server hardware you're running on is at least comparable, and running the same build of Analysis Services.

- Make sure that no-one else has access to the server you're running your tests on. You won't get reliable results if someone else starts running queries at the same time as you.

- Make sure that the queries you're testing with are equivalent to the ones that your users want to have tuned. As we'll see, you can use Profiler to capture the exact queries your users are running against the cube.

- Whenever you test a query, run it twice: first on a cold cache, and then on a warm cache. Make sure you keep a note of the time each query takes to run and what you changed on the cube or in the query for that run.

Clearing the cache is a very important step—queries that run for a long time on a cold cache may be instant on a warm cache. When you run a query against Analysis Services, some or all of the results of that query (and possibly other data in the cube, not required for the query) will be held in cache so that the next time a query is run that requests the same data it can be answered from cache much more quickly. To clear the cache of an Analysis Services database, you need to execute a `ClearCache` XMLA command. To do this in SQL Management Studio, open up a new XMLA query window and enter the following:

```
<Batch xmlns="http://schemas.microsoft.com/analysisservices/2003/
engine">
  <ClearCache>
    <Object>
      <DatabaseID>Adventure Works DW 2008</DatabaseID>
    </Object>
  </ClearCache>
</Batch>
```

Remember that the ID of a database may not be the same as its name — you can check this by right-clicking on a database in the **SQL Management Studio Object Explorer** and selecting **Properties**. Alternatives to this method also exist: the MDX Studio tool allows you to clear the cache with a menu option, and the Analysis Services Stored Procedure Project (`http://tinyurl.com/asstoredproc`) contains code that allows you to clear the Analysis Services cache and the Windows File System cache directly from MDX. Clearing the Windows File System cache is interesting because it allows you to compare the performance of the cube on a warm and cold file system cache as well as a warm and cold Analysis Services cache: when the Analysis Services cache is cold or can't be used for some reason, a warm file system cache can still have a positive impact on query performance.

After the cache has been cleared, before Analysis Services can answer a query it needs to recreate the calculated members, named sets and other objects defined in a cube's MDX script. If you have any reasonably complex named set expressions that need to be evaluated, you'll see some activity in Profiler relating to these sets being built and it's important to be able to distinguish between this and activity that's related to the queries you're actually running. All MDX Script related activity occurs between the `Execute MDX Script Begin` and `Execute MDX Script End` events; these are fired after the `Query Begin` event but before the `Query Cube Begin` event for the query run after the cache has been cleared. When looking at a Profiler trace you should either ignore everything between the `Execute MDX Script Begin` and `End` events or run a query that returns no data at all to trigger the evaluation of the MDX Script, for example:

```
SELECT {} ON 0
FROM [Adventure Works]
```

Designing for performance

Many of the recommendations for designing cubes we've given so far in this book have been given on the basis that they will improve query performance, and in fact the performance of a query is intimately linked to the design of the cube it's running against. For example, dimension design, especially optimising attribute relationships, can have a significant effect on the performance of all queries—at least as much as any of the optimisations described in this chapter. As a result, we recommend that if you've got a poorly performing query the first thing you should do is review the design of your cube (along with the relevant chapters of this book) to see if there is anything you could do differently. There may well be some kind of trade-off needed between usability, manageability, time-to-develop, overall "elegance" of the design and query performance, but since query performance is usually the most important consideration for your users then it will take precedence. To put it bluntly, if the queries your users want to run don't run fast your users will not want to use the cube at all!

Performance-specific design features

Once you're sure that your cube design is as good as you can make it, it's time to look at two features of Analysis Services that are transparent to the end user but have an important impact on performance and scalability: measure group partitioning and aggregations. Both of these features relate to the Storage Engine and allow it to answer requests for data from the Formula Engine more efficiently.

Partitions

A partition is a data structure that holds some or all of the data held in a measure group. When you create a measure group, by default that measure group contains a single partition that contains all of the data. Enterprise Edition of Analysis Services allows you to divide a measure group into multiple partitions; Standard Edition is limited to one partition per measure group, and the ability to partition is one of the main reasons why you would want to use Enterprise Edition over Standard Edition.

Why partition?

Partitioning brings two important benefits: better manageability and better performance. Partitions within the same measure group can have different storage modes and different aggregation designs, although in practice they usually don't differ in these respects; more importantly they can be processed independently, so for example when new data is loaded into a fact table, you can process only the partitions that should contain the new data. Similarly, if you need to remove old or incorrect data from your cube, you can delete or reprocess a partition without affecting the rest of the measure group. We'll explore these manageability benefits in more detail in Chapter 10.

Partitioning can also improve both processing performance and query performance significantly. Analysis Services can process multiple partitions in parallel and this can lead to much more efficient use of CPU and memory resources on your server while processing is taking place. Analysis Services can also fetch and aggregate data from multiple partitions in parallel when a query is run too, and again this can lead to more efficient use of CPU and memory and result in faster query performance. Lastly, Analysis Services will only scan the partitions that contain data necessary for a query and since this reduces the overall amount of IO needed this can also make queries faster.

Building partitions

You can view, create and delete partitions on the **Partitions** tab of the **Cube Editor** in BIDS. When you run the New Partition Wizard or edit the `Source` property of an existing partition, you'll see you have two options for controlling what data is used in the partition:

- Table Binding means that the partition contains all of the data in a table or view in your relational data source, or a named query defined in your DSV. You can choose the table you wish to bind to on the Specify Source Information step of the New Partition Wizard, or in the **Partition Source** dialog if you choose **Table Binding** from the **Binding Type** dropdown box.
- Query Binding allows you to specify an SQL `SELECT` statement to filter the rows you want from a table; BIDS will automatically generate part of the `SELECT` statement for you, and all you'll need to do is supply the `WHERE` clause. If you're using the New Partition Wizard, this is the option that will be chosen if you check the **Specify a query to restrict rows** checkbox on the second step of the wizard; in the **Partition Source** dialog you can choose this option from the Binding Type drop-down box.

It might seem like query binding is the easiest way to filter your data, and while it's the most widely-used approach it does have one serious shortcoming: since it involves hard-coding an SQL `SELECT` statement into the definition of the partition, changes to your fact table such as the deletion or renaming of a column can mean the `SELECT` statement errors when it is run if that column is referenced in it. This means in turn will cause the partition processing to fail.. If you have a lot of partitions in your measure group—and it's not unusual to have over one hundred partitions on a large cube—altering the query used for each one is somewhat time-consuming. Instead, table-binding each partition to a view in your relational database will make this kind of maintenance much easier, although you do of course now need to generate one view for each partition. Alternatively, if you're building query-bound partitions from a single view on top of your fact table (which means you have complete control over the columns the view exposes), you could use a query like SELECT * FROM <View> in each partition's definition.

 It's very important that you check the queries you're using to filter your fact table for each partition. If the same fact table row appears in more than one partition, or if fact table rows don't appear in any partition, this will result in your cube displaying incorrect measure values.

On the Processing and Storage Locations step of the wizard you have the chance to create the partition on a remote server instance, functionality that is called Remote Partitions. This is one way of scaling out Analysis Services: you can have a cube and measure group on one server but store some of the partitions for the measure group on a different server, something like a linked measure group but at a lower level.

This can be useful for improving processing performance in situations when you have a very small time window available for processing but in general we recommend that you do not use remote partitions. They have an adverse effect on query performance and they make management of the cube (especially backup) very difficult.

Also on the same step you have the chance to store the partition at a location other than the default of the Analysis Services data directory. Spreading your partitions over more than one volume may make it easier to improve the IO performance of your solution, although again it can complicate database backup and restore.

After assigning an aggregation design to the partition (we'll talk about aggregations in detail next), the last important property to set on a partition is `Slice`. The `Slice` property takes the form of an MDX member, set or tuple — MDX expressions returning members, sets or tuples are not allowed however - and indicates what data is present in a partition. While you don't have to set it, we strongly recommend that you do so, even for MOLAP partitions, for the following reasons:

- While Analysis Services does automatically detect what data is present in a partition during processing, it doesn't always work as well as you'd expect and can result in unwanted partition scanning taking place at query time in a number of scenarios. The following blog entry on the SQLCat team site explains why in detail: `http://tinyurl.com/partitionslicing`

- It acts as a useful safety mechanism to ensure that you only load the data you're expecting into a partition. If, while processing, Analysis Services finds that data is being loaded into the partition that conflicts with what's specified in the `Slice` property, then processing will fail.

More detail on how to set the Slice property can be found in Mosha Pasumansky's blog entry on the subject here: `http://tinyurl.com/moshapartition`

Planning a partitioning strategy

We now know why we should be partitioning our measure groups and what to do to create a partition; the next question is: how should we split the data in our partitions? We need to find some kind of happy medium between the manageability and performance aspects of partitioning — we need to split our data so that we do as little processing as possible, but also so that as few partitions are scanned as possible by our users' queries. Luckily, if we partition by our Time dimension we can usually meet both needs very well: it's usually the case that when new data arrives in a fact table it's for a single day, week or month, and it's also the case that the most popular way of slicing a query is by a time period.

Therefore, it's almost always the case that when measure groups are partitioned they are partitioned by time. It's also worth considering, though, if it's a good idea to partition by time and another dimension: for example, in an international company you might have a `Geography` dimension and a `Country` attribute, and users may always be slicing their queries by `Country` too—in which case it might make sense to partition by `Country`.

Measure groups that contain measures with the `Distinct Count` aggregation type require their own specific partitioning strategy. While you should still partition by time, you should also partition by non-overlapping ranges of values within the column you're doing the distinct count on. A lot more detail on this is available in the following white paper: `http://tinyurl.com/distinctcountoptimize`

It's worth looking at the distribution of data over partitions for dimensions we're not explicitly slicing by, as there is often a dependency between data in these dimensions and the Time dimension: for example, a given Product may only have been sold in certain Years or in certain Countries. You can see the distribution of member DataIDs (the internal key values that Analysis Services creates for all members on a hierarchy) for a partition by querying the `Discover_Partition_Dimension_Stat` DMV, for example:

```
SELECT *
FROM SystemRestrictSchema($system.Discover_Partition_Dimension_Stat
        ,DATABASE_NAME = 'Adventure Works DW 2008'
        ,CUBE_NAME = 'Adventure Works'
        ,MEASURE_GROUP_NAME = 'Internet Sales'
        ,PARTITION_NAME = 'Internet_Sales_2003')
```

The following screenshot shows what the results of this query look like:

DATABASE_NAME	CUBE_NAME	MEASURE_GROUP_NAME	PARTITION_NAME	DIMENSION_NAME	ATTRIBUTE_NAME	ATTRIBUTE_INDEXED	ATTRIBUTE_COUNT_MIN	ATTRIBUTE_COUNT_MAX
Adventure Works DW 2008	Adventure Works	Internet Sales	Internet_Sales_2003	Promotion	(All)	False	1	1
Adventure Works DW 2008	Adventure Works	Internet Sales	Internet_Sales_2003	Promotion	Promotion Category	True	3	4
Adventure Works DW 2008	Adventure Works	Internet Sales	Internet_Sales_2003	Promotion	Promotion	True	2	15
Adventure Works DW 2008	Adventure Works	Internet Sales	Internet_Sales_2003	Promotion	Promotion Type	True	4	7
Adventure Works DW 2008	Adventure Works	Internet Sales	Internet_Sales_2003	Promotion	Discount Percent	True	2	7
Adventure Works DW 2008	Adventure Works	Internet Sales	Internet_Sales_2003	Promotion	Max Quantity	True	2	3
Adventure Works DW 2008	Adventure Works	Internet Sales	Internet_Sales_2003	Promotion	Min Quantity	True	2	3
Adventure Works DW 2008	Adventure Works	Internet Sales	Internet_Sales_2003	Promotion	End Date	True	9	11
Adventure Works DW 2008	Adventure Works	Internet Sales	Internet_Sales_2003	Promotion	Start Date	True	2	7
Adventure Works DW 2008	Adventure Works	Internet Sales	Internet_Sales_2003	Sales Territory	(All)	False	1	1
Adventure Works DW 2008	Adventure Works	Internet Sales	Internet_Sales_2003	Sales Territory	Sales Territory Group	True	2	5
Adventure Works DW 2008	Adventure Works	Internet Sales	Internet_Sales_2003	Sales Territory	Sales Territory Country	True	2	8
Adventure Works DW 2008	Adventure Works	Internet Sales	Internet_Sales_2003	Sales Territory	Sales Territory Region	True	2	11
Adventure Works DW 2008	Adventure Works	Internet Sales	Internet_Sales_2003	Internet Sales Order ...	(All)	False	1	1
Adventure Works DW 2008	Adventure Works	Internet Sales	Internet_Sales_2003	Internet Sales Order ...	Sales Order Number	False	0	0

There's also a useful Analysis Services stored procedure that shows the same data and any partition overlaps included in the Analysis Services Stored Procedure Project (a free, community-developed set of sample Analysis Services stored procedures): `http://tinyurl.com/partitionhealth`. This blog entry describes how you can take this data and visualise it in a Reporting Services report: `http://tinyurl.com/viewpartitionslice`

We also need to consider what size our partitions should be. In general between 5 and 20 million rows per partition, or up to around 3GB, is a good size. If you have a measure group with a single partition of below 5 million rows then don't worry, it will perform very well, but it's not worth dividing it into smaller partitions; it's equally possible to get good performance with partitions of 50-60 million rows. It's also best to avoid having too many partitions as well—if you have more than a few hundred it may make SQL Management Studio and BIDS slow to respond, and it may be worth creating fewer, larger partitions assuming these partitions stay within the size limits for a single partition we've just given.

Automatically generating large numbers of partitions

When creating a measure group for the first time, it's likely you'll already have a large amount of data and may need to create a correspondingly large number of partitions for it. Clearly the last thing you'll want to do is create tens or hundreds of partitions manually and it's worth knowing some tricks to create these partitions automatically. One method involves taking a single partition, scripting it out to XMLA and then pasting and manipulating this in Excel, as detailed here: `http://tinyurl.com/generatepartitions`. The Analysis Services Stored Procedure Project also contains a set of functions for creating partitions automatically based on MDX set expressions: `http://tinyurl.com/autopartition`. Management of partitions once the cube has gone into production is discussed in Chapter 10.

Unexpected partition scans

Even when you have configured your partitions properly it's sometimes the case that Analysis Services will scan partitions that you don't expect it to be scanning for a particular query. If you see this happening (and we'll talk about how you can monitor partition usage later in this chapter) the first thing to determine is whether these extra scans are making a significant contribution to your query times. If they aren't, then it's probably not worth worrying about; if they are, there are some things to try to attempt to stop it happening.

The extra scans could be the result of a number of factors, including:

- The way you have written MDX for queries or calculations. In most cases it will be very difficult to rewrite the MDX to stop the scans, but the following blog entry describes how it is possible in one scenario: `http://tinyurl.com/moshapart`

- As mentioned in Chapter 4, the `LastNonEmpty` measure aggregation type may result in multiple partition scans. If you can restructure your cube so you can use the `LastChild` aggregation type, Analysis Services will only scan the last partition containing data for the current time period.

- In some cases, even when you've set the `Slice` property, Analysis Services has trouble working out which partitions should be scanned for a query. Changing the attributes mentioned in the `Slice` property may help, but not always. The section on *Related Attributes* and *Almost Related Attributes* in the following blog entry discusses this in more detail: `http://tinyurl.com/mdxpartitions`

- Analysis Services may also decide to retrieve more data than is needed for a query to make answering future queries more efficient. This behavior is called **prefetching** and can be turned off by setting the following connection string properties: `Disable Prefetch Facts=True; Cache Ratio=1`

  More information on this can be found in the section on *Prefetching and Request Ordering* in the white paper *Identifying and Resolving MDX Query Bottleneck* available from `http://tinyurl.com/mdxbottlenecks`

  Note that setting these connection string properties can have other, negative effects on query performance.

You can set connection string properties in SQL Management Studio when you open a new MDX Query window. Just click the **Options** button on the **Connect to Analysis Services** dialog, then go to the **Additional Connection Parameters** tab. Note that in the RTM version of SQL Management Studio there is a problem with this functionality, so that when you set a connection string property it will continue to be set for all connections, even though the textbox on the **Additional Connection Parameters tab** is blank, until SQL Management Studio is closed down or until you set the same property differently.

Aggregations

An aggregation is simply a pre-summarised data set, similar to the result of an SQL SELECT statement with a GROUP BY clause, that Analysis Services can use when answering queries. The advantage of having aggregations built in your cube is that it reduces the amount of aggregation that the Analysis Services Storage Engine has to do at query time, and building the right aggregations is one of the most important things you can do to improve query performance. Aggregation design is an ongoing process that should start once your cube and dimension designs have stabilised and which will continue throughout the lifetime of the cube as its structure and the queries you run against it change; in this section we'll talk about the steps you should go through to create an optimal aggregation design.

Creating an initial aggregation design

The first stage in creating an aggregation design should be to create a core set of aggregations that will be generally useful for most queries run against your cube. This should take place towards the end of the development cycle when you're sure that your cube and dimension designs are unlikely to change much, because any changes are likely to invalidate your aggregations and mean this step will have to be repeated. It can't be stressed enough that good dimension design is the key to getting the most out of aggregations: removing unnecessary attributes, setting AttributeHierarchyEnabled to False where possible, building optimal attribute relationships and building user hierarchies will all make the aggregation design process faster, easier and more effective. You should also take care to update the EstimatedRows property of each measure group and partition, and the EstimatedCount of each attribute before you start, and these values are also used by the aggregation design process. BIDS Helper adds a new button to the toolbar in the **Partitions** tab of the Cube Editor to update all of these count properties with one click.

To build this initial set of aggregations we'll be running the Aggregation Design Wizard, which can be run by clicking the **Design Aggregations** button on the toolbar of the **Aggregations** tab of the Cube Editor. This wizard will analyse the structure of your cube and dimensions, look at various property values you've set, and try to come up with a set of aggregations that it thinks should be useful. The one key piece of information it doesn't have at this point is what queries you're running against the cube, so some of the aggregations it designs may not prove to be useful in the long-run, but running the wizard is extremely useful for creating a first draft of your aggregation designs.

You can only design aggregations for one measure group at a time; if you have more than one partition in the measure group you've selected then the first step of the wizard asks you to choose which partitions you want to design aggregations for. An aggregation design can be associated with many partitions in a measure group, and a partition can be associated with just one aggregation design or none at all. We recommend that, in most cases, you have just one aggregation design for each measure group for the sake of simplicity. However if processing time is limited and you need to reduce the overall time spent building aggregations, or if query patterns are different for different partitions within the same measure group, then it may make sense to apply different aggregation designs to different partitions.

The next step of the wizard asks you to review the `AggregationUsage` property of all the attributes on all of the cube dimensions in your cube; this property can also be set on the **Cube Structure** tab of the Cube Editor.

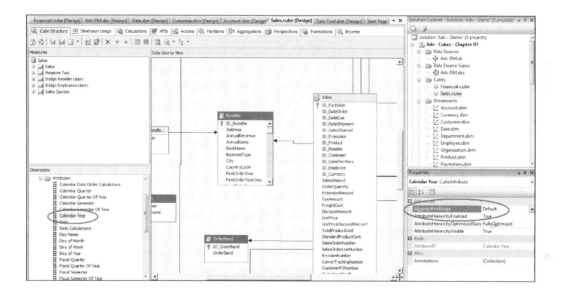

The following figure shows the Aggregation Design Wizard:

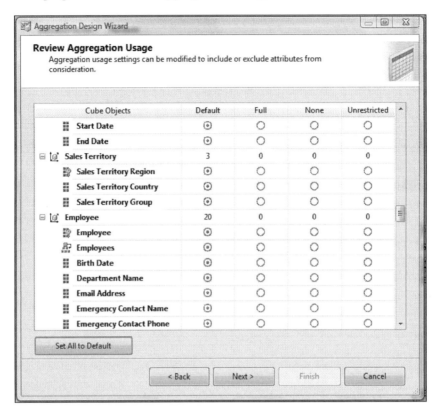

The `AggregationUsage` property controls how dimension attributes are treated in the aggregation design process. The property can be set to the following values:

- **Full**: This means the attribute, or an attribute at a lower granularity directly related to it by an attribute relationship, will be included in every single aggregation the wizard builds. We recommend that you use this value sparingly, for at most one or two attributes in your cube, because it can significantly reduce the number of aggregations that get built. You should set it for attributes that will almost always get used in queries. For example, if the vast majority of your queries are at the Month granularity it makes sense that all of your aggregations include the Month attribute from your Time dimension.

- **None:** This means the attribute will not be included in any aggregation that the wizard designs. Don't be afraid of using this value for any attributes that you don't think will be used often in your queries, it can be a useful way of ensuring that the attributes that are used often get good aggregation coverage. Note that Attributes with `AttributeHierarchyEnabled` set to **False** will have no aggregations designed for them anyway.

- **Unrestricted:** This means that the attribute may be included in the aggregations designed, depending on whether the algorithm used by the wizard considers it to be useful or not.

- **Default**: The default option applies a complex set of rules, which are:
   ° The granularity attribute (usually the key attribute, unless you specified otherwise in the dimension usage tab) is treated as Unrestricted.

   ° All attributes on dimensions involved in many-to-many relationships, unmaterialised referenced relationships, and data mining dimensions are treated as None. Aggregations may still be built at the root granularity, that is, the intersection of every All Member on every attribute.

   ° All attributes that are used as levels in natural user hierarchies are treated as Unrestricted.

   ° Attributes with `IsAggregatable` set to `False` are treated as Full.

   ° All other attributes are treated as None.

The next step in the wizard asks you to verify the number of `EstimatedRows` and `EstimatedCount` properties we've already talked about, and gives the option of setting a similar property that shows the estimated number of members from an attribute that appear in any one partition. This can be an important property to set: if you are partitioning by month, although you may have 36 members on your Month attribute a partition will only contain data for one of them.

On the Set Aggregation Options step you finally reach the point where some aggregations can be built. Here you can apply one last set of restrictions on the set of aggregations that will be built, choosing to either:

- **Estimated Storage Reaches**, which means you build aggregations to fill a given amount of disk space.

- **Performance Gain Reaches,** the most useful option. It does not mean that all queries will run n% faster; nor does it mean that a query that hits an aggregation directly will run n% faster. Think of it like this: if the wizard built all the aggregations it thought were useful to build (note: this is not the same thing as all of the possible aggregations that could be built on the cube) then, in general, performance would be better. Some queries would not benefit from aggregations, some would be slightly faster, and some would be a lot faster; and some aggregations would be more often used than others. So if you set this property to 100% the wizard would build all the aggregations that it could, and you'd get 100% of the performance gain possible from building aggregations. Setting this property to 30%, the default and recommended value, will build the aggregations that give you 30% of this possible performance gain—not 30% of the possible aggregations, usually a much smaller number. As you can see from the screenshot below, the graph drawn on this step plots the size of the aggregations built versus overall performance gain, and the shape of the curve shows that a few, smaller aggregations usually provide the majority of the performance gain.

- **I Click Stop,** which means carry on building aggregations until you click the Stop button. Designing aggregations can take a very long time, especially on more complex cubes, because there may literally be millions or billions of possible aggregations that could be built. In fact, it's not unheard of for the aggregation design wizard to run for several days before it's stopped!

- **Do Not Design Aggregations** allows you to skip designing aggregations.

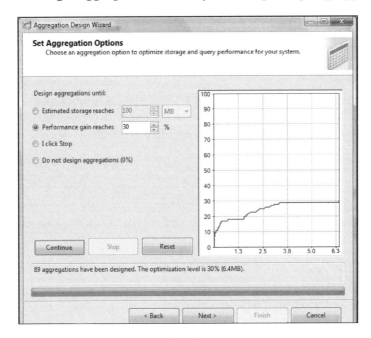

The approach we suggest taking here is to first select **I Click Stop** and then click the **Start** button. On some measure groups this will complete very quickly, with only a few small aggregations built. If that's the case click **Next**; otherwise, if it's taking too long or too many aggregations are being built, click **Stop** and then **Reset**, and then select **Performance Gain Reaches** and enter 30% and Start again. This should result in a reasonable selection of aggregations being built; in general around 50-100 aggregations is the maximum number you should be building for a measure group, and if 30% leaves you short of this try increasing the number by 10% until you feel comfortable with what you get.

On the final step of the wizard, enter a name for your aggregation design and save it. It's a good idea to give the aggregation design a name including the name of the measure group to make it easier to find if you ever need to script it to XMLA.

It's quite common that Analysis Services cube developers stop thinking about aggregation design at this point. This is a serious mistake: just because you have run the Aggregation Design Wizard does not mean you have built all the aggregations you need, or indeed any useful ones at all! Doing Usage-Based Optimisation and/or building aggregations manually is absolutely essential.

Usage-based optimization

We now have some aggregations designed, but the chances are that despite our best efforts many of them will not prove to be useful. To a certain extent we might be able to pick out these aggregations by browsing through them; really, though, we need to know what queries our users are going to run before we can build aggregations to make them run faster. This is where usage-based optimisation comes in: it allows us to log the requests for data that Analysis Services makes when a query is run and then feed this information into the aggregation design process.

To be able to do usage-based optimization, you must first set up Analysis Services to log these requests for data. This involves specifying a connection string to a relational database in the server properties of your Analysis Services instance and allowing Analysis Services to create a log table in that database. The white paper *Configuring the Analysis Services Query Log* contains more details on how to do this (it's written for Analysis Services 2005 but is still relevant for Analysis Services 2008), and can be downloaded from `http://tinyurl.com/ssasquerylog`.

The query log is a misleading name, because as you'll see if you look inside it it doesn't actually contain the text of MDX queries run against the cube. When a user runs an MDX query, Analysis Services decomposes it into a set of requests for data at a particular granularity and it's these requests that are logged; we'll look at how to interpret this information in the next section. A single query can result in no requests for data, or it can result in as many as hundreds or thousands of requests, especially if it returns a lot of data and a lot of MDX calculations are involved. When setting up the log you also have to specify the percentage of all data requests that Analysis Services actually logs with the `QueryLogSampling` property—in some cases if it logged every single request you would end up with a very large amount of data very quickly, but on the other hand if you set this value too low you may end up not seeing certain important long-running requests. We recommend that you start by setting this property to 100 but that you monitor the size of the log closely and reduce the value if you find that the number of requests logged is too high.

Once the log has been set up, let your users start querying the cube. Explain to them what you're doing and that some queries may not perform well at this stage. Given access to a new cube it will take them a little while to understand what data is present and what data they're interested in; if they're new to Analysis Services it's also likely they'll need some time to get used to whatever client tool they're using. Therefore you'll need to have logging enabled for at least a month or two before you can be sure that your query log contains enough useful information. Remember that if you change the structure of the cube while you're logging then the existing contents of the log will no longer be usable.

Last of all, you'll need to run the Usage-Based Optimisation Wizard to build new aggregations using this information. The Usage-Based Optimisation Wizard is very similar to the Design Aggregations Wizard, with the added option to filter the information in the query log by date, user and query frequency before it's used to build aggregations. It's a good idea to do this filtering carefully: you should probably exclude any queries you've run yourself, for example, since they're unlikely to be representative of what the users are doing, and make sure that the most important users queries are over-represented.

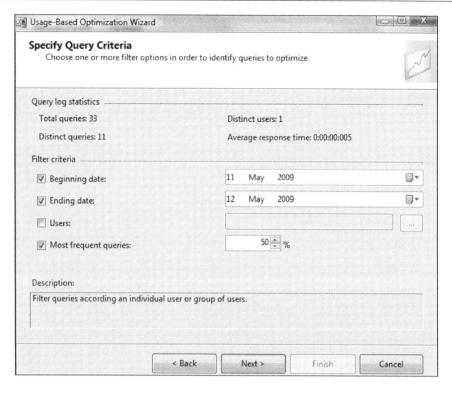

Once you've done this you'll have a chance to review what data is actually going to be used before you actually build the aggregations.

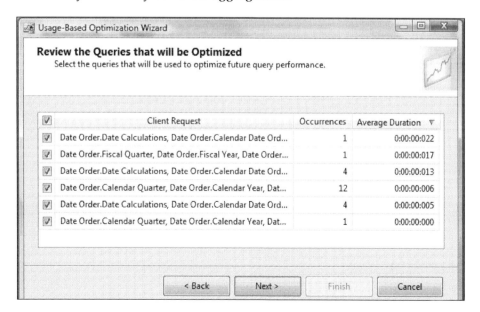

On the last step of the wizard you have the choice of either creating a new aggregation design or merging the aggregations that have just been created with an existing aggregation design. We recommend the latter: what you've just done is optimize queries that ran slowly on an existing aggregation design, and if you abandon the aggregations you've already got then it's possible that queries which previously had been quick would be slow afterwards.

This exercise should be repeated at regular intervals throughout the cube's lifetime to ensure that you built any new aggregations that are necessary as the queries that your users run change. Query logging can, however, have an impact on query performance so it's not a good idea to leave logging running all the time.

Processing aggregations

When you've created or edited the aggregations on one or more partitions, you don't need to do a full process on the partitions. All you need to do is to deploy your changes and then run a **ProcessIndex**, which is usually fairly quick, and once you've done that queries will be able to use the new aggregations. When you run a **ProcessIndex** Analysis Services does not need to run any SQL queries against the relational data source if you're using MOLAP storage.

Monitoring partition and aggregation usage

Having created and configured your partitions and aggregations, you'll naturally want to be sure that when you run a query Analysis Services is using them as you expect. You can do this very easily by running a trace with SQL Server Profiler or by using MDX Studio (a free MDX Editor that can be downloaded from `http://tinyurl.com/mdxstudio`).

To use Profiler, start it and then connect to your Analysis Services instance to create a new trace. On the **Trace Properties dialog** choose the **Blank template** and go to the **Events Selection** tab and check the following:

- **Progress Reports\Progress Report Begin**
- **Progress Reports\Progress Report End**
- **Queries Events\Query Begin**
- **Queries Events\Query End**
- **Query Processing\Execute MDX Script Begin**
- **Query Processing\Execute MDX Script End**
- **Query Processing\Query Cube Begin**
- **Query Processing\Query Cube End**

- **Query Processing\Get Data From Aggregation**
- **Query Processing\Query Subcube Verbose**

Then clear the cache and click **Run** to start the trace.

Once you've done this you can either open up your Analysis Services client tool or you can start running MDX queries in SQL Management Studio. When you do this you'll notice that Profiler starts to show information about what Analysis Services is doing internally to answer these queries. The following screenshot shows what you might typically see:

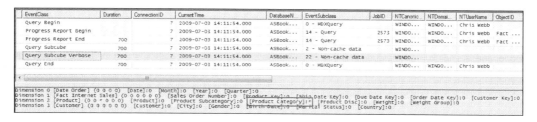

Interpreting the results of a Profiler trace is a complex task and well outside the scope of this book, but it's very easy to pick out some useful information relating to aggregation and partition usage. Put simply:

- The **Query Subcube Verbose** events represent individual requests for data from the Formula Engine to the Storage Engine, which can be answered either from cache, an aggregation or base-level partition data. Each of these requests is at a single granularity, meaning that all of the data in the request comes from a single distinct combination of attributes; we refer to these granularities as "subcubes". The **TextData** column for this event shows the granularity of data that is being requested in human readable form; the **Query Subcube** event will display exactly the same data but in the less friendly-format that the Usage-Based Optimisation Query Log uses.

- Pairs of **Progress Report Begin** and **Progress Report End** events show that data is being read from disk, either from an aggregation or a partition. The **TextData** column gives more information, including the name of the object being read; however, if you have more than one object (for example an aggregation) with the same name, you need to look at the contents of the **ObjectPath** column to see what object exactly is being queried.

- The **Get Data From Aggregation** event is fired when data is read from an aggregation, in addition to any **Progress Report** events.

- The **Duration** column shows how long each of these operations takes in milliseconds.

At this point in the cube optimisation process you should be seeing in Profiler that when your users run queries they hit as few partitions as possible and hit aggregations as often as possible. If you regularly see slow queries that scan all the partitions in your cube or which do not use any aggregations at all, you should consider going back to the beginning of the process and rethinking your partitioning strategy and rerunning the aggregation design wizards. In a production system many queries will be answered from cache and therefore be very quick, but you should always try to optimise for the worst-case scenario of a query running on a cold cache.

Building aggregations manually

However good the aggregation designs produced by the wizards are, it's very likely that at some point you'll have to design aggregations manually for particular queries. Even after running the Usage Based Optimisation Wizard you may find that it still does not build some potentially useful aggregations: the algorithm the wizards use is very complex and something of a black box, so for whatever reason (perhaps because it thinks it would be too large) it may decide not to build an aggregation that, when built manually, turns out to have a significant positive impact on the performance of a particular query.

Before we can build aggregations manually we need to work out which aggregations we need to build. To do this, we once again need to use Profiler and look at either the **Query Subcube** or the **Query Subcube Verbose** events. These events, remember, display the same thing in two different formats - requests for data made to the Analysis Services storage engine during query processing - and the contents of the **Duration** column in Profiler will show how long in milliseconds each of these requests took. A good rule of thumb is that any **Query Subcube** event that takes longer than half a second (500 ms) would benefit from having an aggregation built for it; you can expect that a **Query Subcube** event that requests data at the same granularity as an aggregation will execute almost instantaneously.

The following screenshot shows an example of trace on an MDX query that takes 700ms:

EventClass	ConnectionID	CurrentTime	Databa...	EventSubclass	Duration	JobID
Query Begin	26	2009-05-20 07:02:12.000	Adv...	0 - MDXQuery		
Progress Report Begin	26	2009-05-20 07:02:12.000	Adv...	14 - Query		26354
Progress Report End	26	2009-05-20 07:02:12.000	Adv...	14 - Query	700	26354
Query Subcube	26	2009-05-20 07:02:12.000	Adv...	2 - Non-cache data	700	
Query Subcube Verbose	26	2009-05-20 07:02:12.000	Adv...	22 - Non-cache data	700	
Query End	26	2009-05-20 07:02:12.000	Adv...	0 - MDXQuery	700	

The single **Query Subcube Verbose** event is highlighted, and we can see that the duration of this event is the same as that of the query itself, so if we want to improve the performance of the query we need to build an aggregation for this particular request. Also, in the lower half of the screen we can see the contents of the **TextData** column displayed. This shows a list of all the dimensions and attributes from which data is being requested —the granularity of the request—and the simple rule to follow here is that whenever you see anything other than a zero by an attribute we know that the granularity of the request includes this attribute. We need to make a note of all of the attributes which have anything other than a zero next to them and then build an aggregation using them; in this case it's just the Product Category attribute of the Product dimension.

The white paper *Identifying and Resolving MDX Query Performance Bottlenecks* (again, written for Analysis Services 2005 but still relevant for Analysis Services 2008), available from http://tinyurl.com/mdxbottlenecks, includes more detailed information on how to interpret the information given by the **Query Subcube Verbose** event.

So now that we know what aggregation we need to build, we need to go ahead and build it. We have a choice of tools to do this: we can either use the functionality built into BIDS, or we can use some of the excellent functionality that BIDS Helper provides. In BIDS, to view and edit aggregations, you need to go to the **Aggregations** tab in the cube editor. On the Standard View you only see a list of partitions and which aggregation designs they have associated with them; if you switch to the Advanced View by pressing the appropriate button on the toolbar, you can view the aggregations in each aggregation design for each measure group. If you right-click in the area where the aggregations are displayed you can also create a new aggregation and once you've done that you can specify the granularity of the aggregation by checking and unchecking the attributes on each dimension. For our particular query we only need to check the box next to the Product Categories attribute, as follows:

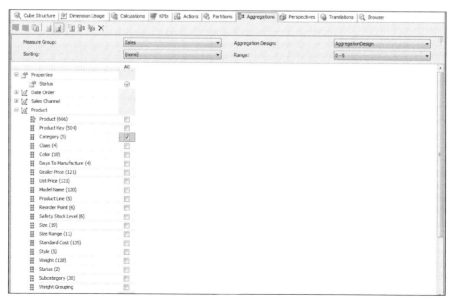

The small tick at the top of the list of dimensions in the **Status** row shows that this aggregation has passed the built-in validation rules that BIDS applies to make sure this is a useful aggregation. If you see an amber warning triangle here, hover over it with your mouse and in the tooltip you'll see a list of reasons why the aggregation has failed its status check.

If we then deploy and run a **ProcessIndex**, we can then rerun our original query and watch it use the new aggregation, running much faster as a result:

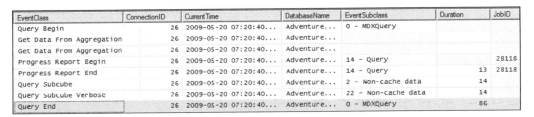

EventClass	ConnectionID	Current Time	DatabaseName	Event Subclass	Duration	JobID
Query Begin	26	2009-05-20 07:20:40...	Adventure...	0 - MDXQuery		
Get Data From Aggregation	26	2009-05-20 07:20:40...	Adventure...			
Get Data From Aggregation	26	2009-05-20 07:20:40...	Adventure...			
Progress Report Begin	26	2009-05-20 07:20:40...	Adventure...	14 - Query		28118
Progress Report End	26	2009-05-20 07:20:40...	Adventure...	14 - Query	13	28118
Query Subcube	26	2009-05-20 07:20:40...	Adventure...	2 - Non-cache data	14	
Query Subcube Verbose	26	2009-05-20 07:20:40...	Adventure...	22 - Non-cache data	14	
Query End	26	2009-05-20 07:20:40...	Adventure...	0 - MDXQuery	86	

The problem with the native BIDS aggregation design functionality is that it becomes difficult to use when you have complex aggregations to build and edit. The functionality present in BIDS Helper, while it looks less polished, is far more useable and offers many benefits over the BIDS native functionality, for example:

- The BIDS Helper Aggregation Design interface displays the aggregation granularity in the same way (ie using 1s and 0s, as seen in the screenshot below) as the **Query Subcube** event in Profiler does, making it easier to cross reference between the two.

- It also shows attribute relationships when it displays the attributes on each dimension when you're designing an aggregation, as seen on the righthand side in the screenshot that follows. This is essential to being able to build optimal aggregations.

- It also shows whether an aggregation is rigid or flexible.

- It has functionality to remove duplicate aggregations and ones containing redundant attributes (see below), and search for similar aggregations.

- It allows you to create new aggregations based on the information stored in the Query Log.

- It also allows you to delete unused aggregations based on information from a Profiler trace.

- Finally, it has some very comprehensive functionality to allow you to test the performance of the aggregations you build (see http://tinyurl. com/testaggs).

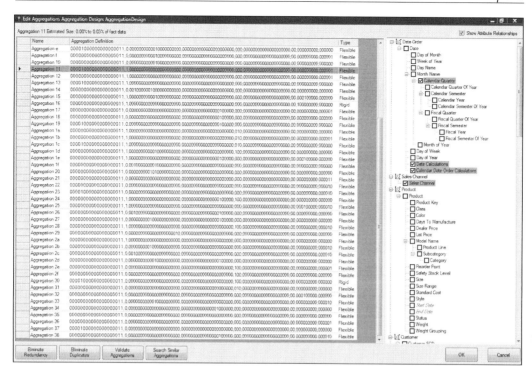

Unsurprisingly, if you need to do any serious work designing aggregations manually we recommend using BIDS Helper over the built-in functionality.

Common aggregation design issues

Several features of your cube design must be borne in mind when designing aggregations, because they can influence how Analysis Services storage engine queries are made and therefore which aggregations will be used. These include:

- There's no point building aggregations above the granularity you are slicing your partitions by. Aggregations are built on a per-partition basis, so for example if you're partitioning by month there's no value in building an aggregation at the Year granularity since no aggregation can contain more than one month's worth of data. It won't hurt if you do it, it just means that an aggregation at month will be the same size as one at year but useful to more queries. It follows from this that it might be possible to over-partition data and reduce the effectiveness of aggregations, but we have anecdotal evidence from people who have built very large cubes that this is not an issue.

- For queries involving a dimension with a many-to-many relationship to a measure group, aggregations must not be built using any attributes from the many-to-many dimension, but instead must be built at the granularity of the attributes with a regular relationship to the intermediate measure group. Taking the example we saw in Chapter 5 of Sales Reasons and Sales Orders, when a query is run using the Sales Reason dimension Analysis Services first works out which Sales Orders relate to each Sales Reason, and then queries the main measure group for these Sales Orders. Therefore, only aggregations at the Sales Order granularity on the main measure group can be used. As a result, in most cases it's not worth building aggregations for queries on many-to-many dimensions since the granularity of these queries is often close to that of the original fact table.

- Queries involving measures which have semi-additive aggregation types are always resolved at the granularity attribute of the time dimension, so you need to include that attribute in all aggregations.

- Queries involving measures with measure expressions require aggregations at the common granularity of the two measure groups involved.

- You should not build aggregations including a parent/child attribute; instead you should use the key attribute in aggregations.

- No aggregation should include an attribute which has `AttributeHierarchyEnabled` set to `False`.

- No aggregation should include an attribute that is below the granularity attribute of the dimension for the measure group.

- Any attributes which have a default member that is anything other than the All Member, or which have `IsAggregatable` set to `False`, should also be included in all aggregations.

- Aggregations and indexes are not built for partitions with fewer than 4096 rows. This threshold is set by the `IndexBuildThreshold` property in msmdsrv.ini; you can change it but it's not a good idea to do so.

- Aggregations should not include redundant attributes, that is to say attributes from the same 'chain' of attribute relationships. For example if you had a chain of attribute relationships going from month to quarter to year, you should not build an aggregation including month and quarter—it should just include month. This will increase the chance that the aggregation can be used by more queries, as well as reducing the size of the aggregation.

MDX calculation performance

Optimizing the performance of the Storage Engine is relatively straightforward: you can diagnose performance problems easily and you only have two options—partitioning and aggregation—for solving them. Optimizing the performance of the Formula Engine is much more complicated because it requires knowledge of MDX, diagnosing performance problems is difficult because the internal workings of the Formula Engine are hard to follow, and solving the problem is reliant on knowing tips and tricks that may change from service pack to service pack.

Diagnosing Formula Engine performance problems

If you have a poorly-performing query, and if you can rule out the Storage Engine as the cause of the problem, then the issue is with the Formula Engine. We've already seen how we can use Profiler to check the performance of **Query Subcube** events, to see which partitions are being hit and to check whether aggregations are being used; if you subtract the sum of the durations of all the **Query Subcube** events from the duration of the query as a whole, you'll get the amount of time spent in the Formula Engine. You can use MDX Studio's Profile functionality to do the same thing much more easily—here's a screenshot of what it outputs when a calculation-heavy query is run:

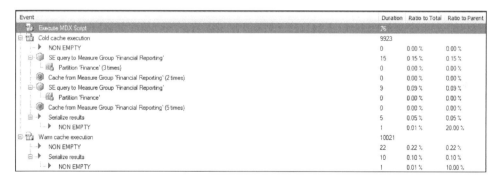

The following blog entry describes this functionality in detail: `http://tinyurl.com/mdxtrace`; but what this screenshot displays is essentially the same thing that we'd see if we ran a Profiler trace when running the same query on a cold and warm cache, but in a much more easy-to-read format. The column to look at here is the `Ratio to Total`, which shows the ratio of the duration of each event to the total duration of the query. We can see that on both a cold cache and a warm cache the query took almost ten seconds to run but none of the events recorded took anywhere near that amount of time: the highest ratio to parent is 0.09%. This is typical of what you'd see with a Formula Engine-bound query.

Another hallmark of a query that spends most of its time in the Formula Engine is that it will only use one CPU, even on a multiple-CPU server. This is because the Formula Engine, unlike the Storage Engine, is single-threaded. As a result if you watch CPU usage in Task Manager while you run a query you can get a good idea of what's happening internally: high usage of multiple CPUs indicates work is taking place in the Storage Engine, while high usage of one CPU indicates work is taking place in the Formula Engine.

Calculation performance tuning

Having worked out that the Formula Engine is the cause of a query's poor performance then the next step is, obviously, to try to tune the query. In some cases you can achieve impressive performance gains (sometimes of several hundred percent) simply by rewriting a query and the calculations it depends on; the problem is knowing how to rewrite the MDX and working out which calculations contribute most to the overall query duration. Unfortunately Analysis Services doesn't give you much information to use to solve this problem and there are very few tools out there which can help either, so doing this is something of a black art.

There are three main ways you can improve the performance of the Formula Engine: tune the structure of the cube it's running on, tune the algorithms you're using in your MDX, and tune the implementation of those algorithms so they use functions and expressions that Analysis Services can run efficiently. We've already talked in depth about how the overall cube structure is important for the performance of the Storage Engine and the same goes for the Formula Engine; the only thing to repeat here is the recommendation that if you can avoid doing a calculation in MDX by doing it at an earlier stage, for example in your ETL or in your relational source, and do so without compromising functionality, you should do so. We'll now go into more detail about tuning algorithms and implementations.

 Mosha Pasumansky's blog, `http://tinyurl.com/moshablog`, is a goldmine of information on this subject. If you're serious about learning MDX we recommend that you subscribe to it and read everything he's ever written.

Tuning algorithms used in MDX

Tuning an algorithm in MDX is much the same as tuning an algorithm in any other kind of programming language—it's more a matter of understanding your problem and working out the logic that provides the most efficient solution than anything else. That said, there are some general techniques that can be used often in MDX and which we will walk through here.

Using named sets to avoid recalculating set expressions

Many MDX calculations involve expensive set operations, a good example being rank calculations where the position of a tuple within an ordered set needs to be determined. The following query includes a calculated member that displays Dates on the Rows axis of a query, and on columns shows a calculated measure that returns the rank of that date within the set of all dates based on the value of the Internet Sales Amount measure:

```
WITH
  MEMBER MEASURES.MYRANK AS
    Rank
    (
      [Date].[Date].CurrentMember
     ,Order
      (
        [Date].[Date].[Date].MEMBERS
       ,[Measures].[Internet Sales Amount]
       ,BDESC
      )
    )
SELECT
  MEASURES.MYRANK ON 0
 ,[Date].[Date].[Date].MEMBERS ON 1
FROM [Adventure Works]
```

It runs very slowly, and the problem is that every time the calculation is evaluated it has to evaluate the `Order` function to return the set of ordered dates. In this particular situation, though, you can probably see that the set returned will be the same every time the calculation is called, so it makes no sense to do the ordering more than once. Instead, we can create a named set hold the ordered set and refer to that named set from within the calculated measure, so:

```
WITH
  SET ORDEREDDATES AS
    Order
    (
      [Date].[Date].[Date].MEMBERS
     ,[Measures].[Internet Sales Amount]
     ,BDESC
    )
  MEMBER MEASURES.MYRANK AS
    Rank
    (
      [Date].[Date].CurrentMember
     ,ORDEREDDATES
    )
```

```
SELECT
  MEASURES.MYRANK ON 0
 ,[Date].[Date].[Date].MEMBERS ON 1
FROM [Adventure Works]
```

This version of the query is many times faster, simply as a result of improving the algorithm used; the problem is explored in more depth in this blog entry: http://tinyurl.com/mosharank

Since normal named sets are only evaluated once they can be used to cache set expressions in some circumstances; however, the fact that they are static means they can be too inflexible to be useful most of the time. Note that normal named sets defined in the MDX Script are only evaluated once, when the MDX script executes and not in the context of any particular query, so it wouldn't be possible to change the example above so that the set and calculated measure were defined on the server. Even named sets defined in the WITH clause are evaluated only once, in the context of the WHERE clause, so it wouldn't be possible to crossjoin another hierarchy on columns and use this approach, because for it to work the set would have to be reordered once for each column.

The introduction of dynamic named sets in Analysis Services 2008 improves the situation a little, and other more advanced techniques can be used to work around these issues, but in general named sets are less useful than you might hope. For further reading on this subject see the following blog posts:

http://tinyurl.com/chrisrank

http://tinyurl.com/moshadsets

http://tinyurl.com/chrisdsets

Using calculated members to cache numeric values

In the same way that you can avoid unnecessary re-evaluations of set expressions by using named sets, you can also rely on the fact that the Formula Engine can (usually) cache the result of a calculated member to avoid recalculating expressions which return numeric values. What this means in practice is that anywhere in your code you see an MDX expression that returns a numeric value repeated across multiple calculations, you should consider abstracting it to its own calculated member; not only will this help performance, but it will improve the readability of your code. For example, take the following slow query which includes two calculated measures:

```
WITH
  MEMBER [Measures].TEST1 AS
      [Measures].[Internet Sales Amount]
    /
    Count
```

```
          (
            TopPercent
            (
                {
                    [Scenario].[Scenario].&[1]
                    ,[Scenario].[Scenario].&[2]
                }*
                [Account].[Account].[Account].MEMBERS*
                [Date].[Date].[Date].MEMBERS
              ,10
              ,[Measures].[Amount]
            )
          )
    MEMBER [Measures].TEST2 AS
        [Measures].[Internet Tax Amount]
      /
        Count
        (
          TopPercent
          (
                {
                    [Scenario].[Scenario].&[1]
                    ,[Scenario].[Scenario].&[2]
                }*
                [Account].[Account].[Account].MEMBERS*
                [Date].[Date].[Date].MEMBERS*
                [Department].[Departments].[Department Level 02].MEMBERS
              ,10
              ,[Measures].[Amount]
            )
        )
SELECT
  {
      [Measures].TEST1
    ,[Measures].TEST2
  } ON 0
  ,[Customer].[Gender].[Gender].MEMBERS ON 1
FROM [Adventure Works]
```

A quick glance over the code shows that a large section of it occurs twice in both calculations—everything inside the Count function. If we remove that code to its own calculated member as follows:

```
WITH
  MEMBER [Measures].Denominator AS
    Count
    (
      TopPercent
      (
        {
          [Scenario].[Scenario].&[1]
          ,[Scenario].[Scenario].&[2]
        }*
        [Account].[Account].[Account].MEMBERS*
        [Date].[Date].[Date].MEMBERS
        ,10
        ,[Measures].[Amount]
      )
    )
  MEMBER [Measures].TEST1 AS
    [Measures].[Internet Sales Amount] / [Measures].Denominator
  MEMBER [Measures].TEST2 AS
    [Measures].[Internet Tax Amount] / [Measures].Denominator
SELECT
  {
    [Measures].TEST1
    ,[Measures].TEST2
  } ON 0
  ,[Customer].[Gender].[Gender].MEMBERS ON 1
FROM [Adventure Works]
```

The query runs much faster, simply because instead of evaluating the count twice for each of the two visible calculated measures, we evaluate it once, cache the result in the calculated measure Denominator and then reference this in the other calculated measures.

It's also possible to find situations where you can rewrite code to avoid evaluating a calculation that always returns the same result over different cells in the multidimensional space of the cube. This is much more difficult to do effectively though; the following blog entry describes how to do it in detail: http://tinyurl.com/fecache

Tuning the implementation of MDX

Like just about any other software product, Analysis Services is able to do some things more efficiently than others. It's possible to write the same query or calculation using the same algorithm but using different MDX functions and see a big difference in performance; as a result, we need to know which are the functions we should use and which ones we should avoid. Which ones are these though? Luckily MDX Studio includes functionality to analyse MDX code and flag up such problems—to do this you just need to click the Analyze button—and there's even an online version of MDX Studio that allows you to do this too, available at: `http://mdx.mosha.com/`. We recommend that you run any MDX code you write through this functionality and take its suggestions on board. Mosha walks through an example of using MDX Studio to optimise a calculation on his blog here: `http://tinyurl.com/moshaprodvol`

Block computation versus cell-by-cell

When the Formula Engine has to evaluate an MDX expression for a query it can basically do so in one of two ways. It can evaluate the expression for each cell returned by the query, one at a time, an evaluation mode known as "cell-by-cell"; or it can try to analyse the calculations required for the whole query and find situations where the same expression would need to be calculated for multiple cells and instead do it only once, an evaluation mode known variously as "block computation" or "bulk evaluation". Block computation is only possible in some situations, depending on how the code is written, but is often many times more efficient than cell-by-cell mode. As a result, we want to write MDX code in such a way that the Formula Engine can use block computation as much as possible, and when we talk about using efficient MDX functions or constructs then this is what we in fact mean. Given that different calculations in the same query, and different expressions within the same calculation, can be evaluated using block computation and cell-by-cell mode, it's very difficult to know which mode is used when. Indeed in some cases Analysis Services can't use block mode anyway, so it's hard know whether we have written our MDX in the most efficient way possible. One of the few indicators we have is the Perfmon counter MDX\Total Cells Calculated, which basically returns the number of cells in a query that were calculated in cell-by-cell mode; if a change to your MDX increments this value by a smaller amount than before, and the query runs faster, you're doing something right.

The list of rules that MDX Studio applies is too long to list here, and in any case it is liable to change in future service packs or versions; another good guide for Analysis Services 2008 best practices exists in the Books Online topic *Performance Improvements for MDX in SQL Server 2008 Analysis Services*, available online here: `http://tinyurl.com/mdximp`. However, there are a few general rules that are worth highlighting:

- Don't use the `Non_Empty_Behavior` calculation property in Analysis Services 2008, unless you really know how to set it and are sure that it will provide a performance benefit. It was widely misused with Analysis Services 2005 and most of the work that went into the Formula Engine for Analysis Services 2008 was to ensure that it wouldn't need to be set for most calculations. This is something that needs to be checked if you're migrating an Analysis Services 2005 cube to 2008.

- Never use late binding functions such as `LookupCube`, or `StrToMember` or `StrToSet` without the `Constrained` flag, inside calculations since they have a serious negative impact on performance. It's almost always possible to rewrite calculations so they don't need to be used; in fact, the only valid use for `StrToMember` or `StrToSet` in production code is when using MDX parameters. The `LinkMember` function suffers from a similar problem but is less easy to avoid using it.

- Use the `NonEmpty` function wherever possible; it can be much more efficient than using the `Filter` function or other methods. Never use `NonEmptyCrossjoin` either: it's deprecated, and everything you can do with it you can do more easily and reliably with `NonEmpty`.

- Lastly, don't assume that whatever worked best for Analysis Services 2000 or 2005 is still best practice for Analysis Services 2008. In general, you should always try to write the simplest MDX code possible initially, and then only change it when you find performance is unacceptable. Many of the tricks that existed to optimise common calculations for earlier versions now perform worse on Analysis Services 2008 than the straightforward approaches they were designed to replace.

Caching

We've already seen how Analysis Services can cache the values returned in the cells of a query, and how this can have a significant impact on the performance of a query. Both the Formula Engine and the Storage Engine can cache data, but may not be able to do so in all circumstances; similarly, although Analysis Services can share the contents of the cache between users there are several situations where it is unable to do so. Given that in most cubes there will be a lot of overlap in the data that users are querying, caching is a very important factor in the overall performance of the cube and as a result ensuring that as much caching as possible is taking place is a good idea.

Formula cache scopes

There are three different cache contexts within the Formula Engine, which relate to how long data can be stored within the cache and how that data can be shared between users:

- **Query Context**, which means that the results of calculations can only be cached for the lifetime of a single query and so cannot be reused by subsequent queries or by other users.

- **Session Context**, which means the results of calculations are cached for the lifetime of a session and can be reused by subsequent queries in the same session by the same user.

- **Global Context**, which means the results of calculations are cached until the cache has to be dropped because data in the cube has changed (usually when some form of processing takes place on the server). These cached values can be reused by subsequent queries run by other users as well as the user who ran the original query.

Clearly the Global Context is the best from a performance point of view, followed by the Session Context and then the Query Context; Analysis Services will always try to use the Global Context wherever possible, but it is all too easy to accidentally write queries or calculations that force the use of the Session Context or the Query Context. Here's a list of the most important situations when that can happen:

- If you define any calculations (not including named sets) in the WITH clause of a query, even if you do not use them, then Analysis Services can only use the Query Context (see http://tinyurl.com/chrisfecache for more details).

- If you define session-scoped calculations but do not define calculations in the WITH clause, then the Session Context must be used.

- Using a subselect in a query will force the use of the Query Context (see http://tinyurl.com/chrissubfe).

- Use of the CREATE SUBCUBE statement will force the use of the Session Context.

- When a user connects to a cube using a role that uses cell security, then the Query Context will be used.

- When calculations are used that contain non-deterministic functions (functions which could return different results each time they are called), for example the Now() function that returns the system date and time, the Username() function or any Analysis Services stored procedure, then this forces the use of the Query Context.

Other scenarios that restrict caching

Apart from the restrictions imposed by cache context, there are other scenarios where caching is either turned off or restricted.

When arbitrary-shaped sets are used in the WHERE clause of a query, no caching at all can take place in either the Storage Engine or the Formula Engine. An arbitrary-shaped set is a set of tuples that cannot be created by a crossjoin, for example:

```
({([Customer].[Country].&[Australia], [Product].[Category].&[1]),
([Customer].[Country].&[Canada], [Product].[Category].&[3])})
```

If your users frequently run queries that use arbitrary-shaped sets then this can represent a very serious problem, and you should consider redesigning your cube to avoid it. The following blog entries discuss this problem in more detail:
http://tinyurl.com/tkarbset
http://tinyurl.com/chrisarbset

Even within the Global Context, the presence of security can affect the extent to which cache can be shared between users. When dimension security is used the contents of the Formula Engine cache can only be shared between users who are members of roles which have the same permissions. Worse, the contents of the Formula Engine cache cannot be shared between users who are members of roles which use dynamic security at all, even if those users do in fact share the same permissions.

Cache warming

Since we can expect many of our queries to run instantaneously on a warm cache, and the majority at least to run faster on a warm cache than on a cold cache, it makes sense to preload the cache with data so that when users come to run their queries they will get warm-cache performance. There are two basic ways of doing this, running CREATE CACHE statements and automatically running batches of queries.

Create Cache statement

The CREATE CACHE statement allows you to load a specified subcube of data into the Storage Engine cache. Here's an example of what it looks like:

```
CREATE CACHE FOR [Adventure Works] AS
({[Measures].[Internet Sales Amount]}, [Customer].[Country].[Country].
MEMBERS,
[Date].[Calendar Year].[Calendar Year].MEMBERS)
```

More detail on this statement can be found here: http://tinyurl.com/createcache

CREATE CACHE statements can be added to the MDX Script of the cube so they execute every time the MDX Script is executed, although if the statements take a long time to execute (as they often do) then this might not be a good idea; they can also be run after processing has finished from an Integration Services package using an Execute SQL task or through ASCMD, and this is a much better option because it means you have much more control over when the statements actually execute—you wouldn't want them running every time you cleared the cache, for instance.

Running batches of queries

The main drawback of the CREATE CACHE statement is that it can only be used to populate the Storage Engine cache, and in many cases it's warming the Formula Engine cache that makes the biggest difference to query performance. The only way to do this is to find a way to automate the execution of large batches of MDX queries (potentially captured by running a Profiler trace while users go about their work) that return the results of calculations and so which will warm the Formula Engine cache. This automation can be done in a number of ways, for example by using the ASCMD command line utility which is part of the sample code for Analysis Services that Microsoft provides (available for download here: http://tinyurl.com/sqlprodsamples); another common option is to use an Integration Services package to run the queries, as described in the following blog entries— http://tinyurl.com/chriscachewarm and http://tinyurl.com/allancachewarm

This approach is not without its own problems, though: it can be very difficult to make sure that the queries you're running return all the data you want to load into cache, and even when you have done that, user query patterns change over time so ongoing maintenance of the set of queries is important.

Scale-up and scale-out

Buying better or more hardware should be your last resort when trying to solve query performance problems: it's expensive and you need to be completely sure that it will indeed improve matters. Adding more memory will increase the space available for caching but nothing else; adding more or faster CPUs will lead to faster queries but you might be better off investing time in building more aggregations or tuning your MDX. Scaling up as much as your hardware budget allows is a good idea, but may have little impact on the performance of individual problem queries unless you badly under-specified your Analysis Services server in the first place.

If your query performance degenerates as the number of concurrent users running queries increases, consider scaling-out by implementing what's known as an OLAP farm. This architecture is widely used in large implementations and involves multiple Analysis Services instances on different servers, and using network load balancing to distribute user queries between these servers. Each of these instances needs to have the same database on it and each of these databases must contain exactly the same data in it for queries to be answered consistently. This means that, as the number of concurrent users increases, you can easily add new servers to handle the increased query load. It also has the added advantage of removing a single point of failure, so if one Analysis Services server fails then the others take on its load automatically.

Making sure that data is the same across all servers is a complex operation and you have a number of different options for doing this: you can either use the Analysis Services database synchronisation functionality, copy and paste the data from one location to another using a tool like Robocopy, or use the new Analysis Services 2008 shared scalable database functionality. We will discuss these options in more detail in chapter 10. The following white paper from the SQLCat team describes how the first two options can be used to implement a network load-balanced solution for Analysis Services 2005: `http://tinyurl.com/ssasnlb`.

Shared scalable databases have a significant advantage over synchronisation and file-copying in that they don't need to involve any moving of files at all. They can be implemented using the same approach described in the white paper above, but instead of copying the databases between instances you process a database (attached in **ReadWrite** mode) on one server, detach it from there, and then attach it in **ReadOnly** mode to one or more user-facing servers for querying while the files themselves stay in one place. You do, however, have to ensure that your disk subsystem does not become a bottleneck as a result.

Summary

In this chapter we've learned how to optimize the performance of our cube so our users' queries execute as quickly as possible. We've looked at how Analysis Services processes queries and what the roles of the Storage Engine and the Formula Engine are; we've seen how building partitions and aggregations can improve the performance of the Storage Engine, and we've also seen how to write MDX to ensure that the Formula Engine works as efficiently as possible. Last of all, we've seen how important caching is to overall query performance and what we need to do to ensure that we can cache data as often as possible, and we've discussed how to scale-out Analysis Services using network load balancing to handle large numbers of concurrent users.

9
Securing the Cube

Security, for an Analysis Services cube, is a very important issue and one that needs to be properly understood and implemented. It's almost always the case that some form of security needs to be in place: the data in the cube may be extremely sensitive. For example, if a cube contains sales data for a whole company, we may need to make sure that each sales person can only view his or her own sales and no-one else's; equally, if a cube contains data regarding the profitability of a company it's likely we'll need to ensure that only the finance department and the board have access to it.

Ignoring security during the initial analysis phase will inevitably lead to problems during the deployment of the solution. We can't stress this enough: security must be planned for in advance; it is such a complex issue that it cannot simply be left until the cube is in production.

In this chapter we will discuss the Analysis Services security model, exploring the different ways to use it and highlighting best practices. As with the rest of the book, this chapter is not about where to click to add a role to a cube. Instead, we'll focus on how to solve the most common security problems, and how we can make the best use of the different security features of Analysis Services.

Sample security requirements

Before diving into technical details, let's outline the sample set of security requirements that we will use in this chapter to illustrate how security can be implemented.

Imagine we are building a BI solution for a multinational company, and we want to give employees and partner companies all over the world access to our cube. Here's what we will need to do:

- We need to restrict access by Country: Canadian users will be able to see only Canadian data, French users will only be able to see data for France, and so on.

- We need to restrict access by Reseller. So if users from the "Roadway Bicycle Supply" reseller query the cube, they will only be able to see their sales and will have no access to other resellers' information. We will demonstrate two different ways to handle this requirement.
- We need to restrict access to certain Measures, both real and calculated.

In a real-world project the security requirements must be agreed with the customer and they **should be specified before we start work on building the cube**. The reason for this is that the cube needs to contain the right information to apply the security rules; if we leave the security analysis until after the cube implementation has finished, we may end up in a situation where the cube doesn't contain some information that is needed for security purposes.

Analysis Services security features

Analysis Services provides a rich set of security features that allow us to control every aspect of how a user can interact with a cube. In this section we'll describe how Analysis Services security actually works, and the different types of permission you can grant to a user.

Roles and role membership

Analysis Services uses roles to manage security. A role is a security group, and users have to be members of one or more roles in order to access the cube. We can grant a role the right to access any cube object or perform any administrative task.

Given our requirements, we will need to create several roles. We will need to create roles to secure countries, so we'll have one role for French users which only allows access to data from France, one for Canadian users that only grants access to Canadian data, and so on. Similarly we will also need to have one role for each reseller who is to access the cube. This may mean, of course, that we end up having a large number of different roles; later on in this chapter we'll show how you can use a single role to handle many different sets of permissions.

Analysis Services uses roles to define security but a role, from the point of view of the security model, is just a container. Security only comes into play when we add users to a role. Therefore, we need to know what kind of users we can add to a role. The answer is that the only users allowed to access a cube through a role are Windows users.

If you are familiar with other Microsoft products, like Internet Information Services or SQL Server itself, you will know that they provide several different ways to authenticate users: Windows integrated security is always one option, but these products often implement some other forms of authentication. This is not the case for Analysis Services—it only supports Windows integrated security and no other form of authentication.

When we talk about "Windows users", we are referring to both domain users and local users from the server where Analysis Services is installed. Local users are often used when the cube is accessible over the internet. In this scenario, there will probably be an Analysis Services server in a DMZ, with a copy of a cube that has been processed on another Analysis Services server from somewhere inside the corporate network and, since the server in the DMZ does not belong to a domain, we will need to use local users in order to access it.

Since we do not want to tie security to specific Windows users, who will come and go over time, it's a good idea to restrict membership of Analysis Services roles to Windows user groups (and preferably domain user groups). We can then control who has access to the cube by adding and removing Windows users from these groups. This level of indirection frees us from the need to make changes in Analysis Services each time a new user needs access to the cube.

So, in order to let users access the cube and enforce security we will need to:

- Define Analysis Services roles, one for each set of permissions our users will have.
- Define domain groups and add them to the roles. For the sake of clarity, we should use the same name for the Analysis Services role and the domain group.
- Add domain users to these groups.

This will only work if users are able to access the cube using Windows integrated security. There are however a lot of situations where integrated security cannot be used, as a result of the presence of firewalls protecting the server or other types of network infrastructure that prevent integrated security from working. In these cases we will need to use Internet Information Services to let the users connect to the cube via HTTP; we'll describe how to do this later on in the chapter.

Securable objects

Here is a list of the objects in an Analysis Services database that can be secured:

- **Data Sources**: We can define whether a role has read access to a data source or to its definition.
- **Cubes**: We can define which cubes can be queried by each role.

- **Dimensions**: We can define which members on a hierarchy can be queried by a role. We can also change the default member of a hierarchy for a specific role. This applies to all hierarchies on all dimensions, including the Measures dimension.

- **Cells**: We can apply security at the cell level, defining which cells in the cube can be queried by each role. When we refer to a cell, we are referring to a point in the multidimensional space of the cube that contains a value.

Obviously, different securable objects will have different permissions we can set. For example, we can grant permission to execute Drillthrough queries at the cube level, while this would make no sense for a specific dimension.

There are two basic types of permission we can grant a user in Analysis Services: permission to perform administrative tasks such as process a cube, and permission to access data within a cube. Here's a brief overview of what type of permission can be granted on each securable object:

Object	Administrative Security	Data Security
Data Source	Read Definition	Read
Cube	Process	Read
		Read / Write
		Drillthrough, Local Cube
Cell Data		Read
		Read Contingent
		Read / Write
Dimensions	Read Definition	Read / Write
	Process	
Dimension Data		Member selection
		Default Member

Administrative rights are relatively straightforward and allow users to perform tasks such as processing a cube. Data security is much more complex and controls what access a role has to data in the cube; as such, we'll spend much more time discussing data security and how it can be implemented.

Creating roles

A new role can be created by right-clicking on the **Role** node in the **Solution Explorer** pane in BI Development Studio. The new role will get a default name, but can subsequently be renamed. Upon creation, we can define the role's permissions in each of the following tabs in the Role Editor:

- **General**: Here we can provide a text description of what the role does, and define administrative permissions for the entire Analysis Services database. These permissions are not usually granted to regular users, only to administrators.
- **Membership**: On this tab we can add local and domain users and groups to the role. As stated before, we will only use domain user groups so as not to tie the security to specific users. Local users and local groups are useful only when users need to connect to the cube via HTTP through IIS.
- **Data Source**: On this tab we can grant access to data sources. This is only necessary when using the data mining functionality in Analysis Services; as data mining is outside the scope of this book, we can ignore this tab.
- **Cubes**: Here we can grant the right to access cubes and set various cube-level administrative permissions.
- **Cell Data**: Here we can define security at the cell level, allowing the role to access data in individual cells within the cube.
- **Dimensions**: On this tab we can set various administrative permissions on our dimensions.
- **Dimension Data**: On this tab we can configure dimension security, allowing the role to access data for specific members on dimension hierarchies.

Membership of multiple roles

It's possible that a user can belong to more than one role, so as a result we need to understand what happens when a user is a member of multiple roles that have different permissions.

If you have worked with security in Windows then you will probably know about the "deny wins over grant" rule. This means that, if a user belongs to a group that grants access to a resource and at the same time belongs to another group where access to that resource is explicitly denied, then the user will not have access to that resource because the deny in the second group wins over the grant in the first one.

In Analysis Services there is no such rule. When a user is a member of multiple roles, that user will have all of the permissions granted to them in each of the roles—the permissions of each role are unioned together. For example, if a user belongs to a role that can only see data for Canada and no other Country, and another role that can only see data for France, that user will be able to see data for both Canada and France. Similarly, if a developer is a member of a role that gives them full administrative permissions then this will guarantee that they can perform all administrative tasks and see all data in all cubes, even if they are also members of roles with more limited permissions. This might seem strange but, like it or not, this is how Analysis Services security works.

Testing roles

If we, as developers, have full administrative permissions then we need a way of simulating membership of more restrictive roles so that we can test they work properly. There are three ways of doing this:

- We can set the following two connection string properties when connecting to the cube. Connection string properties can be set in SQL Management Studio in the **Additional Connection Properties** tab of the connection dialog.

    - **Roles**: This property takes a comma delimited set of role names; when this property is set the user will then connect to the server as if they were a member of these roles. In order to use this option, the user needs to be either an administrator or belong to the roles in question.

    - **EffectiveUserName**: This property takes a Windows username in the form DomainName\Username; when this property is set the user will then connect to the server impersonating this user. To use this property the user must be an administrator.

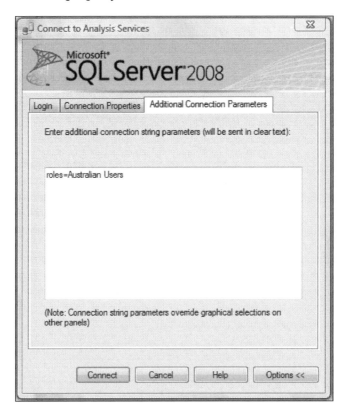

- In BI Development Studio, in the **Browser** tab of the **Cube Editor**, we can set the connection string properties above by clicking on the Change User button in the toolbar. This is the easiest way to test security.

- Running the client tool (for example Excel) as a different user, by using the **Run As** option on the right-click menu in Windows. Note that in Windows Vista this option is only visible if you hold down the *Shift* key while right-clicking.

Administrative security

Administrative permissions can be granted at two levels in Analysis Services: at the server level and at the database level. To become an Analysis Services server administrator, a user must be a member of the special, server-wide Administrators role. Users can be added to this role when Analysis Services is installed, or by right-clicking on an instance in the **Object Explorer** pane in SQL Management Studio, selecting **Properties** on the right-click menu, and going to the **Security** page in the Analysis Services Properties dialog. Server administrators have no restrictions on what they can do; also, certain tasks, such as creating databases, can only be performed by server administrators. As a result it's likely that we'll have to be a member of this role while we're developing our cube.

Database-level administrative permissions are granted in the database roles we've just been introduced to in the preceding sections. By checking the **Full Control box** on the **General** tab we can grant a role full administrative permissions to the database. This means members of the role can create new objects, edit existing objects, process objects and so on. In the unlikely event that we need finer grain control over administrative permissions, you can grant the following two permissions on either the entire database or individual objects:

- **Read Definition:** Allows members of a role to read the XMLA definition of an object, without being able to modify it or read data associated with it. If a user needs to be able to view an object in SQL Management Studio or BI Development Studio (while connected to the database in Online mode), they need to be a member of a role which has this permission.

- **Process:** Allows members of a role to process an object.

Data security

There are three different types of data security that we can implement: we can grant members of a role the permission to access entire cubes; and we can control access to data within a cube by granting or denying access to individual cells (Cell Security) or individual members on dimension hierarchies (Dimension Security).

Granting read access to cubes

Before a user can access any data in a cube, they need to be a member of a role that has Read permissions on that cube. A role can be granted Read permission on a cube by selecting **Read** on the **Access** dropdown box next to the cube name on the **Cubes** tab of the Role Editor.

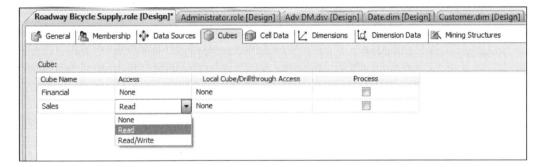

If we have set up writeback on our cube, we can also control whether the Role can write data back to the cube by granting the Read/Write permission instead. Last of all, if we want members of the role to be able to run Drillthrough queries and create local cubes, we can grant permission to do this by choosing the appropriate option from the **Local Cube/Drillthrough Access** dropdown box.

Cell security

Cell security is configured using three MDX expressions returning Boolean values. These three expressions let us define which cells in the cube can be read or written back to: they are evaluated for every cell in the cube and if they return `true` then we can read or write to the cell, if they return `false` then we cannot.

Let's look at an example. If, for example, we check the **Enable Read Permissions** box on the **Cell Data** tab in the Role Editor, and enter the following expression into the Allow Reading of **Cube Content** box:

```
[Sales Territory].[Sales Territory Country].CurrentMember IS [Sales
Territory].[Sales Territory Country].&[Canada]
```

Then we are stating that the user will be able to see only the cells where the `CurrentMember` on the Sales Territory Country hierarchy of the Sales Territory dimension is Canada. If we then query the cube, under this role, we will see this:

Row Labels	Sales Amount
⊞ Europe	#N/A
⊞ N/A	#N/A
⊟ North America	#N/A
⊟ Canada	16,355,770.46
Canada	16,355,770.46
⊟ United States	#N/A
Central	#N/A
Northeast	#N/A
Northwest	#N/A
Southeast	#N/A
Southwest	#N/A
⊞ Pacific	#N/A
Grand Total	#N/A

There are several interesting things to point out in this screenshot:

- Even if the role is able to access data only for **Canada**, users will see that data for other countries exists. For all the cells the role can't read, the value returned is **#N/A**; however, this can be changed by setting the **Secured Cell Value** connection string property.

- Granting access to a Country also grants access to all of the Regions in that Country. This is because there is an attribute relationship defined between Country and Region, so when a Region is selected in a query the `CurrentMember` on Country changes to be the Country that Region is in. Granting access to members on an attribute therefore grants access to lower granularity attributes that have a direct or indirect relationship with that attribute. This does not happen on higher granularity attributes though, so values for the North America member and the Grand Total (which is the All Member on the hierarchy) cannot be accessed.

This last point raises another question: what will happen if a user queries the cube through this role without selecting anything from the Sales Territory hierarchy? We can see the answer in the left-hand screenshot below—the `CurrentMember` on Sales Territory is the default member, which is the **All** Member, which of course the role cannot access data for. It's only when the user specifically selects Canada in the query, as in the righthand screenshot, that any data is visible.

Cell level security can be used to control access to `Measures` too. For example, using this expression for the Read permissions:

```
([Measures].CurrentMember IS [Measures].[Sales Amount])
OR
([Measures].CurrentMember IS [Measures].[Tax Amount])
```

We get this result:

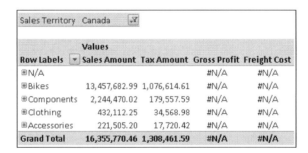

Let's now take a look at Read Contingent permissions, and see how they are different from Read permissions. If we want our users to be able to see the Sales Amount for all Countries but Total Product Cost only for Canada, we could use the following expression:

```
[Measures].CurrentMember IS [Measures].[Sales Amount]
OR (
    [Measures].CurrentMember IS [Measures].[Total Product Cost]
    AND
```

```
    [Sales Territory].[Sales Territory Country].CurrentMember
     IS [Sales Territory].[Sales Territory Country].&[Canada]
) OR
[Measures].CurrentMember IS [Measures].[Gross Profit]
```

Notice that we added the Gross Profit measure too, since we want our users to be able to see the Gross Profit for wherever he can access the Total Product Cost. Remember that Gross Profit is a calculated measure equal to Sales Amount minus Total Product Cost.

However, querying the cube, we get this result:

Row Labels	Values		
	Sales Amount	Total Product Cost	Gross Profit
North America	79353361.17	#N/A	#N/A
Canada	16355770.46	15347621.87	1,008,148.59
Bikes	13,457,682.99	12,828,017.74	629,665.25
Components	2,244,470.02	2,048,263.43	196,206.59
Clothing	432,112.25	355,195.20	76,917.05
Accessories	221,505.20	116,145.49	105,359.71
United States	62997590.72	#N/A	#N/A
Bikes	53,832,611.26	#N/A	3,287,244.5
Components	7,434,097.31	#N/A	685,297.16
Clothing	1,170,944.86	#N/A	207,501.56
Accessories	559,937.30	#N/A	264,095.36
Grand Total	79353361.17	#N/A	#N/A

We can see that the Read expression worked correctly, but the users can see Sales Amount and Gross Profit in places where they cannot see the Total Product Cost. Clearly, by subtracting Sales Amount from Gross Profit, they will be able to determine the Total Product Cost.

We can solve this problem by making the Read expression more complex, making sure that Gross Profit is only accessible when both Sales Amount and Total Product Cost are accessible, but doing this for all of the calculated measures in the cube would involve a lot of work. What we really want to do is apply a more general rule: we want to let our users access values for a calculated member only when they can access all of the values that calculated member is derived from. This is what Read Contingent security allows us to do.

If we remove the expression controlling access to Gross Profit from the Read security and add it to the Read Contingent textbox, then we will get the following result:

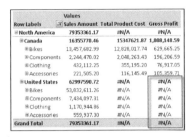

We can now see that users can only access values for Gross Profit when they can access values for both Sales Amount and Total Product Cost.

Dimension security

Dimension security allows us to control access to members on a hierarchy. It's less flexible than cell security but it's much easier to configure and manage, and in most cases security requirements can and should be implemented with dimension security rather than cell security.

Let's go back to our first requirement: we want our users to only be able to see sales for Canada, and no other country. We showed how to use cell security to do this and we have seen that, when browsing the cube, while users do see other countries they only see **#N/A** in the cells containing non-Canadian data. We can achieve the same result rather more elegantly using Dimension Security so let's describe how.

Here's the **Dimension Data** tab from the Role Editor, for the Sales Territory Country attribute from the Sales Territory dimension:

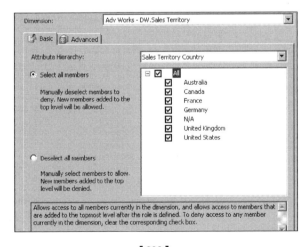

First of all, notice that there are two options to choose from on the left: **Select all members** and **Deselect all members**. They might seem to be two shortcuts to avoid having to click on each box in the treeview on the righthand side, but there is more to them than that.

- **Select all members** means that all the members in the hierarchy will be accessible through the role by default, and we have to specifically uncheck the members that we do not want to be accessible.

- **Deselect all members** means that no members will be accessible by default, and we have to specifically check any members we do want to be accessible.

The difference between the two becomes clear when, during the life of the dimension, new members appear in the hierarchy, for example because new countries appear in the underlying dimension table. If we used the **Select all members** option then these new members would automatically be accessible to the role until we edited the role and unchecked them; if, however we used the **Deselect all members** option then these new members would not be accessible until we edited the role and specifically checked them. We can think of these two options as setting the default behavior for how to handle new members in the hierarchy; in most cases it makes sense to use the **Deselect all members** option.

Armed with this knowledge, we can now choose **Deselect all members** and then check Canada. Here's what now happens when we query the cube through the role:

Row Labels	Values		
	Sales Amount	Total Product Cost	Gross Profit
⊟North America	79,353,361.17	73,901,073.99	5,452,287.18
⊟Canada	16,355,770.46	15,347,621.87	1,008,148.59
Canada	16,355,770.46	15,347,621.87	1,008,148.59
⊟Bikes	13,457,682.99	12,828,017.74	629,665.25
⊞Mountain Bikes	5,338,237.22	4,810,190.50	528,046.71
⊞Road Bikes	6,649,827.43	6,504,781.60	145,045.83
⊞Touring Bikes	1,469,618.34	1,513,045.64	-43,427.3
⊞Components	2,244,470.02	2,048,263.43	196,206.59
⊞Clothing	432,112.25	355,195.20	76,917.05
⊞Accessories	221,505.20	116,145.49	105,359.71
Grand Total	109,819,515.28	97,265,576.06	12,553,939.22

The Sales Territory hierarchy now appears as if Canada was the only Country on it. However, even if we don't filter on Country in the Excel worksheet we will still see data because all of the members on the hierarchy above Canada are still there.

However, if we look at the screenshot above carefully we can see something wrong. The Sales Amount for Canada is $16,355,770,46 USD but the Sales Amount for North America is $79,353,361.17 and the Grand Total is $109,819,515.28. We've managed to deny access to the other countries in the hierarchy but their values are still contributing to the totals at the Group level and Grand Totals. This is a potential security loophole because, once again, a user might be able to derive a value they should not have access to from values they can see.

To stop this happening, go to the **Advanced** tab in the Dimension Data security window:

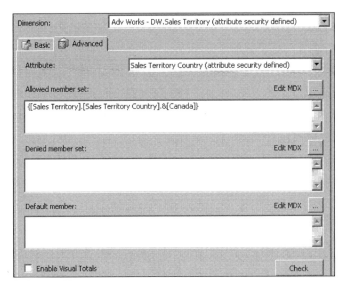

Look at the checkbox at the bottom of the page: **Enable Visual Totals**. This small checkbox controls one of the most powerful features of the Analysis Services security engine. By enabling Visual Totals we can force Analysis Services to aggregate up data using only the members that are accessible through this role. This will mean that the North America Region and the Grand Totals in our example will now return the same values as Canada, as shown in the following screenshot:

Row Labels	Values		
	Sales Amount	Total Product Cost	Gross Profit
North America	16,355,770.46	15,347,621.87	1,008,148.59
Canada	16,355,770.46	15,347,621.87	1,008,148.59
Canada	16,355,770.46	15,347,621.87	1,008,148.59
Bikes	13,457,682.99	12,828,017.74	629,665.25
Mountain Bikes	5,338,237.22	4,810,190.50	528,046.71
Road Bikes	6,649,827.43	6,504,781.60	145,045.83
Touring Bikes	1,469,618.34	1,513,045.64	-43,427.3
Components	2,244,470.02	2,048,263.43	196,206.59
Clothing	432,112.25	355,195.20	76,917.05
Accessories	221,505.20	116,145.49	105,359.71
Grand Total	16,355,770.46	15,347,621.87	1,008,148.59

We now have the exact result we wanted: members of the Role can only see data for Canada.

What is the price of checking this box? It is, potentially, a high one. As we know, Analysis Services makes extensive use of aggregations during query processing to improve performance. If we use the **Enable Visual Totals** option, then aggregations at granularities above the hierarchy we set it on can no longer be used, because they contain values calculated using the entire hierarchy and not the subset of it that the role exposes. This means that when Analysis Services receives a query that contains the **All** member on the Sales Territory Country attribute or any member above it, it will not be able to use certain aggregations and so performance may be worse. It's worth pointing out that there are situations where the **Enable Visual Totals** box can remain unchecked, for example because the need to display unfiltered values at higher granularities is greater than any potential security concerns.

Let's now take a look at some of the other options on the **Advanced** tab of the Dimension Data Security window. We can see in the last screenshot that there are three panes. The first two let us define an MDX set of allowed and denied members; this is simply the MDX representation of the selections made on the **Basic** tab that we discussed before: the role will have access to all of the members in the allowed set except for any members specified in the denied set. The third pane lets us define a default member on the hierarchy specifically for the role, which may be necessary when the role denies access to the original default member.

A common requirement is to be able to deny access to an entire level in a hierarchy. In our example, we might want to give a role access to the Group and Country levels on the Sales Territory user hierarchy but not the Region level; this would mean that users could not drill down below the Country level at all. To do this, all we need to do is to deny access to all of the members on the Sales Territory Region attribute hierarchy except the **All** member: Select the **Deselect all members** option and then select the **All** member. The **Allowed Member Set** pane on the **Advanced** tab would therefore contain the expression:

```
{[Sales Territory].[Sales Territory Region].[All]}
```

The Basic tab will look like this:

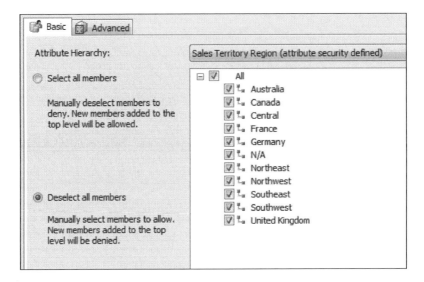

Although it's also another fairly common requirement, it isn't actually possible to deny access to an entire dimension in a role. The only thing we can do is deny access to all of the members on the hierarchy, either by setting the Allowed Member set to an empty set:

{ }

or by only allowing access to the **All** member on every hierarchy. Once we've done this the dimension itself will remain visible, but there will be no members available on any of the hierarchies and so user will not be able to select anything on it. It gives us the result we want, even if the end result isn't very elegant.

Applying security to measures

The **Dimension Data Security** tab can be used to secure the measures dimension in the same way as any other dimension. However, when we look at the measures dimension we might be a little surprised to see that only real, not calculated measures can be secured:

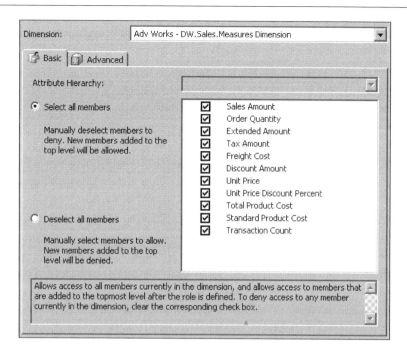

So, if we deny access to the Total Product Cost measure what will happen to any calculated members that depend on it? Here's a screenshot to show us:

Row Labels	Values	
	Sales Amount	Gross Profit
⊟ North America	16,355,770.46	#VALUE!
⊟ Canada	16,355,770.46	#VALUE!
Canada	16,355,770.46	#VALUE!
⊞ N/A		#VALUE!
⊟ Bikes	13,457,682.99	#VALUE!
⊞ Mountain Bikes	5,338,237.22	#VALUE!
⊞ Road Bikes	6,649,827.43	#VALUE!
⊞ Touring Bikes	1,469,618.34	#VALUE!
⊞ Components	2,244,470.02	#VALUE!
⊞ Clothing	432,112.25	#VALUE!
⊞ Accessories	221,505.20	#VALUE!
Grand Total	16,355,770.46	#VALUE!

Since one of the measures needed to perform the calculation is not available, the result of the calculation will not be accessible through the role. Nevertheless, the value displayed is very different from what we saw with Cell Security.

The cube returns **#VALUE** which indicates that there is an error in the definition of the calculated measure, which is, strictly speaking, true—the Total Product Cost measure does not exist as far as this role is concerned.

One possible approach for avoiding this problem is outlined here: `http://tinyurl.com/ChrisDimSecurity`, but this is rather complex. An alternative would be to adapt the Date Tool technique from Chapter 4 and create a new, empty physical measure group containing real measures whose value we can overwrite with MDX Script assignments, as described here: `http://tinyurl.com/SSAS-MeasureTool`.

When is security evaluated?

More details on when security is evaluated during the cube initialization process can be found here: `http://tinyurl.com/moshascriptinit`. The basic rule is that dimension security is evaluated before the MDX Script is evaluated, and cell security is evaluated after the MDX Script. This means that it is safe to reference named sets and calculated members in cell security expressions but not in dimension security expressions. This is a simplification of what actually happens, however: in some cases it does appear to be possible to reference MDX Script objects from dimension security expressions but it can lead to some unexplained behavior so we do not recommend doing this.

Dynamic security

Armed with the knowledge we've learned up to now, we might think we're ready to create the roles that we need to handle our reseller-related requirements. If you remember, we need to grant each reseller access to the cube and allow them to see their own sales data but not that of any other reseller. It sounds very much like what we've just done for countries, and indeed we can take the same approach and set up dimension security on the Reseller dimension with one role for each reseller.

This solution works fine if we only have a small number of resellers that need access to the cube. However, a quick look at the Reseller dimension will show that we have 702 resellers, so potentially we would need to create 702 roles in order to let all these resellers have access to our cube. Moreover, if we needed to change something in the role definition, for example because a new measure has been added and we don't want resellers to have access to it, we will need to update 702 different roles. The obvious solution, as simple as it is, is not powerful enough.

In order to solve this problem we will need to use **dynamic security**. The security roles we have seen so far have been static. This means that we have defined the set of accessible cells and members using MDX expressions that will return the same results for all the users belonging to the role. If we can write a single MDX expression that will return different results for each user, then we will be able to use only one role for all the reseller users. This is exactly what we'll do when we implement dynamic security.

Dynamic security uses one very important function: UserName. This function returns the name of the user (not the role) that is currently querying the cube. The user name will be preceded by the domain name, separated with a slash, as is standard in Windows logon names. So, a possible return value for UserName is SQLBOOK\Alberto. The UserName function can be used in any MDX expression used to define security, and it is the key to writing MDX expressions that return different results for each user.

There is another function, which we will not show in our examples, which can be used to pass user information into MDX from the outside world: CustomData. The CustomData MDX function returns a string value which is the value assigned to the CustomData connection string property. Strictly speaking, CustomData is not a security-related function, because any user can set this connection string property to any value and there is no validation at all carried on by Analysis Services. However, if the cube we are building will be queried only by other applications, in a multi-tier environment, then it might be convenient to run all the cube queries under the same user account and, in this case, UserName will always return the same value. The particular application querying the cube could set the CustomData connection string property to simulate impersonation of a different user for each query. Remember that CustomData should not be used in security if the cube is directly accessible by users, because it would represent a potentially serious vulnerability.

Even if it is very powerful, there are some issues to watch out for with dynamic security that need to be well understood. Over the next few pages we will cover the most important ones, as well as showing some concrete examples of how to implement dynamic security.

Dynamic dimension security

Let's take a look at how we'd go about implementing dynamic dimension security for resellers. If you recall, we want to define a single role that will be used by all of our resellers. In this role, we want to apply dimension security so that each reseller sees only their own sales.

First of all, we need to somehow model the relationship between resellers and the users who should have access to those resellers in our dimensional model. We might be tempted to add a new column to the reseller dimension table containing a username, but this only allows us to associate one username with one reseller. It's very likely, though, that many different users will need to have access to the same reseller and, probably, that a single user will need to have access to more than one reseller. Modeling this relationship with a bridge table will give us much more flexibility than adding another column to the dimension table will do. Our bridge table might look something like this:

User Name	Reseller
SQLBOOK\Alberto	Rewarding Activities Company
SQLBOOK\Chris	Roadway Bicycle Supply
SQLBOOK\Chris	Requisite Part Supply
SQLBOOK\Marco	Roadway Bicycle Supply

This table allows us to model the many-to-many relationship between users and the resellers they have access to. Since we need to write an MDX expression to return the set of allowed members, we will need to build a new measure group from this bridge table. Here's what we need to do to add the objects we need to our cube:

- Create a new table, `Security.Users`, in our relational data source containing all the users needed to model reseller security

- Create a new bridge table `Security.Bridge_ResellerUsers` that models the many-to-many relationship between users and resellers, as shown in the table

- Create a new Analysis Services dimension, `ResellerUsers`, based on `Security.Users`

- Create a new measure group based on `Security.Bridge_ResellerUsers`

- Create regular dimension relationships between the two dimensions, `ResellerUsers` and `Reseller`, and this new measure group

The relational data source, for the security section, will look like this:

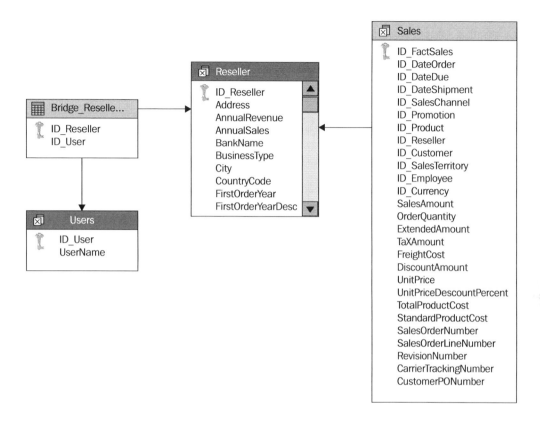

Both the new dimension containing reseller users and the new measure group should not be made visible to end users: they cannot be used in users' queries, and their presence might be confusing to them. However, as it's useful to be able to see them for debugging purposes, we might be tempted to create them as visible and then use security to deny end users access to them. Unfortunately, as we found earlier, we can't deny access to an entire dimension using dimension security, so setting their visibility is the only thing we can do.

> Setting an object's `Visible` property to **False** to hide it from end users is not the same thing as using security to deny access to it. Even if an object is not visible, it can still be used in a query and results returned for it.

After we've completed these steps, the **Dimension Usage** tab will look like this:

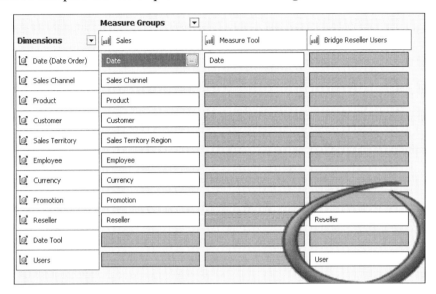

Now that we've added these structures to the cube, it will be very easy for us to write an MDX expression that returns the set of resellers each user has access to. The `UserName` function will return a string containing the user name, and what we need is a way to transform it into a member on the User dimension to use it as a filter on the measure group we built from the bridge table. We'll be able to use the `StrToMember` function for this purpose: it takes a string containing the unique name of a member and returns the corresponding member object.

Where possible, always specify the `Constrained` flag in the second parameter of the `StrToMember` function. Even though it is optional, using it has two benefits: it improves the performance of the function and, more importantly, it prevents MDX injection attacks. However, in this case we can't use it because we are dynamically generating the string we're passing into `StrToMember`, which violates the restrictions that the `Constrained` flag imposes.

The set definition we'll use is this:

```
NonEmpty (
    Reseller.Reseller.Members,
    (
        StrToMember ("[Users].[User].[" + UserName () + "]"),
        [Measures].[Bridge Reseller Users Count]
    )
)
```

This expression filters the set of members from the Reseller hierarchy, returning only those members where the Bridge Reseller User measure group contains a value for the member on the User hierarchy of the User dimension that has a name that's the same as the string returned by `UserName`. Enabling Visual Totals, we end up with this role definition:

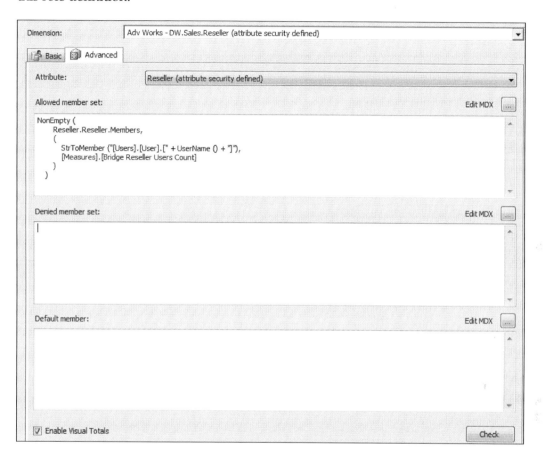

Note that users have access to the **All** member too: enabling Visual Totals will make sure the user only sees totals for the members that the user has access to. Here's what the users **Chris** and **Marco** will see when they connect to the cube through the role:

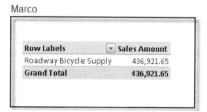

We can see that the two different users see different members on the Reseller dimension. Both users can see the reseller **RoadWay Bicycle Supply** but Marco can't see **Requisite Bicycle Supply**.

Dynamic security with stored procedures

The example we've just looked at uses data-driven security: it stores data on access rights inside the cube itself. Sometimes, though, we will be faced with more complex requirements: we might, for example, have to call external authentication procedures through web services. This is definitely something that cannot be handled using MDX expressions alone.

In such cases, we can create a .NET assembly to handle the security logic and then call the assembly from an MDX expression. A .NET function, when called from inside Analysis Services, is called a **Stored Procedure**; note that Analysis Services stored procedures should not be confused with SQL Server stored procedures—they're really just a way of creating custom MDX functions. Having the ability to call .NET code from inside MDX will, though, let us use the full power of .NET programming to define very complex security models.

In this section we are going to:

- Create a new class library containing security authentication code in C#
- Upload this library to Analysis Services
- Call our stored procedure from MDX to return the Allowed Members set for dimension security

The first thing we need to do in our new C# project is to add a reference to the msmgdsrv assembly, which gives us access to the Microsoft.AnalysisServices. AdomdServer namespace. We are not going to explain what everything in this assembly does; it's enough to say that it allows us to interact with the Analysis Services server object model in .NET.

In this example we're going to secure the Sales Territory Country attribute hierarchy on the Sales Territory dimension. The full code is available with the rest of the samples for this book, so we won't repeat it here, but the most important part is the function that returns the set of countries accessible to a user:

```
public static Set SecuritySet ()
{
  try
  {
    string userName = (new Expression ("UserName ()")
                          .Calculate (null)).ToString ();
```

```
MemberCollection members = Context.CurrentCube
                .Dimensions["Sales Territory"]
                .AttributeHierarchies["Sales Territory Country"]
                .Levels[1]
                .GetMembers ();

        SetBuilder sb = new SetBuilder ();
        foreach (Member m in members)
        {
          if (RegionsForUsers.isRegionEnabled (m.Caption, userName))
            {
              TupleBuilder tb = new TupleBuilder ();
              tb.Add (m);
              sb.Add (tb.ToTuple ());
            }
        }
        return sb.ToSet ();
      }
    catch (Exception)
    {
      return null;
    }
  }
```

Let us comment this code:

- The return value is a `Set`, an MDX set object, from `Microsoft.
  AnalysisServices.AdomdServer`. This means that the return value of
  the function can be used directly in our MDX expression; it is much more
  efficient than returning a string from the function, and then casting that
  string to a set using the `StrToSet` function.

- The local variable `userName` is calculated using the AdomdServer
  `Expression` object. `Expression` takes any valid MDX expression and, when
  evaluated, will return the value of the MDX expression. We use it to return
  the value of the `UserName` MDX function.

- The local variable `members` is assigned the set of all members from Sales
  Territory Country. We use this variable to iterate over all members of the
  hierarchy and decide whether they will be visible or not.

  ○ `Context` is an AdomdServer object that exposes the context of
     the current query; among other things, it lets us interact with the
     cube currently being queried. `Context.CurrentCube` exposes
     dimensions, measure groups and other metadata.

- ° `Dimensions` is a collection of all the dimensions on the cube. We use it to select the Sales Territory dimension.

- ° `AttributeHierarchies` is a collection containing all the hierarchies of a dimension, from which we select the Sales Territory Country hierarchy

- ° `Levels` contains the levels in the hierarchy. For user hierarchies it might contain several levels, for attribute hierarchies it normally contains two levels: one is the `All` level, the second one is the level of the other members on the hierarchy. We are interested in the second level, to get the different countries.

- ° `GetMembers` returns the list of all the members at the specified level.

- Since we want to return a set, we use the AdomdServer helper object `SetBuilder`, which lets us create a set and add items to it.

- We then iterate over each country in the `Members` collection and, for each one, we call a simple function called `RegionsForUsers.isRegionEnabled` that will return true or false, indicating whether the user is allowed to see that country or not. In our example the code is very simple, as it simply looks up values from a static array. In your implementation the code will almost certainly be more complex, perhaps querying a table in a relational database to determine which countries users can see.

- Since a set is made up of tuples, for every country we want to return we need to use the AdomdServer helper object `TupleBuilder` to create a simple tuple containing only that country member, and then pass that to the `SetBuilder`.

- At the end, `SetBuilder.ToSet` will create the set of all allowed countries and return it to the caller.

Having written the stored procedure, we can compile it and add it to the assemblies referenced by the Analysis Services project in BI Development Studio. This can be done by right-clicking on the Assemblies node in the Solution Explorer and choosing New Assembly Reference. BI Development Studio will copy the necessary files to the server during the next cube deployment. Once we have done this, we still need to call the function from the **Dimension Security** pane. In order to call a function from a stored procedure in MDX, we need to reference it in the form:

```
AssemblyName.FunctionName
```

In our case the expression is

```
SecurityUDF.SecuritySet()
```

All we then need to do is insert this expression inside the Allowed Members set of the Sales Territory Country hierarchy. When the expression is evaluated Analysis Services will recognize it as a stored procedure and call the function from the assembly. The function will return the set of countries accessible by the current user, and that is the set that will be used for dimension security.

> We recommend that you only use stored procedures for dynamic security in situations where it is not possible to store security information inside the cube, as stored procedures are hard to write, test and debug. The following blog entry contains some best practices for writing them: `http://tinyurl.com/moshasproc`, you can also find a lot of code examples in the Analysis Services Stored Procedure Project: `http://tinyurl.com/assproc`. For information on how to go about debugging a stored procedure, see `http://tinyurl.com/debugassproc`.

Dimension security and parent/child hierarchies

Parent/Child hierarchies handle dimension security in a different and much more complex way compared to standard dimensions. When a dimension contains a parent/child hierarchy:

- We cannot set up security directly on the key attribute—it will not appear on the dropdown list of hierarchies on the **Dimension Data Security** tab in the Role editor.

- Granting access to a member on a parent/child hierarchy will grant access to all of that member's descendants on the hierarchy.

- Granting access to a member on a parent/child hierarchy will grant access to all of its ancestors, so that the user can reach the selected member in the hierarchy. Enabling Visual Totals will ensure that these ancestor members only display values derived from the accessible members.

Let's take, as an example of a dimension with a parent/child hierarchy, the Employee dimension. What we want to do is implement dynamic dimension security on this dimension in a similar way to how we've implemented it on regular dimensions in the previous section. We want to create a bridge table to model the relationship between users and the employees whose data they need to have access to.

As we've already seen, setting up security is as easy or as hard as finding the right set expression to enter in the **Allowed Member Set** pane. Unfortunately, in the case of parent/child hierarchies, finding the right set expression can be pretty hard.

Let's start with the requirements: we want to link users and employees using this table:

UserName	Employee
SQLBOOK\Alberto	Syed E. Abbas
SQLBOOK\Alberto	Garrett R. Vargas
SQLBOOK\Alberto	Amy E. Alberts
SQLBOOK\Chris	Stephen Y. Jiang
SQLBOOK\Marco	Amy E. Alberts
SQLBOOK\Marco	Lynn N. Tsoflias
SQLBOOK\Marco	Jillian . Carson

Here's a visual representation of what this means when the employees are shown in the context of the parent/child relationship:

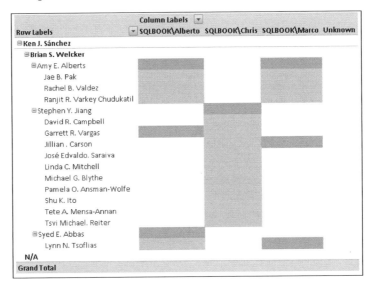

In the picture the dark gray cells show where security user has been explicitly granted access to an `Employee`; the light gray cells show where a user has been granted access to an `Employee` indirectly, through being granted access to one of the Employee's ancestors. We can see, for example, that Alberto has access to Amy E. Alberts and so gets full access to that member's children; he also has access to Garret R. Vargas but not to that member's parent or siblings.

Now, here's the difficult part: how do we write an MDX set expression so that
Analysis Services will grant access to only the members we've specified? Our first
idea might be to filter the parent/child hierarchy using an expression like this:

```
NonEmpty (
    Employee.Employees.Members,
    (
        [Measures].[Employee Count],
        [Users].[User].[SQLBOOK\Marco]
    )
)
```

Unfortunately this will not work. The reason is that not only the Employees we want
Marco to have access to will have a value for the Employee Count measure, their
ancestors will too, due to the aggregation performed by the Parent/Child hierarchy.
A picture will show this much better:

Employee Count Row Labels	Column Labels SQLBOOK\Alberto	SQLBOOK\Chris	SQLBOOK\Marco
⊟Ken J. Sánchez	3	1	3
⊟Brian S. Welcker	3	1	3
Amy E. Alberts	1		1
⊟Stephen Y. Jiang	1	1	1
Garrett R. Vargas	1	.	
Jillian . Carson			1
⊟Syed E. Abbas	1		1
Lynn N. Tsoflias			1
Grand Total	3	1	3

If we focus on Marco's column, we will see that the three highlighted cells contain
a value, and they represent the employees we've explicitly granted access to. Their
ancestors have values too, as a result of aggregation, so our set definition will return
a set containing Ken J.Sanchez and Brian S. Welcker, members which Marco should
not have access to. Since, as we know, granting access to a member grants access to
all of the descendants of that member, and since Ken J. Sanchez is the top member in
the hierarchy, this means that Marco will have access to all of the employees on the
hierarchy. In fact, it follows that with this set expression if a user is explicitly granted
access to any member on the hierarchy then they will be implicitly granted access to
all members on the hierarchy.

Let's try again. In order to return the correct set of members we need to make Analysis Services ignore the presence of the parent/child hierarchy, at least initially. To do this, we need to filter on the key attribute and not the parent/child hierarchy. If we try this set:

```
NonEmpty (
    [Employee].[Employee] .[Employee].Members,
    (
        [Measures].[Employee Count],
        [Users].[User].[SQLBOOK\Marco]
    )
)
```

We're getting closer to what we want: it returns only the three employees that Marco should have access to, just from the wrong hierarchy—and Analysis Services won't, of course, allow us to apply dimension security to the key attribute when there is a parent/child hierarchy.

> Notice that we used the set expression `Employee.Employee.Employee.Members` and not `Employee.Employee.Members` in the first parameter of the `Nonempty` function. This is very important because `Employee.Employee.Members` returns a set containing the **All** member and `Employee.Employee.Employee.Members` does not. We do not want the **All** member to appear in the set: if it does the technique will not work, for the same reason that the previous set expression did not.

All we need now is a way to take the members this set expression returns and find the equivalent members on the parent/child hierarchy. Luckily, we can do this easily with the `LinkMember` function.

`LinkMember` takes a member and finds the member on another hierarchy that has the same key value. This expression:

```
LinkMember (
    Employee.Employee.[Amy E. Alberts],
    Employee.Employees
)
```

Takes the member `Amy E.Alberts` from the `Employee` hierarchy and returns the same member but on the parent/child hierarchy. What we need is to iterate over the set of members we've got from the key attribute (the `Employee` hierarchy) and use `LinkMember` to convert each of them into the equivalent members on the parent/child hierarchy (the `Employees` hierarchy), and for this we can use the `Generate` function.

`Generate` takes two sets: the first is the "source" set, the second one contains an MDX set expression that is evaluated for each member of the first set. In order to reference the current item from the first set, we can use the `CurrentMember` function on the hierarchy used in the first set. Here's what the complete set expression looks like:

```
Generate (
    NonEmpty (
        [Employee].[Employee] .[Employee].Members,
        (
            [Measures].[Employee Count],
            [Users].[User].[SQLBOOK\Marco]
        )
    ), {
        LinkMember (
            Employee.Employee.CurrentMember,
            Employee.Employees
        )
    }
)
```

This is what each part of the expression actually does:

- The first set in the `Generate` function is the expression we have already seen: it returns the set of `Employee` members from the key attribute that the user has access to

- `Generate` iterates over this first set, and for each member it evaluates the `LinkMember` expression

- The `LinkMember` function takes `Employee.Employee.CurrentMember` to return the current Employee from the first set, and finds the equivalent member on the parent/child hierarchy, `Employee.Employees`

- The result of each evaluation of the `LinkMember` function is added to the final set that the `Generate` function returns

Finally, we just need to replace the reference to **SQLBOOK\Marco** with an expression that dynamically evaluates the user based on the value returned by the `UserName` function. We already learned how to write this before:

```
StrToMember ("[Users].[User].[" + UserName () + "]")
```

The final expression is:

```
Generate (
    NonEmpty (
        [Employee].[Employee] .[Employee].Members,
        (
```

```
            [Measures].[Employee Count],
            StrToMember ('[Users].[User].[' + UserName () + ']')
        )
    ), {
        LinkMember (
            Employee.Employee.CurrentMember,
            Employee.Employees
        )
    }
)
```

Copying this expression in the Allowed Member set of the parent/child hierarchy and enabling Visual Totals will do exactly what we need. Now, when Marco accesses the cube he will see this:

Row Labels	Sales Amount
⊟Ken J. Sánchez	27,033,801.81
⊟Brian S. Welcker	27,033,801.81
⊟Amy E. Alberts	15,546,187.34
Jae B. Pak	8,503,338.65
Rachel B. Valdez	1,800,764.33
Ranjit R. Varkey Chudukatil	4,509,888.93
⊟Stephen Y. Jiang	10,065,803.54
Jillian . Carson	10,065,803.54
⊟Syed E. Abbas	1,421,810.93
Lynn N. Tsoflias	1,421,810.93
Grand Total	**27,033,801.81**

Bear in mind that enabling Visual Totals on dimension security on a parent/child hierarchy can have a significant impact on query performance. Parent/child hierarchies can have no aggregations within the hierarchy itself—the only member that can benefit from aggregations is the **All** member. Denying access to some members in the hierarchy will invalidate any aggregations that have been built at the All level, and this means that every single query at that level (and this includes queries that don't mention the Employee dimension at all) or above will have to aggregate values up through the parent/child hierarchy. We already discouraged the reader from using parent/child hierarchies. The performance impact of security on parent/child hierarchies is yet another reason not to use them in large cubes.

Dynamic cell security

We can implement dynamic security for cell security in much the same way as we have seen with dimension security. In this section we'll use the same bridge table we used in the previous sections to model the relationship between users and resellers they have access to; our requirements will be as follows:

- Members of the role will have complete access to all measures, except for Gross Profit

- For Gross Profit, users will only have access to values for it for resellers they have been granted access to based on the data in our bridge table

- We also need to hide the **All** member of the Reseller dimension to ensure that users cannot derive values for cells they don't have access to.

We can use this expression to control Read access in the **Cell Data** tab:

```
NOT (
    Measures.CurrentMember IS Measures.[Gross Profit]
    AND (
        StrToMember ("[Users].[User].[" + UserName() + "]"),
        Measures.[Bridge Reseller Users Count]) = 0
        OR
        Reseller.Reseller.CurrentMember IS Reseller.Reseller.[All]
    )
)
```

The usage of NOT is very common in cell security expressions: it's usually easier to define the cells that users are not allowed access to. The expression may be read as follows: "if the user is not querying Gross Profit, then show everything. Otherwise, if the reseller they are querying is not present in the bridge table for that user, or the reseller is the **All** member, then deny access to the cell".

The result will be as follows:

Row Labels	Values Sales Amount	Gross Profit
Riding Associates	10,349.13	#N/A
Riding Cycles	282,701.32	#N/A
Riding Excursions	419.46	#N/A
Riverside Company	31,960.34	#N/A
Road Way Sales and Rental	758.94	#N/A
Roadway Bicycle Supply	**436,921.65**	**-33,724.76**
Roadway Bike Emporium	148,098.29	#N/A
Road-Way Mart	2,485.70	#N/A
Roadway Supplies	1,778.43	#N/A
Rodeway Bike Store	132,143.71	#N/A
Roving Sports	17,320.33	#N/A
Rugged Bikes	208,802.87	#N/A

The user is allowed to see Sales Amount for all resellers but not Gross Profit, which is only available for Roadway Bicycle Supply.

As we see, the expression is very complex and evaluating this for every cell in the query can have a negative impact on query performance. If we want to optimize the performance of cell security expressions, we can leverage the MDX script—which, as we know, is evaluated before cell security.

In this case we can define a new hidden calculated measure, HideGrossProfit, to hold the logic for our cell security expression. In the initial calculated measure definition we give it a default value of False; thc, we use SCOPE statements to overwrite its value for the parts of the cube where it should return True.

```
CREATE MEMBER CurrentCube.Measures.HideGrossProfit AS
    False,
Visible = 0;


SCOPE (Measures.HideGrossProfit);
  SCOPE (StrToMember ("[Users].[User].[" + UserName() + "]"));
        THIS = (Measures.[Bridge Reseller Users Count] = 0);
  END SCOPE;
  SCOPE (Reseller.Reseller.[All]);
        THIS = True;
  END SCOPE;
END SCOPE;
```

Note the highlighted SCOPE statement, which is the key to making this technique work: we are scoping on a dynamically evaluated member expression.

Having created this calculated member, we can then reference it in a much-simplified cell security expression as follows:

```
NOT (
    Measures.CurrentMember IS Measures.[Gross Profit]
    AND HideGrossProfit
)
```

Now that the security logic is handled in MDX Script the query performance improvement is significant: instead of being re-evaluated for every cell, the expression determining which cells a user has access to is evaluated only once, when the MDX Script is executed. Another benefit of moving the logic to the MDX Script is that it is much easier to define complex expressions and perform debugging there.

One last problem to solve with this technique is that the evaluation of the SCOPE statement requires that each user of the cube, regardless of whether they are a member of the dynamic role, be present in the Users dimension. If they aren't the cube will raise an error, because we'll be attempting to use the SCOPE statement on a member that doesn't exist. This can be worked around by altering our SCOPE statement to use a named set, and then in the named set definition return an empty set if the STRTOMEMBER function returns an error as follows:

```
CREATE MEMBER CurrentCube.Measures.HideGrossProfit AS False, Visible =
0;

CREATE SET CurrentCube.UserSet AS
IIF(
IsError(StrToMember ("[Users].[User].[" + UserName() + "]"))
, {}
, {StrToMember ("[Users].[User].[" + UserName() + "]")});

SCOPE (Measures.HideGrossProfit);
    SCOPE (UserSet);
        THIS = (Measures.[Bridge Reseller Users Count] = 0);
    END SCOPE;
    SCOPE (Reseller.Reseller.[All]);
        THIS = True;
    END SCOPE;
END SCOPE;
```

In our experience, there are very few scenarios where cell data security is really necessary; the scenarios where dynamic cell security is necessary are rarer still. This is true, though, if and only if security has been correctly designed from the beginning of the project: when security is added onto a cube as an afterthought, very often cell security is the only approach possible.

Accessing Analysis Services from outside a domain

So far we've seen that, in order to let a user access a cube, that user needs to be a user on the same domain as Analysis Services. We have seen that roles are based on Windows users and groups, and that Analysis Services does not implement any other forms of authentication.

Nevertheless, it is possible to let users outside a domain access Analysis Services if we set up HTTP access via Internet Information Server (IIS). This method uses a DLL called MSMDPUMP.DLL that acts as a bridge between IIS and Analysis Services; when called, this DLL connects to Analysis Services and impersonates a Windows user, which can be a domain user or a local user on the server hosting Analysis Services and IIS. The DLL is placed in a virtual directory in IIS; the client application then connects to the DLL via IIS and IIS therefore handles the authentication. Using integrated Windows authentication is the recommended option, but it is also possible to use other methods such as anonymous access or basic authentication, for example. For security reasons, it is much better to make users connect to IIS using HTTPS and not HTTP: this will avoid sending query results and possibly user credentials over the network as clear text.

Another benefit of HTTP access is that it allows users to connect to Analysis Services even in situations where a firewall blocks access to ports 2382 (for SQL Server Browser) or 2383 (the default port on which Analysis Services listens for client connections).

A complete walkthrough of how to set up HTTP connectivity is outside the scope of this book; the following blog entry contains links to all of the relevant white papers and collects a lot of other useful information on the subject: http://tinyurl.com/MSMDPUMP.

When HTTP connectivity is set up, we will be able to connect to Analysis Services using any client application, but instead of giving the Analysis Services server name in the connection, we give the URL of the virtual directory and the DLL:

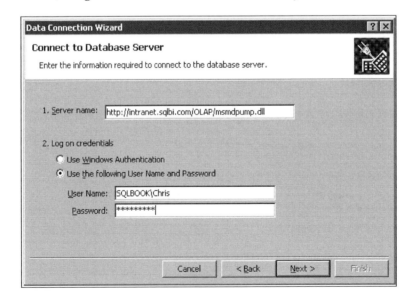

Accessing a cube via HTTP can result in slower query performance when compared to a standard TCP/IP connection, because the translation from TCP/IP to HTTP will require time and will increase packet size. Nevertheless, when the user cannot connect directly to Analysis Services, using IIS is the only other option available.

Managing security

So far, we have only discussed how to set up security from the point of view of the developer. However, once the roles have been defined, security will still need to be managed: new users will appear, some users will disappear, and users may change which roles they are members of.

This task is not generally managed by the developers of the Analysis Services cube, it is usually handled by someone else such as a network administrator or a DBA whose job it is to look after the cube once it has gone into production. So, the question is: how should these people add new users to a role? The answer should not be that they need to open BI Development Studio or SQL Management Studio and edit the roles directly. If we have followed our rule to only add Windows groups as role members, then it will be possible to add or remove users purely by adding and removing these members from domain groups. This will mean that whoever is managing security will not need administrative access to the cube itself; it will also mean they do not need to learn how to use potentially unfamiliar tools such as SQL Management Studio.

A different and more complex situation is when the Analysis Services developer works in a domain that is not the same as the domain where Analysis Services is installed. In this case we cannot define the relationship between roles and Windows groups in BI Development Studio, because we do not even have access to the domain where those roles exist. The only thing we can do is to create empty roles and let whoever is managing security create associations between roles and groups once the Analysis Services database has been deployed. What's more, when this happens we can no longer deploy our cube from BI Development Studio because doing so would overwrite the properly configured roles on the server with the empty roles in our solution. Instead we will need to use the Analysis Services Deployment Wizard to deploy our solution: it gives us the option to either deploy only roles that do not exist already on the server, or to not deploy any of the roles in our solution at all.

Managing dynamic security adds another set of challenges, because as we've seen dynamic security requires us to store our security permissions somewhere outside the cube, probably in a relational database table. We don't want whoever's managing our security permissions to have to write a SQL statement every time these permissions change; there should be an application they can use for this purpose. In some cases we may be importing this permissions data from our OLTP database, which means there will probably be an application in place to manage permissions already. However, in other cases we may need to build a custom .NET application to manage dynamic security permissions: it would need to update the permissions table and, if we are using the security measure group approach, it would need to process that measure group and the User dimension.

Security and query performance

Applying security to a cube comes at a cost to query performance. However, since we don't usually have a choice about whether to apply security or not, we then need to understand which security features have the least impact on performance when choosing which ones to use. In this final section we'll give some details on the relative impact on query performance of each type of security.

Cell security

Cell security has by far the biggest negative impact on query performance, and for this reason alone it should only be used when there is no other option. Also remember that there are two different types of cell security, Read and Read Contingent; Read Contingent cell security has more impact on query performance than Read. The reason why cell security is so bad is because it prevents Analysis Services from using many important query optimization techniques (for example, in many cases it appears to completely prevent the use of the Formula Engine cache, so the results of calculations are not cached from query to query), even when users are querying cells they do have access to.

Dimension security

Dimension security has less impact on performance than cell security, although it can still lead to noticeably slower queries.

As we've already noted, enabling Visual Totals can prevent the use of aggregations at higher levels of granularity, which means Analysis Services may need to do more aggregation at query time. Setting the `AggregationUsage` property of the attribute that we're securing to **Full** and setting it to **None** for any attributes at a higher granularity might, as a result, be a good idea to make sure we don't build any aggregations that the role cannot use.

Dimension security does not stop Analysis Services from caching the result of MDX calculations, but it does limit its ability to share cached calculated values between users. Only users that have exactly the same set of permissions and are members of exactly the same roles can share cached calculated values. So, for example, if user A ran a query that included a calculated measure, as we saw in Chapter 8 in most cases the second time user A ran the same query the calculated measure's values would be retrieved from the Formula Engine cache. However, if user B then connected to the cube and ran the same query, that query would only be able to retrieve values from the Formula Engine cache if user B had exactly the same security rights as user A. On cubes with very complex calculations the ability to share values in the Formula Engine cache between users can make a big difference to the overall performance of the cube.

Dynamic security

Dynamic security can slow down the process of connecting to a cube, if the MDX expressions we're using to determine what data a user can see take a long time to be evaluated. In almost all cases a purely data-driven approach, where security information is stored within the cube itself, will perform noticeably better than approaches that use Analysis Services stored procedures, so this is another good reason to avoid using stored procedures for security.

Dynamic dimension security also completely prevents Analysis Services from sharing values in the Formula Engine cache between users. Unlike regular dimension security, with dynamic dimension security a user can never access values in the Formula Engine cache that are there as a result of queries run by other users. As a result, on cubes with very complex calculations, we recommend you try to use regular dimension security unless the number of roles that would be required is genuinely too many to manage.

Summary

In this chapter we have learned that:

- The only form of authentication supported by Analysis Services is Windows authentication. If access need to be granted from outside the domain the Analysis Services server belongs to, then it is possible to configure HTTP access to Analysis Services via IIS.

- Analysis Services security is based on roles. Only Windows users and groups can be members of roles.

- If a user belongs to multiple roles, they will have all of the permissions granted to them by every role they are a member of; there is no concept of "deny wins over grant".

- We can use cell security to secure individual cell values within the cube. Cell security can cause poor query performance and should only be used if there is no other option.

- Dimension security lets us allow or deny access to members on a hierarchy. Using the **Enable Visual Totals** option then controls whether values at higher granularities are calculated based on all of the members on the hierarchy or just the members that the user has access to.

10
Productionization

When the Analysis Services cube is finished, its life—from the developer's point of view—is over. Nevertheless, its real life, from the user's point of view, has just begun. During the development phase we probably didn't care too much about what would happen once the cube was in production, but of course there are a whole new set of problems that must be dealt with when a cube has gone live. We are going to address these problems in this chapter.

The focus is on the following topics:

- **Making changes to a cube once it has gone into production**: Changes will still need to be made to the cube once it's in production, but we need to be very careful about how we make them in case we accidentally break reports, overwrite properties, or unprocess objects.

- **Managing partitions**: Partitioning our cube is good for two reasons—to improve query performance and to reduce the amount of processing we need to do. In production, new data will need to be loaded into the cube on a regular basis and this means we'll need a way of automatically creating new partitions when they are necessary.

- **Processing**: Having a lot of data to process forces us to find the most efficient way of processing it. If, as is usually the case, we don't have enough time available to do a full process on our Analysis Services database every time we need to load new data into it, then we need to understand what other options are available for cube and dimension processing.

- **Copying databases from one server to another**: On larger implementations we'll have several instances of Analysis Services, for example in a network load balanced cluster. In this scenario we will not want to process the same database more than once; instead we'll need to look at the methods we can use for copying a newly processed database from one instance to another.

Making changes to a cube in production

The first problem we'll face once a cube has gone into production is how to make changes to it without causing disruption to our users. In a development environment we can generally make any changes to a cube we like because we are the only users of our cube; however, we need to be more careful when deploying changes to the cube into production for two reasons:

- Some changes we make may result in cubes or dimensions becoming unprocessed. Adding a new calculated measure to a cube doesn't require any processing at all; adding a new dimension to a cube means that the cube will need a full process. If we have a lot of data in our cube a full process might take a long time, and our users will probably not want to have to wait to run their queries while this happens.

- It's likely that our BI Development Studio solution will not match the deployed version of the cube in some important respects. We saw in Chapter 9 that roles may be added or updated on an Analysis Services database after it has been deployed; similarly, we may be using different data sources in our development environment compared to our production environment, and, as we'll see later in this chapter, it's possible that the measure groups in deployed cubes will contain extra, dynamically created partitions. When we deploy a solution in BI Development Studio we have to deploy every object in it—and if we overwrite the roles, data sources or partitions on the production server, we will end up denying access to users and dropping data from the cube.

One method we definitely do not want to use for deploying changes to a cube in production is to edit the cube directly in online mode. Although this might seem a quick and easy option, it will of course mean we are bypassing any source control we are using. For the same reason we don't recommend making changes by running XMLA statements to update an object's definition.

There are two safe, commonly-used techniques for deploying changes to a production environment:

- We can use Visual Studio's project configurations feature, as detailed in this blog entry: `http://tinyurl.com/gregprojconfig`. For a single project this allows us to configure different property settings, such as the connection strings used in a data sources, for different build types such as development or production. This is a very powerful feature, but it still does not solve the problem of overwriting roles or partitions on the production server.

- The recommended approach is to use the Deployment Wizard, which allows us complete control over what actually gets deployed to the production server. To use it, first we have to build our project in BI Development Studio; we can then run the wizard, point it to the `.asdatabase` file that is created in our project's `bin` directory when we did the build, and then choose what happens to roles, partitions, connection strings, and various other properties.

Managing partitions

As we saw in Chapter 8, partitioning a measure group simply involves slicing it up into smaller chunks that are both easier to maintain and to query. In that chapter we already introduced and explained the basic concepts of partitioning; now we are interested in how to manage partitions when the cube is up and running.

Measure groups are usually partitioned by the time dimension, for example with one partition holding one month of data. Although there are rare cases where we might want to partition a measure group based on a different dimension (for example, geography is sometimes used), the vast majority of projects we have worked on use time as the slicer. This follows from the fact that new data usually needs to be loaded into the measure group at regular intervals in time, and this new data needs to be processed and stored alongside the existing data.

Clearly, since partitioning is so closely linked to the concept of time, we need to be able to build and process new partitions dynamically when we have new data to load. We could certainly build extra partitions in our Analysis Services database to handle our future needs—maybe create 48 empty monthly partitions to last for four years—but not only would this be time-consuming to do, it would also mean that in four years' time someone would need to remember to create some more partitions. And even then, we'd still need a way of processing only the partition that contained the latest data, rather than all partitions.

 Note that if our partitioning strategy is not dynamic, for example if we're partitioning by geography, then this section is of no relevance. Static partitions can safely be defined inside BI Development Studio because they do not change over time.

In this section we'll demonstrate how you can use SQL Server Integration Services plus some .NET code to create partitions dynamically. Here's a breakdown of what we're going to be doing:

- We'll create a template partition within our measure group that we will use as the basis for all of the new partitions we are going to create.

- We'll create an Integration Services package that loads data from a configuration database, uses this data to decide if any new partitions need to be created, and then creates them by copying the template partition and modifying its properties.

- There will be two types of partition slice: data for the most recent twelve months will be stored in twelve monthly partitions, while older data will be stored in yearly partitions. This will give us the opportunity to show how to handle more advanced problems such as merging partitions.

- The measure group will contain different aggregation designs for the different types of partition, monthly and yearly, and our package will apply the right aggregation design to any new partitions it creates.

Once again, all of the code for this chapter will be available as part of the sample projects and databases for the book; we're going to highlight only the most interesting parts of that code here.

Relational versus Analysis Services partitioning

The fact tables upon which we build our Analysis Services measure groups are normally partitioned. Partitioning in the relational database follows rules and needs dictated by the relational data structure. A common relational partitioning model is by month, so each partition holds a month of data; when data gets too old it is deleted or moved somewhere else, to leave space for new data.

Partitioning in Analysis Services is different in several respects:

- Partitions in the same measure group can, and often do, have different slices. For example, as in our case, older data may be partitioned at the year level, while more recent data may be partitioned at the month level. As we said, in the relational database partitioning is normally done with only one type of slice.

- Similarly, different partitions may have different aggregation designs. Older data tends to be queried less often and at a higher level, and so partitions containing older data may need different aggregations from partitions containing newer data.

- Sometimes not all the data from the relational database needs to be loaded into the cube. Very old data might be useful in the relational database for relational reporting purposes but dropped from the cube, for example to make it faster to process, query, or take a backup.

- We may change our partitioning strategy if our requirements change. If, for example, it turns out that a lot of queries are being run at the month level for old data, we might change our partitioning strategy so that we used monthly partitions for all of our data. This, of course, would not require any changes to the relational database although it would mean that we would have to process all of the newly-created partitions, which might take a long time.

Building a template partition

The first step towards implementing a dynamic partitioning strategy is to create a template partition in our measure group. Since, in a partitioned measure group, all of the partitions are identical except for the slice of the fact data they contain and possibly the aggregation design they use, what we're going to do is to create a single partition that will be used as a blueprint by our Integration Services package. When the package creates a real partition in the measure group, it will make a copy of the template partition and change some of its properties so that it will contain, when processed, the appropriate slice of the fact data.

We will be implementing dynamic partitioning on the **Sales** measure group in our sample cube here. To do this, we need to make sure there is only one partition in that measure group and we need to change its **Binding type** to **Query Binding**. Since this is only a template partition we don't want it to be able to store any data, so we need to add a condition to the WHERE clause in the SELECT statement that this partition is bound to, such as WHERE 1=0, as shown in the following screenshot. This will ensure that, if it is processed, no rows will be read during processing and that it will contain no data.

If we want to use the Design Aggregation Wizard at this point, we will need to either remove the WHERE clause from the query, deploy the cube, and process it before launching the wizard; or set the EstimatedRows property on the partition to the average number of rows we expect to have in each partition.

Generating partitions in Integration Services

The technique we are going to use to build partitions in Integration Services requires the creation of a script task and some .NET code that uses **AMO** (**Analysis Management Objects**) to connect to the cube and create or delete partitions. AMO is a .NET class library that contains the objects necessary to perform administrative tasks on an Analysis Services database. Since script tasks do not by default contain a reference to the AMO library, the first thing we need to do after creating our script task is right-click on the **References** node in the **Project Explorer** in the **Script Editor** window, and add a reference to the **Analysis Management Objects** component. Full documentation for AMO can be found at *Books Online*, so we won't go into any detail on what each object does.

Here is an outline of what happens within the script task:

- First, we retrieve information on what partitions exist in our fact table from the relational database. This will tell us what partitions need to be present in our measure group.

- Then we connect to Analysis Services and our measure group, and find out what partitions currently exist there.

- Next, we work out what Analysis Services partitions should be present in the measure group based on what relational partitions are currently present in the fact table.

- The next, and most complex, step is to compare the list of Analysis Services partitions that should be present with the list of partitions that currently exist, and apply any changes that are necessary. This will include deleting old partitions, merging existing partitions, and creating new partitions. When creating new partitions we simply take the template partition and call the Clone method on it to create a new, identical partition.

- Each new Analysis Services partition is bound to a dynamically generated SQL query that will return all of the data from the relational partitions it covers, and other properties such as Slice are also set appropriately.

Once this has happened we will need to process any new partitions, which we'll see how to do in the next section in this chapter.

At this point the package looks like this:

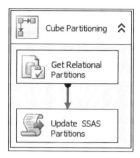

Here's what the cube looks like immediately after the deployment, with only the empty template partition present:

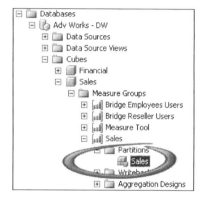

If we run the package to create partitions up to June 2004, this is the result:

The package has added a lot of new partitions:

- Yearly partitions, for the years 2001, 2002, and 2003. Note that the 2003 partition does not contain a whole year but only the months from January to June. Other months are covered by monthly partitions.

- Monthly partitions, for the last 12 months up to June 2004.

The Sales partition, the template partition, is still there and still empty.

 In our simple implementation we use only a single template partition. A more complex implementation could use two different template partitions: one for monthly partitions and one for yearly partitions, perhaps with different aggregation designs associated to them.

If we script the **Sales of Year 2003** partition into an XMLA query editor window in SQL Management Studio we can see its definition and understand what the package has done; here's the part of the definition where all the important properties are set:

```
<ObjectDefinition>
    <Partition>
        <ID>Sales of Year 2003</ID>
        <Name>Sales of Year 2003</Name>
        <Annotations>
            <Annotation>
                <Name>MonthsInsidePartition</Name>
                <Value>200301200302200303200304200305200306</Value>
            </Annotation>
            <Annotation>
                <Name>PartitionType</Name>
                <Value>YEAR</Value>
            </Annotation>
        </Annotations>
        <Source xsi:type="QueryBinding">
            <DataSourceID>Adv DM</DataSourceID>
            <QueryDefinition>
              SELECT * FROM CubeSales.Sales WHERE
              OrderYearMonth=200301
              UNION ALL
              SELECT * FROM CubeSales.Sales WHERE
              OrderYearMonth=200302
              UNION ALL
              SELECT * FROM CubeSales.Sales WHERE
              OrderYearMonth=200303
              UNION ALL
              SELECT * FROM CubeSales.Sales WHERE
              OrderYearMonth=200304
```

```
            UNION ALL
            SELECT * FROM CubeSales.Sales WHERE
            OrderYearMonth=200305
            UNION ALL
            SELECT * FROM CubeSales.Sales WHERE
            OrderYearMonth=200306
        </QueryDefinition>
      </Source>
    </Partition>
</ObjectDefinition>
```

There are two things to point out here:

- In order to store the list of relational partitions that are covered by this Analysis Services partition, we used an Annotation. **Annotations** are string values that can be stored inside many Analysis Services objects programmatically, and we can use them to store additional information not covered by the standard Analysis Services properties.

  In this case we have used annotations to store both the partition type (Yearly or Monthly) and the list of months that are stored inside the partition. For the month names, we used a string consisting of multiple six character groups in the form YYYYMM. These annotations are used when we rerun the package, in order to determine which months each partition covers without having to parse the source query.

- The QueryDefinition tag contains the SQL query that will be sent to the relational data source (in our case SQL Server) when the partition is processed. The query has been constructed to use the partition key in the most effective way: each SELECT statement returns data from exactly one partition and the results are UNIONed together.

Now, if we run the script again, moving a month forward, the script will update the partitioning structure once again. Here's what the log of the Integration Services package shows:

```
Year partition Sales of Year 2001 is already ok.
Year partition Sales of Year 2002 is already ok.
Merging partition Sales of Month 200307 into Sales of Year 2003
Partition Sales of Month 200308 is already ok.
Partition Sales of Month 200309 is already ok.
Partition Sales of Month 200310 is already ok.
Partition Sales of Month 200311 is already ok.
Partition Sales of Month 200312 is already ok.
Partition Sales of Month 200401 is already ok.
Partition Sales of Month 200402 is already ok.
Partition Sales of Month 200403 is already ok.
```

```
Partition Sales of Month 200404 is already ok.
Partition Sales of Month 200405 is already ok.
Partition Sales of Month 200406 is already ok.
Partition Sales of Month 200407 has been created.
```

The script has detected that the following changes need to be made and made them:

- The 2003 yearly partition needs to be extended by one month to include July 2003. Since this month is already present as a monthly partition, it is merged into the 2003 partition. This operation does not require that the 2003 partition be reprocessed: Analysis Services is able to merge two already-processed partitions without the need for any further processing.

    When merging two partitions, Analysis Services will use the aggregation design of the destination partition (in this case the 2003 yearly partition) but will disable any aggregations that are not present in the source partition (July 2003 here). A ProcessDefault on the destination partition will rebuild the invalidated aggregations.

- A new monthly partition, for July 2004, is needed and so it has been created.

After having performed the merge operation, the script updates all the annotations inside the partition and also the SELECT statement the partition is bound to. This ensures that the next time this partition is processed it will contain the correct data.

There is no way to delete data from within an existing partition without reprocessing it. In the scenario above, when we created a new monthly partition for July 2004 we might also have wanted to delete one month of data from the yearly partition for 2001 to maintain a consistent time window of data in the measure group. This would have meant we had to reprocess the 2001 partition, though, a potentially expensive operation. Instead, what the script does is only delete a partition at the start of the time window when it contains a whole year's data. This has the added benefit that any "Same Period Previous Year" calculations that use the ParallelPeriod MDX function (described in Chapter 6) will always work properly for the second year in the time window.

Managing processing

During development we can process cubes or dimensions whenever we want; in a production environment processing needs more thought though. On a very simple project we might be able to get away with doing a full process on our entire Analysis Services database if it only takes a few minutes to complete. However, we usually have large data volumes to manage and a limited amount of time to perform any processing, so a full process simply isn't feasible—we need to think carefully how we can only process the data that needs to be processed, and do that processing in the most efficient way possible.

Analysis Services processing can be broken down into two different tasks:

- **Dimension Processing** involves loading data into a dimension and building indexes on it.

- **Partition Processing** is more complex. Before we can query a cube, all of the dimensions in the cube need to be processed and we need to process the cube itself too. A cube is made up of measure groups and a measure group is made up of partitions, and since partitions are where the data in a cube is actually stored then when we talk about processing a cube what we are really talking about is processing all of the partitions in a cube. Processing a partition involves loading data into it, building indexes, and building any aggregations specified in the aggregation design associated with this partition.

MOLAP, HOLAP, or ROLAP?

So far we've assumed that we're always going to use MOLAP storage mode for all of our partitions. That's because 99% of the time we will be! **MOLAP** storage involves storing all data in Analysis Services' own data structures; it gives us the fastest query performance but involves the longest processing times. **ROLAP** storage leaves all data in the relational database, and when MDX queries are run then Analysis Services generates SQL statements to retrieve the data it needs; querying is relatively slow as a result but processing is very fast. **HOLAP** storage is a cross between the two and involves storing aggregations and indexes in MOLAP mode but everything else in ROLAP mode.

ROLAP storage for partitions is only very rarely useful, for when we really do need to see real-time data inside a cube, and even then the poor query performance of ROLAP partitions means it can only be used with relatively small data volumes. Since fast query performance is the number one priority for any Analysis Services cube the extra time needed for processing MOLAP partitions is usually a price worth paying. We have never seen a scenario where HOLAP storage is the right choice, so we can safely ignore it.

Similarly, MOLAP storage is almost always the right choice for dimensions. As we saw in Chapter 5, ROLAP storage is usually only used for very large fact dimensions that would take too long to process in MOLAP mode.

Dimension processing

In this section we'll discuss the various different types of processing that can be performed on a dimension and what they actually do. For obvious reasons we'll want to choose the option that loads the data we need into the dimension in the quickest and most efficient way. However, when processing a dimension we also need to be aware of the side effects that this processing might have on any cubes that the dimension is present in. If, for example, we perform a Process Update on a dimension, then this might invalidate aggregations that include hierarchies from this dimension, meaning they need to be rebuilt too. In this case and others, the side effects are more significant than dimension processing itself: the processing of a single dimension is usually a relatively fast operation while rebuilding aggregations can take much longer.

 Clicking on the **Impact Analysis** button in the **Process** dialog in either SQL Management Studio or BI Development Studio will list all of the objects that are affected by any type of processing on any object.

Here is a complete list of all of the options we have for dimension processing, along with a brief description of what each one does and any side effects:

Type	Description
Full	The dimension's structure is deleted and rebuilt, and all dimension data is reloaded from scratch. In addition, all measure groups related to this dimension, and all partitions in these measure groups, require a Full process before they can be queried.
Add	Compares the contents of the relational dimension table with the contents of the Analysis Services dimension, adds any new members that are found but does not delete or update existing members: this means that you run the risk that important changes to existing dimension members are not made. It does not invalidate existing partition data or aggregations. Also known as incremental processing, this option is not visible in SQL Management Studio or BI Development Studio. For more information on how to use process Add, see http://tinyurl.com/gregprocessadd.
Data	Loads data into the dimension but does not process dimension indexes. It has the same side effects as Process Full.
Index	Usually used after Process Data, it builds the bitmap indexes of the dimension and does not require any access to the relational database.

Type	Description
Update	Compares the contents of the relational dimension table with the contents of the Analysis Services dimension and then deletes any members from the Analysis Services dimension that no longer exist in the relational table, updates any members that have changed and adds any new members.
	Since existing members on hierarchies with at least one flexible attribute relationship in the chain of attribute relationships down to the key attribute can change, then all aggregations including these hierarchies will be dropped. They can be rebuilt later by running a Process Default on affected cubes or measure groups.
	Over time the performance of a dimension will degrade after multiple Process Updates. As a result, if you do use Process Update regularly it's a good idea to schedule an occasional Process Full, for example at a weekend or public holiday when it will cause minimal disruption.
Unprocess	Deletes all structures and data for the dimension.
Default	Performs whatever processing is necessary to bring the dimension up to a fully processed state.

With these options in mind, here, in order of increasing complexity, are some of the possible strategies we can use for processing dimensions:

- We can run a Process Full on all of our dimensions, which of course means we then have to run a Process Full on all of our cubes. As we have already said this is the simplest option but is only feasible if we have enough time to do this—and can be sure that we will have enough time in the future as the data volumes in our data warehouse grow. Remember that adding hardware can have a dramatic impact on processing performance, and may be cheaper than developing and maintaining a more complex processing solution.

- We can run a Process Update on any dimensions that have changed their contents, and then run a Process Default on our cube to rebuild any invalidated aggregations.

- If existing members on dimensions never change we can run a Process Add to add any new members that appear. Although Process Add can be much more difficult to configure than Process Update, it can perform significantly better and in scenarios where we are only making Type 2 changes to a dimension then it is safe to use; the fact that it does not invalidate existing partition data or aggregations is also very important.

- If existing members do change but we don't mind waiting for these changes to appear in the Analysis Services dimension, then we can run regular Process Adds and then run a Process Update or even a Process Full on a less regular basis. This can, for example, be useful if we need to add new members to a dimension during the day with minimal impact to our users but can wait until our nightly processing window for our dimensions to be completely updated.

For very large dimensions consisting of several million members or a large number of attributes, splitting a Process Full up into separate Process Data and Process Index operations may allow us to make better use of available memory. Whether it does or not will depend on the structure of our dimension and our server's hardware; thorough testing is necessary to determine whether it is worth doing this. Similarly, as mentioned in Chapter 2, setting the `AttributeHierarchyOptimizedState` and `AttributeHierarchyOrdered` properties to `False` may also improve processing performance at the expense of, respectively, query performance and member ordering.

Last of all, remember that many structural changes to a dimension (for example adding a new hierarchy) will mean that a Process Full is necessary. As a result such structural changes will need to be carefully planned for.

Partition processing

As with dimensions, partitions can be processed in several ways. Processing a large partition is a very slow, CPU intensive operation and as a result partition processing normally takes longer than dimension processing; we therefore have to think more carefully about how to process our partitions in the most efficient way. Luckily, partition processing is also a lot less complex than dimension processing in that processing a partition has no side effects on any other objects.

The following table lists the different options for processing a partition:

Type	Description
Full	The partition is completely rebuilt. All data inside the partitions is deleted and reloaded from the relational database; indexes and aggregations are rebuilt. It is equivalent to an Unprocess, followed by a Process Data, followed by a Process Index.
Add	Also known as incremental processing, this adds new data to the partition. After we've specified a table or SQL query containing new fact rows, Analysis Services creates a new partition, fully processes it, and then merges the new partition with the existing one.
	Over time the performance of a partition will degrade after multiple Process Adds. Once again it's a good idea to schedule an occasional Process Full if we are using Process Add regularly.

Type	Description
Data	Behaves the same as Process Full but does not process indexes and aggregations.
Index	Builds indexes and aggregations for the partition. This is normally used after a Process Data.
Default	Does whatever processing is necessary to bring the partition up to a fully processed state. If the partition itself is in an unprocessed state, then a Process Full is performed. If, on the other hand, the partition is processed but some indexes or aggregations inside of it are not processed, then only those indexes and aggregations will be processed.
Unprocess	Deletes all structures, data, indexes, and aggregations from the partition.

There are a different set of issues to consider when choosing a partition processing strategy compared to a dimension processing strategy. Dimension data changes naturally, and these changes are something we have to plan for. On the other hand, existing data in our fact tables does not usually change over time. New rows will appear in our fact tables and recently added rows may be updated, but unless older data is incorrect or we need to recalculate measure values based on new business requirements then this older data is normally static.

Let's take a look at some scenarios where the different partition processing options can be used:

- For new partitions, or where data in existing partitions needs to be completely reloaded, we have to do a Process Full. The important thing here is to set the slices for our partitions so that when we do need to do a Process Full we do the minimum amount of processing necessary. For example, if new data is loaded into our fact tables every month, then every month we can create a new Analysis Services partition to hold that new month's data and run a Process Full on just that new partition. Assuming that the data for previous months does not change, no other partitions need to be processed.

- Process Add is normally only used with Standard Edition of Analysis Services, where we are only allowed to have one partition per measure group and so strategies such as the one described in the previous bullet are not possible. With only one partition to store all of our data, a Process Full will involve reloading all of the data from our fact table whether it is new or not and could take a long time. Using Process Add to load only new rows is going to take much less time, even if we still need to schedule an occasional Process Full as noted above.

- If our partitions are very large, then processing data and building aggregations might require a great deal of memory. It might be better to perform a Process Data simultaneously for all the partitions that need to be processed and then, when this has finished and the memory has been released, we can run a Process Index on them. In this way we can separate the two processing steps and reduce memory pressure on the server while also having greater control over when load is placed on the relational database.

  It is very difficult to say whether this approach will benefit processing performance—thorough testing is necessary. If memory is not an issue and we have a powerful server, then processing both data and indexes at the same time might increase parallelism because when the CPUs are waiting on the I/O operations involved in a Process Data, they can be used to build aggregations and indexes instead.

- If dimensions have been updated using Process Update, then some aggregations on existing, processed partitions may no longer be valid and will need to be rebuilt. In this case running a Process Default on all these partitions will rebuild only the invalid aggregations. Therefore if we are using Process Update and loading data into newly-created partitions at the same time, then our workflow needs to be as follows:

  ° Run a Process Update on all dimensions that need it.

  ° Build any new partitions that are necessary and perform any other partition management tasks.

  ° Run a Process Default on all the partitions in the cube. This will have the same effect as running a Process Full on the new partitions, and rebuild any invalid aggregations on the existing partitions.

In order to be able to query a cube we also need to run a Process Structure on it, which usually takes just a few seconds. This can be run the first time a cube is deployed to production and will only be necessary afterwards if the cube's structure is changed. If we do this and do not process any partitions then the cube can be queried but will contain no data; we can then process partitions individually and as each partition finishes processing its data will appear in the cube. This behavior can be useful in a development environment if we want an exact copy of our production cube but don't want to load all of the data into it. In this case we can run a Process Structure on the cube and then a Process Full on just one or two partitions.

Processing an object will lead to the Storage Engine caches related to that object and the entire Formula Engine cache being cleared: if the data in the cube has changed then any data in the cache may no longer be valid. This is especially important if we have to perform any kind of processing during the day because query performance will suffer as a result, and the more often we process the less benefit we will get from caching.

Lazy Aggregations

Lazy Aggregations is a processing option for partitions. Normally when we run a Process Full on a partition it can be queried when both the Process Data and Process Index steps have completed. If we want the partition to be available sooner, we can set the `Processing Mode` property on the partition to **Lazy Aggregations**. This means that the partition becomes available as soon as the Process Data step has completed; the Process Index step will then be run in the background as and when resources are available. The price we pay for having the partition available earlier is that, while aggregations and indexes are not built, queries against the partition will perform worse.

Using the **Lazy Aggregations** option we lose control over when the aggregations and indexes for a specific partition will be built because it will depend upon several factors, most of which are out of our control. Also Lazy Aggregations interfere with our ability to synchronize a cube, as we will see later. As a result we do not recommend the use of this option.

Processing reference dimensions

As we saw in Chapters 1 and 4, materialized reference relationships result in a join being made between the fact table and the intermediate dimension table in the SQL generated for partition processing. This highlights the important point that materialized reference relationships are resolved during partition processing and not dimension processing.

Apart from the negative impact that materialized relationships have on partition processing performance, using them also carries a less obvious but more serious penalty: if the intermediate dimension in the relationship ever changes its structure, we have to run a Process Full on all of our partitions.

Consider the scenario we looked at in Chapter 4, where a Region dimension joins to a measure group through a Country attribute on a Customer dimension using a referenced relationship. If that relationship is materialized, then during partition processing the Customer dimension table will be joined to the fact table and the key of the Country that each Customer lives in will be stored in the partition. But what happens if we run a Process Update on the Customer dimension and Customers change the Country they live in? The materialized referenced relationship data on existing partitions will not be refreshed, so Region values for these partitions will be incorrect. Even worse, if we then create new partitions and run a Process Full on them these new partitions will contain the correct materialized relationship data, so Region values will be completely inconsistent. Only a Process Full on all partitions can ensure that queries using the Region dimension will return correct data.

This problem does not occur if the referenced relationship is not materialized. As a result, this is one more good reason not to use materialized referenced relationships.

Handling processing errors

In an ideal world Analysis Services processing would never fail. Certainly, as we argued in Chapter 1, we should always try to ensure that all data integrity issues are handled during the ETL for our relational data warehouse rather than in Analysis Services. However, in the real world there will always be some problems with the data in our data warehouse, and we need to configure Analysis Services processing to handle them.

What happens for each Analysis Services object when there is a processing error is controlled by its ErrorConfiguration property. The default setting is for processing to fail whenever an error occurs, but we can override this for different types of error and either ignore the error completely, ignore anything up a given number or errors and then fail processing, or log the error to a text file and continue processing. We also have two options that govern what happens when we ignore an error: we can either ignore the problematic fact table or dimension table row completely or assign the values from them to a special, automatically generated member called the Unknown Member on a hierarchy. The existence and visibility of unknown members is controlled by the UnknownMember property of a dimension: it can either be set to **None**, **Visible**, or **Hidden**.

We can also set these properties for each processing operation by clicking on the **Change Settings** button in the **Process** dialog, and then going to the **Dimension Key Errors** tab.

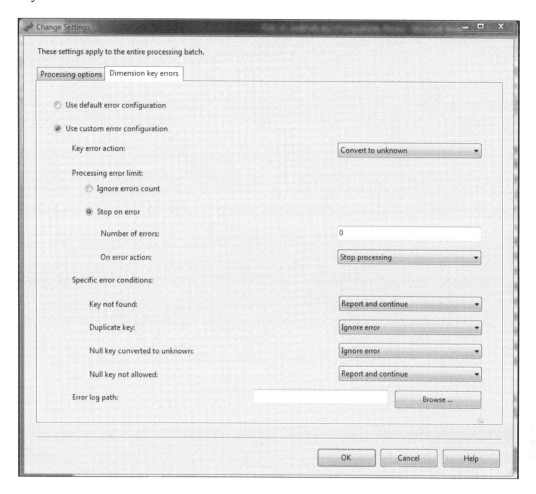

We recommend handling processing errors by setting the ErrorConfiguration property on objects rather than having to remember to set them every time we do processing. Discarding rows when they contain errors is probably a bad thing to do since it means our cube could potentially contain incorrect values; it is usually better to assign these values to a visible Unknown Member. This way even if we can't see these values assigned correctly for a particular hierarchy the totals seen at the All Member will still be correct and, when browsing the cube, we'll be able to see where exactly these errors are occurring. Remember, though, this use of Unknown Members is purely an insurance policy in case errors get past the checks we have implemented in our ETL.

We probably don't want processing to completely fail either if an error is encountered; it's better to let processing continue and then reprocess objects later once we have fixed the data problems. Therefore we should ignore the number of errors generated, use the **Report and Continue** option for each type of error, and then log these errors to a text file.

Managing processing with Integration Services

Just as we used Integration Services to manage our partitions, we can also use it to manage our dimension and partition processing very easily. Using Integration Services gives us the following benefits:

- It gives us complete control over the order in which objects are processed and the type of processing used. It's very easy to implement even very complex processing strategies using the Integration Services control flow.

- Using Integration Services' own logging features (which we should already be using in our ETL) we will be able to record exactly what gets processed, how long each step takes, and any errors that are raised.

- If processing fails, for whatever reason, Integration Services makes it very easy to do things such as send an email to the cube administrator to tell them that this has happened.

- As we have seen, in Integration Services we can use a script task to automatically manage our partitions using AMO. As a result it makes sense to manage partition processing in the same place.

There are four main methods we can use to manage processing within Integration Services:

- Using the Analysis Services Processing Task is our recommended method. It's very easy to configure and allows us to process multiple objects either sequentially or in parallel, in a single batch. However, there may be scenarios where we might not choose to use it. For example, the list of objects that we can set the task to process is static and cannot be changed, even with Integration Services expressions. In some cases we might only want to run a Process Update on a large dimension if we know its structure has changed; we could certainly build this kind of conditional logic into the control flow and have one Analysis Serviced Processing Task for each dimension, but there may well be easier ways of doing this such as writing AMO code.

- We can also execute XMLA processing commands directly using the Execute Analysis Services DDL Task. This gives us complete flexibility with our processing options, but XMLA commands are not easy for humans to read and therefore they are difficult to maintain. We can generate XMLA processing commands very easily by right-clicking on the object we want to process in the **Object Explorer** pane in SQL Management Studio, selecting **Process**, and then in the **Process** dialog clicking the **Script** button instead of the **OK** button.

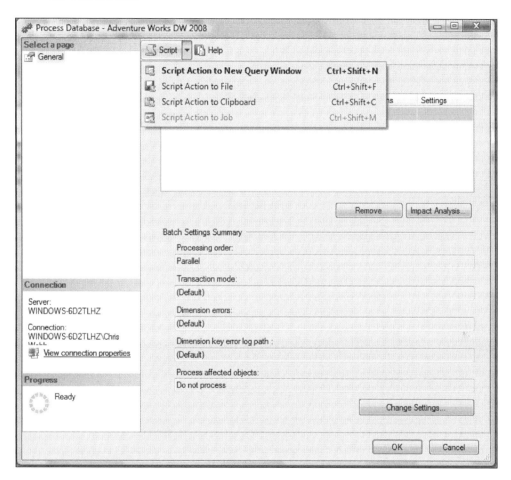

- We can write .NET code using AMO to process objects, just as we did to create and delete partitions. While this works usually gives us no particular advantages over the other methods, it will take slightly longer to develop and will be harder to maintain. It's a good option when we have very complex logic determining what needs processing, and it would be too difficult to implement this logic in the control flow.

- External applications, for example the ASCMD utility described below, that can manage processing can be invoked using the Execute Process Task.

The ASCMD utility is a command-line tool that can execute XMLA, MDX, or DMX commands against Analysis Services. A detailed list of its functionality can be found in its readme here: `http://tinyurl.com/ascmdreadme` and the Analysis Services 2008 version can be downloaded from here: `http://tinyurl.com/ascmddownload`. It's extremely useful in situations where we can't use Integration Services, but if we do have a choice then using Integration Services is always the easiest option.

A simple Integration Services package that performs processing might look something like this:

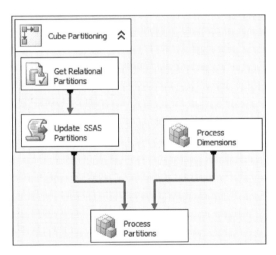

In this example we're running our partition management tasks simultaneously with our dimension processing, where we're running a Process Update on each dimension that may have changed. After both of these operations have completed, we then use another processing task to process, in parallel, all of the measure groups in our cube with a Process Default so that new partitions are fully processed and any existing partitions with invalid aggregations have their aggregations rebuilt.

Push-mode processing

So far, when we've processed dimensions or partitions we've been sending XMLA commands to Analysis Services to initiate this. Analysis Services then generates whatever SQL is necessary and runs it against a relational data source, and loads the data returned by these queries into the object that is being processed. This is known as **pull-mode** processing: Analysis Services is pulling data from a data source.

There is also another, much less often used, method for processing objects: push-mode processing. In **push-mode** processing we can use Integration Services to push data from a data flow into a partition or dimension, using a Partition Processing or a Dimension Processing destination. No SQL is generated by Analysis Services in this case—we are pushing data into Analysis Services ourselves.

Push-mode processing is useful when we need to load data into Analysis Services from data sources that are not officially supported and for which Analysis Services would not be able to generate valid SQL (such as text files, or databases like MySQL). It is also an alternative to running a Process Add on a partition, or a Process Add or a Process Update on a dimension, in situations where data needs to be loaded into Analysis Services; however, like Process Add and Process Update, regular use can lead to performance degradation and so running a Process Full occasionally is necessary.

Proactive caching

The proactive caching features in Analysis Services allow processing to be kicked off automatically in response to changes in the relational data. When they were first introduced in Analysis Services 2005 they were very heavily hyped but the truth is that they are almost never used in a production environment. This isn't because there are any major problems with the functionality, but because there are easier ways of handling the requirement for "real-time" data.

In an environment where Analysis Services cubes are built on top of a traditional data warehouse, when we know when data is loaded into the data warehouse, it's easier to schedule Analysis Services processing as part of the overall data warehouse ETL. That way we can kick off processing when we're sure that the fact and dimension tables have finished loading, and have finished successfully. Even if the cube needs to be updated regularly during the day, scheduling that processing at regular intervals using SQL Server Agent and Integration Services means that we can be sure when that processing will take place, that it does not take place too often and therefore impact query performance, and be able to log and handle any errors appropriately.

We only recommend the use of proactive caching on less formal Analysis Services implementations, for example when cubes are built on tables in an OLTP database. In these cases, where there is no ETL or data warehouse in place and where data volumes are relatively small, using proactive caching is often easier than having to develop and maintain an Integration Services package.

Analysis Services data directory maintenance

By default, all of the files used by Analysis Services to store MOLAP data are stored in the Analysis Services data directory. The location of this directory is set during installation, and can be changed by changing the value of the `DataDir` server property.

As with any other type of file handled by Windows, the files in the Analysis Services data directory are prone to fragmentation. During processing a lot of files are created, written, and deleted, and if the disk is very fragmented these files may be split across different portions of the disk, slowing down access to them.

A regular defragmentation of the drive on which the data directory exists will improve the overall speed of the disk subsystem, which will of course have benefits for Analysis Services query and processing performance. As a result we suggest regular disk defragmentation of the Analysis Services data directory's drive as part of the server's maintenance plan, making sure of course that it only takes place at a time when we are not processing or when users are not querying the cube.

Backup

It may be stating the obvious, but after processing has finished we should always back up our Analysis Services database. This can be done very easily from Integration Services using an Execute Analysis Services DDL task; once again, we can generate the XMLA command needed to back up a database by right-clicking on it in SQL Management Studio, selecting **Back Up**, and then pressing the **Script** button on the **Back Up Database** dialog.

Copying databases between servers

There are several scenarios where we may need to copy an Analysis Services database from one server with one on a different server. Here are a couple of examples:

- We have several frontend servers directly accessible by users in the DMZ area of the network, and one backend server inside the internal network. When the cube is processed on the internal server, it needs to be duplicated to the frontend servers so that it can be queried by our users.

- We have two powerful Analysis Services servers and several cubes. Half of the cubes are processed on one server and half are processed on the other. When both servers have finished processing, the databases are synchronized between the two servers, so they both have the same data and can share the query load.

Using Analysis Services 2008 we have three options to synchronize data between servers:

- **Use the Synchronize XMLA command**: This is the preferred method in most situations. When executed, the `Synchronize` command tells one Analysis Services instance to synchronize a database with a database on another instance. During the synchronization process Analysis Services checks for any differences between the version of the database on the destination database and the version on the source server. Updated objects are copied over the network from the source server to the destination server until the destination is identical to the source.

  The XMLA needed for a `Synchronize` command can be generated in SQL Management Studio by right-clicking on **Databases** node of an instance in the **Object Explorer** pane, running the Synchronize Database wizard and at the end choosing to generate script rather than running the synchronization immediately. This XMLA command can be run from an Execute Analysis Services DDL Task in Integration Services.

  The synchronization operation might be slow in situations where there is a lot of data in a cube or where there are a lot of differences between the source and the destination. However, the major advantage of using this approach is that users can continue to query the destination server while synchronization takes place, although when synchronization has completed there will be a (usually short) period where new users cannot connect and new queries cannot be run, while the old version of the database is replaced by the new version.

  Note that synchronization cannot be used at the same time as lazy aggregation building is taking place because there is a risk of database corruption.

- **Use backup/restore**: Even if this approach seems crude when compared with the more elegant Synchronize XMLA command, it has some advantages. For a start, we're going to be backing up our database anyway after it has been processed so using the backup to copy the database to another server will require little extra development. Secondly, we can take the same backup file and copy it to multiple destination servers, where they can be restored in parallel.

  A problem with this approach is that if we try to restore over our existing database on the destination server then we cannot query that database while the restore is taking place. One way of working around this would be to restore to a different database to the one that users are currently querying, and then to redirect all new queries to this second database after the restore has completed. This would be feasible if the only client tool used was Reporting Services, where connection strings can be parameterized, but not if a client tool like Excel was used. Another issue is that we have to copy the entire database over the network even if there is only a small amount of new data, and if the backup file is very large then this might take a relatively long time and require extra disk space.

- **Use Attach/Detach**: This method simply involves detaching the database from the source server, copying the database files over to the destination server, detaching the old version of the database on the destination server and then reattaching the new version of the database. Since attaching and detaching a database is a very fast operation this method involves the minimum of downtime; it also has the advantage that if a database is attached to one instance with its `ReadModeMode` property set to **ReadOnly**, then the same database files can be attached to multiple other instances in the same way.

  The main problem with this approach is that when we detach a database it cannot of course be queried at all, and any open connections to it are closed. This may lead to errors in some client tools and, at best, all users will have to reconnect to the server once the attach operation has completed.

Our recommendation is to use the `Synchronize` command if it runs fast enough and doesn't result in queries being blocked for too long. If we can't use `Synchronize` because it takes too long, or we don't mind that connections will be dropped, then attach/detach is the best option.

Summary

In this chapter we have discussed several topics including:

- How to deploy changes to a database already in production, using Visual Studio configurations or the Deployment Wizard.

- Automating partition management using Integration Services and AMO code to create, merge and delete partitions.

- Processing strategies. Although we always want to minimize the amount of time spent processing, there is no one processing strategy that is appropriate for all projects. In most cases a Process Update will handle any updates to dimensions; this can then be followed by a Process Default on our partitions, which will rebuild any aggregations that have been invalidated by dimension processing on existing partitions, and fully process any newly created partitions.

- How processing can be managed using Integration Services. The Process Analysis Services Task is the easiest way of doing this, but other Control Flow tasks such as the Execute Analysis Services DDL Task can also be used. It's also possible to push data directly into partitions and dimensions in the Integration Services Data Flow.

- Methods for copying databases between different instances of Analysis Services. The `Synchronize` command is the easiest way of doing this, but attaching and detaching databases is another option.

11
Monitoring Cube Performance and Usage

We need to be able to monitor activity on Analysis Services if we're going to be able to detect possible performance issues, to provide good service levels and to optimize individual queries or processing operations. In order to learn how to do this, first of all we need to know how Analysis Services interacts with the operating system. Resources consumed by Analysis Services are controlled by the operating system and we need to understand these relationships. After an introduction to the tools and performance counters provided by the operating system, we will look at the Analysis Services Memory Manager and how it can be configured. In the last part of this chapter we will examine how to monitor specific operations in Analysis Services like processing and querying.

Analysis Services and the operating system

The first concept we have to understand when learning about monitoring is that Analysis Services is a process running as a service on a Microsoft Windows operating system. Running as a service, it usually starts when the operating system starts and is running even when no users are connected. The process name is `msmdsrv.exe` and knowing this name is very important because it allows us to recognize the Analysis Services process in lists of all processes running on a server, for example when we're using the **Task Manager** as in the following screenshot. Notice that there are in fact two Analysis Services processes running here—later in this chapter we will see how to recognize which instance is linked to which process.

However, let's first concentrate on the following screenshot:

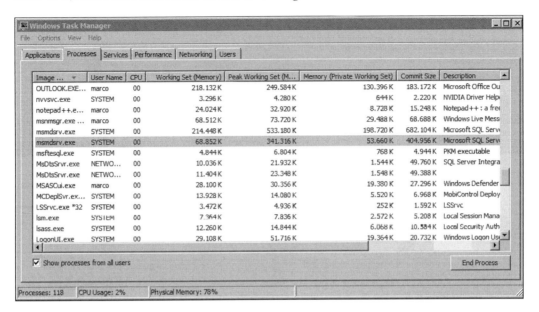

As Analysis Services is a Windows process, the first thing we can analyze is the interaction between that process and the hosting operating system. It's the operating system that provides a running process the resources that it needs, and that are shared with other processes: CPU, memory, and I/O.

Resources shared by the operating system

It is important to understand the interaction between Analysis Services and the resources provided by the operating system, because at the end of the day almost every bottleneck causes by an abnormal consumption of resources by a process.

We will examine the behavior of Analysis Services using several tools. It is important to point out that we should run our tests when there is no other activity on our server, so we can reduce the amount of noise in our measurements. The only exception is when we're trying to reproduce real-world conditions, such as processing a partition when we have both SQL Server and Analysis Services running on the same server.

CPU

Analysis Services consumes CPU during two operations: processing and querying. Many of the operations performed by Analysis Services can scale on multiple cores. We won't go into any detail here about the extent to which each single operation can scale on multiple cores, simply because this might be subject to change in future releases or service packs. However, Analysis Services can scale up because it runs multiple operations in parallel (for example, in Enterprise Edition multiple objects can be processed in parallel), but also because a single operation (for example, processing a single partition) can be executed across several threads.

During partition processing, CPU is used mainly to build aggregations. If a partition doesn't have any aggregations designed, then CPU usage will be minimal. However, as we will explain in more detail later on, CPU consumption will only be high during partition processing if there is enough RAM available for Analysis Services, and memory paging is kept to a minimum. If we don't have enough physical memory for Analysis Services, we will see long processing times even if there is little CPU usage. In general, having high CPU usage during processing is a good thing because it generally means that there are no other bottlenecks in memory or I/O operations. If we want to reduce processing times when we already have high CPU usage, we need to either reduce the number of aggregations in the cube design or add more CPU cores on the server running Analysis Services.

During querying, CPU is used by Analysis Services to perform calculations on the data that has been requested by a query. Most of these calculations scale on a multi-core server, but sometimes (and this happens more often than during processing) it might not be possible to parallelize an operation across several threads. In such cases a single query cannot take advantage of a multi-core server. For example, the Formula Engine is single-threaded whereas the Storage Engine is multi-threaded. If the query has complex MDX calculations, the Formula Engine can only use a single CPU. This scenario can be recognized by observing the CPU usage of the msmdsrv.exe process while a single MDX query is executing. If there is a bottleneck in the Formula Engine, the process does not consume more than the equivalent of one core. In other words, on an 8 core server we will see a constant consumption of 1/8th of our available CPU, that's to say 12 to 13%.

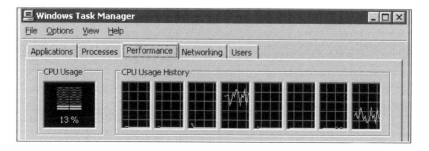

In such cases, there are two ways we can try to optimize query response time. On one hand we can try to change our cube design or our MDX query to enable greater parallelism during query execution; on the other, we can try to reduce the time needed for a sequential operation, for example, by reducing the size of an intermediate fact table used in a many-to-many dimension relationship, or by rewriting MDX to use bulk mode instead of cell-by-cell mode, as discussed in Chapter 8.

In general, Analysis Services can consume a lot of CPU resources during processing and, depending on the conditions, also while running queries. We need to bear this in mind when specifying servers for Analysis Services to run on, or when deciding if Analysis Services should be installed on the same server as other CPU-intensive applications.

Memory

Analysis Services uses memory for a lot of different purposes. It is not a goal of this book to explain all the details of Analysis Services' memory settings or how to tune them; in any case, for most scenarios the default settings are good enough. However, it is important to understand what happens when Analysis Services requests memory from the operating system, because that memory is not always physical RAM and this could have important consequences like increased paging of memory to disk.

Analysis Services, like any other process in Windows, requires memory from the operating system, which in turn provides blocks of virtual memory. Each process has a separate address space that is called a **virtual address space**. Each allocation made by a Windows process inside the virtual address space gets a part of the operating system virtual memory, and that might correspond to either physical RAM *or* disk paging file. The decision as to whether a page of memory (which corresponds to 4K) is in physical RAM or is moved to the paging disk file is up to the operating system. This concept is very important, especially when we have several other services running on the same server, like Reporting Services, Integration Services, and the relational engine of SQL Server itself.

The memory allocated by Analysis Services might be paged to disk due to other process activities and this is partially controlled by some memory settings. An explanation of these settings is available in books online at `http://tinyurl.com/ssas2008memory` and a guide to their optimization can be found in the *Analysis Services Performance Guide* white paper at `http://tinyurl.com/ssas2008perfguide`. We will also cover a few of these settings later, talking about memory differences between 32 bit and 64 bit systems.

In order to understand how much virtual and physical memory a process is using, it is important that we know how to read the numbers provided by Task Manager.

The total amount of virtual memory requested by a process is displayed in a column called **VM Size** in the Task Manager up to Windows XP/Windows Server 2003. Starting from Vista/Windows Server 2008, it has been renamed **Commit Size**.

The total amount of physical RAM used by a process is displayed in a column called **Mem Usage** in Task Manager up to Windows XP/Windows Server 2003. Starting from Vista/Windows Server 2008, it has been renamed **Working Set (Memory)**.

> A better column to watch in Vista/Windows Server 2008 if we want to monitor the physical RAM consumed by a process is **Memory (Private Working Set)**, which is a subset of the **Working Set (Memory)** counter that includes only the data that cannot be shared with other processes. However, these two numbers shouldn't be too different for Analysis Services.

The virtual memory manager in Windows is a complex system that aims to optimize the usage of physical memory, sharing data between processes whenever it is possible, but in general isolating each virtual address space from all the others in a secure manner. For these reasons it is not easy to interpret the counters we just mentioned and it could be useful to recap how virtual memory allocation works in Windows.

As we mentioned, data can be shared across different processes. For example if two different processes use the same DLL, the physical memory containing DLL code is shared between both processes using read-only pages, regardless of the virtual position of the code in each virtual address space. However, this feature is not particularly important for Analysis Services because most of the memory is consumed for data and it is private to the process. For this reason, for the rest of this section we will concentrate on private memory and not on shared memory.

When a process allocates private memory, as Analysis Services does when it requires space for its data, it is requested from virtual memory. When that memory is written the operating system ensures that the page is in physical RAM. When there is not enough RAM to hold all the virtual memory pages used by running processes, the operating system moves older pages from RAM to disk. These pages will be recalled from disk as soon as a process needs to read or write data there. This activity is called **memory paging** and we want it to happen as little as possible. One way to stop it happening would be to remove the paging file from the operating system. This is possible using the **No paging file** setting, but we *do not recommend* using this option on a server running SQL Server or Analysis Services.

There has been a lot of discussion over the years about what the "right" size for the Windows paging file is, and there have been a number of suggestions made that are simply wrong. There are, for example, several formulas around based on the amount of physical RAM, and the most common uses what is reported in the **Virtual Memory** dialog box, which is 1.5 times the physical RAM in the system. However, most of these suggestions are baseless and inherited from an era where the RAM of a server were measured in hundred of Megabytes.

Today we might have tens of Gigabytes of RAM and paging 1.5 times this amount of data seems crazy, even just for the time required to read and write that much data (we are talking about minutes, not seconds, here). There are only two conditions that justify a big paging file size: if we need a full memory dump in the event of a system crash/blue screen then the size of the paging file must be at least the amount of physical RAM; and, if a kernel memory dump is required, then a variable amount of paging file is required, up to the amount of physical RAM but generally lower than that.

Where only a small memory dump is required as a result of a blue screen, the size of the paging file only has an impact on the performance of the dump. Having a few Gigabytes should be enough even on servers with tens of Gigabytes of RAM. If you want to work out what a good paging file size would be for your server, we suggest reading `http://tinyurl.com/PagingSize` and `http://support.microsoft.com/kb/889654`, and also `http://tinyurl.com/VirtualMemory`, which is a more complete description of virtual memory, written by Mark Russinovich.

Thus, we have a paging file and we need to optimize its use; ideally Analysis Services should not use it at all. If Analysis Services were the only process running on the system, it would be sufficient to set its memory limits to a value that doesn't exceed the amount of physical RAM of the system. In fact, the default settings of Analysis Services are below this limit, but they don't take into account that other memory-hungry processes may run concurrently on the same machine. For example, it's quite common to have both SQL Server and Analysis Services running on the same machine. Think what would happen when we processed a cube, which of course would mean that Analysis Services would need to query the fact table in SQL Server: both services require memory and paging to disk could be unavoidable. There is a difference between SQL Server and Analysis Services in terms of memory management, in that SQL Server can adapt the amount of virtual memory it requests from the operating system to the amount of physical RAM available to it. Analysis Services is not as sophisticated as SQL Server and does not dynamically reduce or increase the size of its requests for memory to the operating system based on current available physical memory.

Another reason for paging physical memory to disk is the System File Cache. By default, Windows uses the available unused physical memory as System File Cache. This would be not an issue if the concept of "unused" was really of memory not used by anyone. If applications or file sharing result in a lot of sustained cached read I/O, the operating system gives physical RAM to the file cache and paginates the memory of idle processes if necessary. In other words, if we were working on a 16 GB RAM server and we copied a 20 GB file containing a backup file to an external disk, we could paginate all the memory used by Analysis Services if it was not in use during the copy. To avoid this kind of situation we could reduce the size of the paging file (if virtual memory cannot be paginated to disk, it has to be kept in physical RAM) or use the SetCache utility that is discussed here: http://tinyurl.com/SetCache.

The memory requested by a process is always requested as virtual memory. In situations where the virtual memory allocated by Analysis Services is much larger than the available physical RAM, some Analysis Services data will be paged to disk. As we said, this could happen during cube processing. We should avoid these situations by configuring Analysis Services' memory settings (more on which we discuss later) so that they limit the amount of memory that can be allocated by it. However, when no other processes are asking for memory, we might find that having limited Analysis Services' memory usage in this way we are preventing it from using extra memory when it needs it, even when that memory is not used by anything else.

Later in this chapter we will explore the available memory options for Analysis Services and see how to monitor its memory usage.

I/O operations

Analysis Services generates I/O operations both directly and indirectly. A direct I/O request from Analysis Services is made when it needs to read data from or write data to disk; and when it sends query results back to the client, which involves an inter-process communication, typically made through network I/O operations. The indirect I/O requests generated by Analysis Services come from paging disk operations, and it is very important to be aware that they can happen, because they cannot be seen using the performance counters we might typically monitor for Analysis Services. Paging operations are not visible to the Analysis Services process and can be seen only by using the appropriate operating system performance counters, like **Memory: Pages / sec**.

As we said, there are two different types of directly generated I/O operation that we need to worry about when monitoring Analysis Services. First, there are disk-related operations, which are made when Analysis Services processes cubes and dimensions (mainly to write data to disk) and when Analysis Services reads cube data to answer queries. Monitoring reads to disk is important if we are to spot situations where more RAM or more aggregations are needed to improve performance. Another I/O operation generated by Analysis Services is the transfer of query results to the client. Usually this is not a slow operation, but if a query returns a very large number of cells in a cellset (for example, a list of one million of customers with several measure values for each one) the query response time might be affected by the time needed to transfer the cellset from the server to the client. Take a look at network traffic to understand if this is a possible issue.

Most of the I/O operation bottlenecks for Analysis Services operations are related to disk access. It is out of scope of this book to talk about hardware configurations. However, it is important to highlight that for Analysis Services a set of local disks (especially if in RAID 0 or 10) could be much faster than accessing volumes on a SAN. Getting the same bandwidth for a SAN as we can get with local disks could be very expensive, and bandwidth is very important when Analysis Services needs to do something like scan all the partitions in a measure group. An interesting Microsoft whitepaper about hardware optimization for a multi-terabyte data warehouse and cube is available at http://tinyurl.com/SsasHw.

Tools to monitor resource consumption

The first tools we're going to look at for monitoring resource consumption are Task Manager and Performance Monitor. These tools are available on any server we might use to host an Analysis Services instance and they can also be used to monitor any other process that might compete with Analysis Services for the use of system resources.

Windows Task Manager

The Windows Task Manager is a utility, included with any current Microsoft Windows operating system, which provides information about running applications and their system resource usage (for example CPU, memory, and network activity). Task Manager also allows us to kill a process and change its priority. However, we are only interested in the monitoring features of this tool. As we mentioned before, there have been some changes and improvements in Task Manager moving from the XP/2003 version to the Vista/2008 version. From here on, we will only focus on this latest release of the tool.

The **Services** tab displays a list of services along with the process ID (**PID**) of each service. In the following screenshot we can see that there are two instances of Analysis Services running on the same machine: one is named **MSOLAP$K8** – a named instance called K8—and has the **PID 2568**, the other is named **MSSQLServerOLAPServices**, is the default instance and has the **PID 2768**.

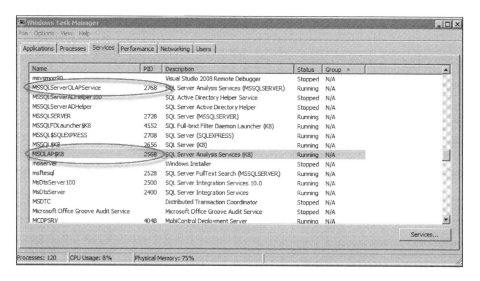

On the **Processes** tab we can distinguish between the two running **msmdsrv.exe** processes based on the PIDs that we have seen on the **Services** tab. The following screenshot also shows several other columns (chosen through the **View / Select Columns** menu) with information about CPU and Memory usage that we'll now explain.

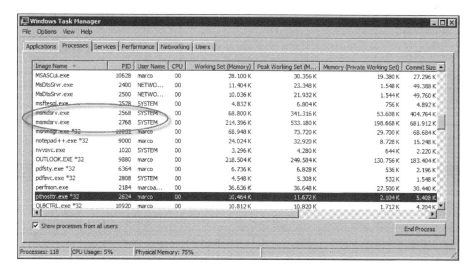

The **CPU** column shows what percentage each process uses of the total processing power available on the system. On a dual core machine, a single thread can consume up to 50%; but the same thread can only consume up to 25% on a quad-core system. Analysis Services scales well on multiple cores in most scenarios, so we should expect to see very high CPU values for Analysis Services during cube processing and query resolution.

Working Set (Memory) and **Commit Size** are the most important counters that we can analyze and correspond to the physical RAM and virtual memory used by the process. As we said before, **Memory (Private Working Set)** is a value that, for Analysis Services, should be slightly lower than **Working Set (Memory)**. Therefore, for our purposes, they can be used almost at the same way. What is interesting is the comparison between virtual memory usage and physical RAM usage. When virtual memory usage is higher than physical RAM usage, probably part of the Analysis Services cache has been paged to disk. This condition is not an issue if Analysis Services does not have a high workload, but if it happens when users are running queries and does not improve over time (the physical RAM usage should grow to almost match the virtual memory usage), then we should investigate the cause of the issue. The server might have insufficient physical RAM or there could be other processes that are consuming physical RAM at the same time. In both cases, adding RAM would be the best way to solve the problem. We can also mitigate the issue by moving other processes to different servers, if we can afford to do so, or by reducing the amount of memory available to Analysis Services (which we'll see how to do later in this chapter). **Page Faults Delta** is another counter that we can monitor to check which process is responsible for any paging activity.

Performance counters

The Windows operating system gathers data about system performance and exposes it through performance counters, which can be displayed through a **Microsoft Management Console (MMC)** snap-in called Performance Monitor. In reality, performance counters are available through a set of APIs and there are third-party tools that can access them too. However, in this book our goal is to highlight what the most important performance counters to monitor are on a server running Analysis Services. We will use Performance Monitor, but the concepts we are going to explain are valid regardless of the tool used to display them. Moreover, in this section we will cover only operating system counters, but there are also other counters specific to Analysis Services instances that we will look at later on in this chapter.

Performance Monitor can be found by clicking the **Administrative Tools |
Performance** shortcut in Windows XP/2003, and by clicking the **Administrative
Tools | Reliability and Performance Monitor** shortcut in Windows Vista/2008.
There are differences in the user interface of these two tools but they are not
significant for the purposes of this chapter. Performance Monitor can display
performance counter data captured in real-time, or it can be used to display a trace
session of performance counter data recorded using the Data Collector Sets feature of
Reliability and Performance Monitor in Windows Vista/2008 (a similar feature was
named **Performance Logs** and **Alerts** in the Performance management console in
Windows XP/2003). Using this trace data is very useful for monitoring a production
server to detect bottlenecks and measure average workload. We suggest reading the
documentation available at `http://tinyurl.com/CollectorSet` to understand
how to make good use of Data Collector Sets.

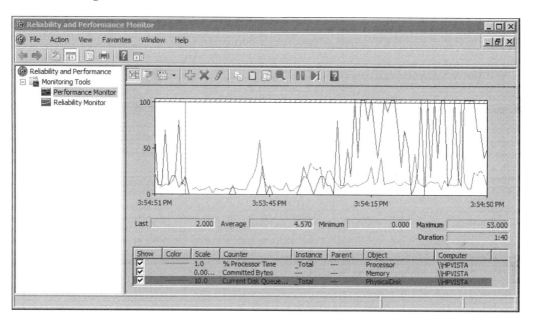

The memory counters are divided in two groups. A first set of counters, included
in the **Memory** category, provides information about the overall consumption of
memory regardless of the consumer (it could be a process, a driver, or the operating
system itself).

- **Pages/sec** is the number of pages read from and written to disk to resolve
  hard page faults. An access to a page of virtual memory that has been paged
  to disk generates this type of event; the cause is insufficient physical RAM to
  satisfy all the memory requests.

- **Committed Bytes** is the amount of virtual memory requested by all running processes. If this value is higher than the amount of available physical RAM, data has been paged to disk. However, if the Pages/sec rate is low or null, data paged to disk is not used often and as long as it does not need to be accessed, there will be no performance problems caused by this situation.

- **% Committed Bytes in Use** is the ratio of Committed Bytes to **Commit Limit**, which is the maximum amount of virtual memory that can be allocated (a value slightly below the sum of physical RAM and paging file).

A second group is made up of performance counters that are available for any running process. This group is included in the **Process** category and includes a few counters that we have already seen in Task Manager, as well as other counters that are useful for analyzing the state of an Analysis Services instance.

- **Virtual Bytes** is generally not so useful, because it represents the amount of virtual memory used for both private allocations and file mapping (including executable files).

- **Page File Bytes** and **Private Bytes** are usually very similar for Analysis Services, and correspond to the **Commit Size** counter we have seen in Task Manager.

- **Page File Bytes Peak** is very important because it reports the maximum value reached by Page File Bytes since the start of process execution, regardless of when we started monitoring. If this value is higher than Page File Bytes, there has been a reduction in the amount of memory requested by Analysis Services, but since this peak has been reached before this usually implies that it could be reached again in the future.

- **Working Set** corresponds to the **Working Set (Memory)** value in Task Manager

- **Working Set–Private** corresponds to the **Memory (Private Working Set)** value in Task Manager

- **Working Set Peak** is the maximum value reached by Working Set since the start of process execution, regardless of when we started monitoring. This value can be higher than the actual Working Set counter because, even if a process has not released memory previously allocated, part of that memory may have been paged as a result of memory activity by other processes. If this happens with Analysis Services, we could investigate what other processes are requesting memory concurrently on the same server.

The Disk I/O counters at the operating system level are divided up into two categories: **LogicalDisk** and **PhysicalDisk**. The difference between these counters is significant when there are multiple partitions on a physical disk or when we use operating system support to create RAID volumes. When the RAID service is provided by the disk controller, the physical disk and logical disk should be the same unless we have several partitions on a disk.

Logical and Physical Disk Performance counters can be enabled or disabled by using the **DiskPerf** command line utility available from the operating system. We can check the state of these counters by simply running this utility without parameters from the command line.

Here are the important counters available in these categories:

- **Current Disk Queue Length** represents the current number of queued requests to the disk. If this number is constantly above the number of spindles plus 2, the disk subsystem could be improved by adding spindles (to a RAID 0/10 configuration) or by using faster disks. If this number is below that limit, even if there is a continuous workload on the disk, it will not be the primarily cause of any performance issues.

- **%Disk Time** is a counter which should represent the percentage of time spent accessing disk, but the calculation used could provide a value higher than 100%.

- **Disk Read Bytes/sec** is important to determine if the speed of the disk subsystem corresponds to its theoretical limits. There could be issues that make this value lower: disk fragmentation, RAID overhead (for example during a RAID rebuild), under-dimensioned LUN channels, and so on. If this number is near to the physical limits of the disk, we can improve performance by reducing data, distributing data to different disks, or by using faster disks.

- **Disk Write Bytes/sec** is also important to determine if the speed of the disk subsystem corresponds to its theoretical limits. Write performance is extremely important for Analysis Services processing operations. Other than the issues we already described for the Disk Read Bytes/sec counter, a common source of issues during writing is the use of a RAID 5 volume. Writing on RAID 5 volumes is slower than normal volumes, and write performance is inversely proportional to the number of spindles in a RAID 5 configuration.

Know your hardware configuration!

Too many times we have seen performance issues caused by a lack of knowledge about hardware configuration. For example, RAID 5 disks are very common but they can be a performance nightmare for ETL and cube processing. The data we collect from performance counters only makes sense if we can compare it to the known physical limits of our hardware. Therefore, we need to know how to interpret terms as LUN, RAID and spindles; we also need to know exactly what hardware we're using in our own environment.

For disk-related terminology, the following glossary is a good place to start: http://tinyurl.com/DiskGlossaryTerms. A description of all possible RAID levels is available at http://en.wikipedia.org/wiki/Standard_RAID_levels and http://en.wikipedia.org/wiki/Nested_RAID_levels.

If we wanted to see data on I/O operations broken down by process, we can use some of the counters available in the **Process** category.

- **IO Data Bytes/sec** is the amount of data transferred in I/O operations. For Analysis Services this includes reads and writes to files and communication between client tools and Analysis Services. Monitoring it can help us understand if a lack of CPU activity while queries are running on Analysis Services is the result of I/O operations or not.

- **IO Write Bytes/sec** is the amount of data transferred in write I/O operations

- **IO Read Bytes/sec** is the amount of data transferred in read I/O operations

Finally, we have the **Processor** category of counters, which provides data on the usage of each processor as well as aggregated values for all processors on the server. When monitoring Analysis Services the only significant counter is % **Processor Time**, which allows us to compare the CPU usage of Analysis Services to the total CPU usage of all processes on the server. If, for example, Analysis Services is consuming 50% of CPU and overall CPU usage is at 100%, then Analysis Services is sharing the CPU with other processes. In this kind of situation, to free up resources for Analysis Services we either need to move other processes to a different server, or we can add more processing power to the server. To monitor the CPU usage of Analysis Services we can use the % **Processor Time** counter from the **Process** category, and select the msmdsrv process.

Resource Monitor

With Windows Vista and Windows Server 2008 a new tool has been introduced to allow us to monitor the core performance counters easily: **Resource Monitor**, which can be found by opening the **Reliability and Performance Monitor** shortcut in **Administrative Tools**, or by clicking the **Resource Monitor** button in the **Performance** tab of **Task Manager**. The following screenshot shows **Resource Monitor**:

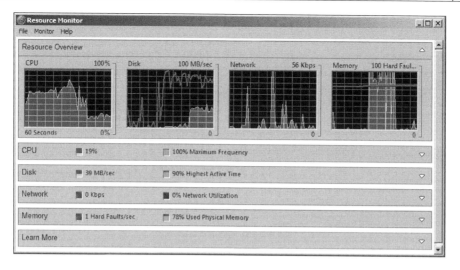

As well as giving us a concise view of the most important performance counters on a server, for each type of resource (**Memory**, **CPU**, and **I/O**, which is divided into **Disk** and **Network**) we can drill down into the details of each process's resource consumption, as shown in the following screenshot:

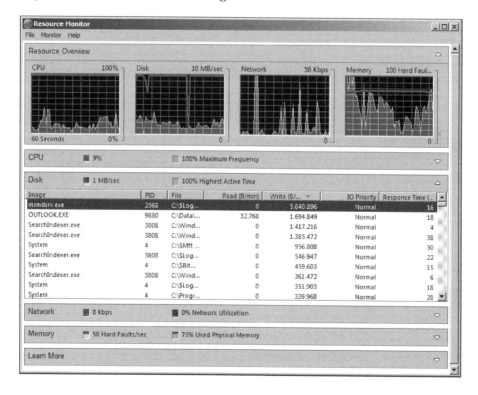

In the case of the **Disk** section, the details show one line for each open file. The **Network** section shows each open connection; **Memory** has a line for each process and **CPU** has a line for each process or service running on the system (if a single process hosts several services, their consumption is split across several lines – however, Analysis Services is hosted in a dedicated process and so this is not relevant for us).

The only limitation of **Resource Monitor** is that we cannot choose the columns we want to display, like we can do with Windows Task Manager. However, the columns that are shown are well chosen and should cover most of our immediate needs when we have to monitor a server running Analysis Services.

Analysis Services memory management

Analysis Services has its own Memory Manager, which provides allocation services for all of its components, distributing the memory that it allocates from the operating system. It is important to understand the implications of this for virtual and physical memory, because in extreme conditions Analysis Services might continue to allocate virtual memory even if there is no more physical RAM available, thus increasing disk paging, and possibly carrying on until it reaches the limit of allocatable virtual memory (for example when paging disk cannot increase over a certain quota). Even if we don't get a memory allocation error, if allocation requests go out of control we'll end up with a very slow system because it will always be busy paging memory to disk.

Memory differences between 32 bit and 64 bit

Having talked about memory, it is important to make a distinction between the 32 bit and 64 bit versions of Analysis Services. Nowadays, any serious Analysis Services deployment should use the 64 bit version. However, we might still encounter legacy servers, or simply small deployments running on virtual machines that use a 32 bit operating system. For all these reasons, it makes sense to discuss the differences between the 32 bit and 64 bit versions of Analysis Services regarding memory management.

Regardless of the physical RAM installed on a system, if Analysis Services is running on a 32 bit operating system it can only address a maximum of 2 GB or 3 GB of virtual memory (it depends on whether we set the /3GB switch in the boot.ini file – see http://support.microsoft.com/kb/833721 for further details). This limit can be an issue for scalability and performance. First of all, even if there was more physical memory available, a process cannot use more virtual memory than is available in its virtual address space. Unlike SQL Server, the Analysis Services memory manager cannot use services like AWE to access more memory. So as we can see, it is important that the memory manager doesn't try to allocate more virtual memory than can be addressed because this will cause errors in Analysis Services.

With the 64 bit version of Analysis Services, there are no practical limits for virtual memory allocation. However, this doesn't prevent memory allocation errors, because we can still reach the limit of virtual memory that can be allocated, which is the sum of the total physical memory and paging file. This condition is much more frequent on a 64 bit server than on a 32 bit one, but if we understand how this can happen we can also apply the right countermeasures.

Controlling the Analysis Services Memory Manager

The default settings of the Analysis Services Memory Manager work well in most cases. However, there might be scenarios where more tuning is required to optimize performance or simply to prevent low memory conditions.

The main server properties that control the Analysis Services Memory Manager are shown in the following screenshot :

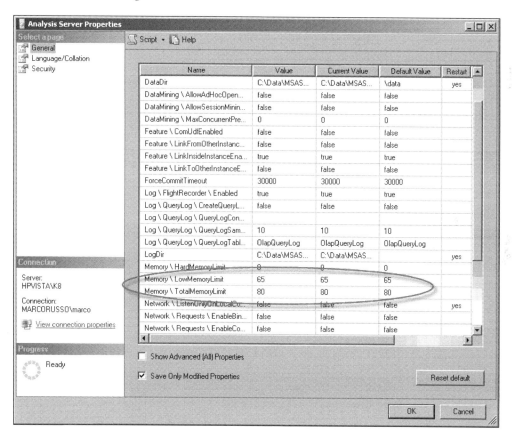

All Analysis Services server property values are held in a configuration file called **msmdsrv.ini**. Whenever we edit server property values in SQL Server Management Studio the changes are written back to this file. Some Analysis Services server properties can only be seen by clicking the **Show Advanced (All) Properties** checkbox, but even then there are still some properties in **msmdsrv.ini** which aren't visible at all in SQL Server Management Studio. The only way to access these properties is to edit the **msmdsrv.ini** file manually. However, all the settings we discuss in this book are visible in SQL Server Management Studio.

In the **Memory** category there are two important properties: **LowMemoryLimit** and **TotalMemoryLimit**. For these properties, values greater than 100 are absolute values (scientific notation is supported in msmdsrv.ini) in bytes. Values of less than 100 are interpreted as a percentage, where the reference value of 100% is calculated as the minimum of the physical memory and the virtual memory available for a process. So, for example a value of 100 would be interpreted as follows: on a 32 bit server with 8 GB of RAM, there is still a 2 GB limit on addressable memory (or 3GB if we have /3GB option enabled) so it would be interpreted as 2 GB; on a 64 bit server with 8 GB of RAM it would be interpreted as 8 GB; on a 32 bit server with only 1 GB RAM it would be interpreted as 1 GB. Here's what each of these properties actually represents:

- **LowMemoryLimit** defines the point at which the server is low on memory. The default setting for a single instance installation is 65 (65%), and that is appropriate in most cases, but if we had other processes on the same machine we might want to use a lower value. If we want to know the actual value that a percentage setting represents, we can look at the **MSAS Memory / Memory Limit Low KB** performance counter.

- **TotalMemoryLimit** is the maximum percentage of virtual memory that Analysis Services will use. The default is 80 (80%) and again this is appropriate in most cases. If we want to know the actual value that a percentage setting represents is, we can look at the **MSAS Memory / Memory Limit High KB** performance counter.

The Analysis Services Memory Manager will carry on requesting memory from the operating system until memory usage reaches the value specified in TotalMemoryLimit. At the same time, though, it also tries to reduce memory usage when it reaches the LowMemoryLimit: when memory usage is between LowMemoryLimit and TotalMemoryLimit, Analysis Services tries to reduce memory requests and to free up memory previously allocated.

However, it takes time to free up memory and there are also some types of internal allocations that cannot be freed up. For these reasons, it is not always possible to control the memory allocated by Analysis Services and increasing the gap between `LowMemoryLimit` and `TotalMemoryLimit` gives Analysis Services more leeway to react to changes in memory usage. Making the gap between these two properties' values too small is not a good idea, and the default values in Analysis Services 2008 generally provide a good balance (Analysis Services 2005 had a `LowMemoryLimit` of 75%, which proved to be too high in some cases).

Finally, remember that the properties we have looked at here only control the Analysis Services Memory Manager, and not any other virtual memory allocations made by components related to Analysis Services: for example, an Analysis Services stored procedure could allocate its own memory directly from the operating system, outside of the control of the Memory Manager.

Other Memory Manager Settings

The Memory Manager can be fine-tuned using other server properties like `MidMemoryPrice` and `HighMemoryPrice`. More details on these properties, and the inner workings of the Memory Manager, can be found in Chapter 27 of *Microsoft SQL Server 2008 Analysis Services Unleashed*, by Gorbach, Berger and Melomed.

The most important thing to remember is that Analysis Services requests virtual memory from the operating system and cannot control whether it is using physical RAM or not. This is intentional. Analysis Services might have a pattern of use very different from SQL Server (which has a completely different model to handle memory allocation) and paging memory to disk could be a good compromise during periods of low usage, especially if other services like SQL Server are running on the same server. However, if paging activity becomes an issue, we can try to reduce the number memory requests made by Analysis Services to the operating system. First, we can set the `LowMemoryLimit` property to a lower value, making the Memory Manager more aggressive in freeing up memory. If this is not enough, we set the `TotalMemoryLimit` property to a lower value too. Changing these properties doesn't require restarting the service.

Out of memory conditions in Analysis Services

So far, we have explained how to control the Analysis Services Memory Manager at a high level, but we also said that in most cases it is better to not change the default settings except in certain circumstances. Another reason why we might want to change these settings is when we find Analysis Services has run out of memory. This can happen when the operating system cannot provide the memory requested by Analysis Services, as in the following scenarios:

- Processes other than Analysis Services are consuming virtual memory. Regardless of the actual use of memory made by Analysis Services, if other processes consume virtual memory, new allocations might be denied to Analysis Services when it requests them.

- Analysis Services consumes too much memory, using up all the virtual memory available. This might happen under heavy load and we cannot completely control this by changing the memory settings of Analysis Services.

If we experience out of memory conditions, increasing the size of the paging file is a workaround that will at least prevent Analysis Services from crashing, even if it will not help performance. If the problem is caused by too many concurrent processes, another solution could be limiting the memory usage of these other processes (for example, SQL Server does have settings to limit its memory allocation). However, if the cause of the out of memory condition is a program or a service other than Analysis Services with memory leaks, a better idea would be to investigate on the cause of the excessive memory allocations, replacing the leaking application version with a fixed version or at least isolating it on another server.

As we said, it's not all that common to find an Analysis Services instance that consumes too much memory, because `TotalMemoryLimit` is based on available physical RAM and virtual memory is typically larger than physical RAM. Therefore, if there are no other processes that are consuming significant amounts of RAM and Analysis Services is the only "big service" running on a server, a reasonable amount of paging file should be enough to avoid such situation. However, in the real world we hardly ever find servers with only a single service running on them.

The `TotalMemoryLimit` is not an absolute limit for the Analysis Services Memory Manager: as we said, virtual memory allocated by other libraries (such as stored procedures) used by Analysis Services is not under the control of the Memory Manager. The Memory Manager itself might be unable to respect the `TotalMemoryLimit` setting. Under heavy load, memory requests cannot be avoided; sometimes memory requests come too fast to allow cleaning of older, rarely-used allocations in a timely manner.

In both cases, the result is that the memory allocated exceeds the `TotalMemoryLimit`. This is not an issue in itself, but it could break the balance of memory usage between all the processes running on the server. Therefore, we cannot assume that Analysis Services will always respect the limit we have defined, especially when the gap between `LowMemoryLimit` and `TotalMemoryLimit` is tight.

Here are some possible causes of the type of heavy load on Analysis Services that could result in abnormal virtual memory consumption:

- Parallel processing – if a server has many processors available, parallel processing of cubes and dimensions will require a larger amount of memory. To reduce memory usage we can try to decrease the amount of parallelism during processing.

- Too many queries and/or concurrent users – in this case we should check the usage of cache and aggregations (adding more aggregations and rewriting queries and calculations if necessary), and make sure that sufficient memory is available to Analysis Services to support the number of concurrent sessions.

- Security – security has implications on Analysis Services' ability to share cache between users, which means more work is likely to be taking place for each query. Using the Enable Visual Totals option with Dimension Security also has an impact on aggregation usage. In both cases we should check if we can make structural changes to the cube or to how we have implemented security that can improve aggregation and cache usage.

A final consideration is that an out of memory condition should be prevented by dealing with memory issues in advance. Memory issues cause paging, and paging causes bad performance. Therefore, monitoring operating system performance counters is the first step to ensuring that Analysis Services performs as well as possible.

Sharing SQL Server and Analysis Services on the same machine

Many Analysis Services installations share a server with SQL Server. This happens mainly because of licensing: the license required for Analysis Services is in fact a SQL Server license, so having both installed on the same machine requires only one server license to be purchased. However, this configuration has a hidden cost: since memory and sometimes CPU must be shared between these services, many of the scenarios we describe in this chapter are much more likely to occur.

It is not always true that it is a good idea to install Analysis Services on a different server to SQL Server, though. If we don't have a multi-terabyte data warehouse and the hardware necessary to support it, chances are that the bandwidth available between two servers could be a bottleneck compared with the faster transfer rate that we could have if Analysis Services and SQL Server were installed on the same server. This is particularly important during cube processing. There is also the question of cost. Often Analysis Services and SQL Server use neither CPU nor disks at the same time, and only require a modest amount of memory to cache data. Nowadays, 64-bit servers allow us to double the memory on a server at a fraction of the cost necessary to provide a new server with the same amount of RAM. In our experience, adding RAM to a server has a much better ROI than investing in a new server. In the end, having both services on the same server results in faster processing and cheaper hardware cost, although it can of course increase the chance of memory issues.

As we have seen in previous sections, we can try to control the memory usage of Analysis Services and SQL Server on servers that host both services. However, our suggestion is to make changes only if it is really necessary. SQL Server has a default setting that allocates memory if no other processes are claiming it. When Analysis Services is running and requests memory, SQL Server might release some of the memory it has previously allocated because it can detect when a system starts pagination. This is not true for Analysis Services. Memory allocated by Analysis Services up to the `LowMemoryLimit` threshold is never released. However, it could be paginated. Sometimes, it is better to page a section of the Analysis Services cache than drop it completely and have to recalculate the values it contains for future queries. Therefore, even if Analysis Services allocated memory and SQL Server pushed some of this memory out to a paging file, this is not a bad thing in itself. Only if paging activity (measured at the operating system level) is continuous, for example because both Analysis Services and SQL Server are used intensively at the same time, then we might want to try to limit the memory used by one or both services. Last of all, remember that any attempt to optimize memory settings should be tested properly: we should compare system performance before and after making any changes, measuring the impact on things like query response time and not only looking at how they affect performance counter values.

Monitoring processing performance

Processing Analysis Services dimensions and partitions is a resource-intensive operation. It should use all of the resources—CPU, memory, and disk I/O - available to Analysis Services. For this reason, it is important to be able to understand the impact of process operations on the operating system, as we have seen earlier on in this chapter.

When a database goes into production, Analysis Services processing usually takes place on a rigid schedule. We should monitor processing for two reasons:

- **Optimize processing times** – usually we want to reduce the time required to process partitions and dimensions
- **Check for any increase in the processing window over time** – the amount of time processing takes could increase over time, especially if we are running a Full Process on our database. We want to ensure that the amount of time processing takes won't exceed our assigned processing timeslot. To do that, we need to log information about the start and finish time of each processing operation, as well as details on the number of rows processed too, if possible.

Analysis Services doesn't provide a ready-to-use logging system for processing operations. However, there are a number of ways to gather this data and make it available for analysis.

Monitoring processing with trace data

Analysis Services generates trace data about its internal operations. This data allows us to analyze the start and end times of many operations, including processing operations. There are several tools that we can use to retrieve this data.

SQL Server Profiler

The first tool we'll look at is the SQL Server Profiler, which despite its name is a tool that can collect both SQL Server and Analysis Services trace data. After connecting to Analysis Services to initiate a new trace session, we have to choose the events we want to capture and where to save them (for example, either to a file or to SQL Server table).

The events that we need to monitor for processing operations are shown in the following screenshot:

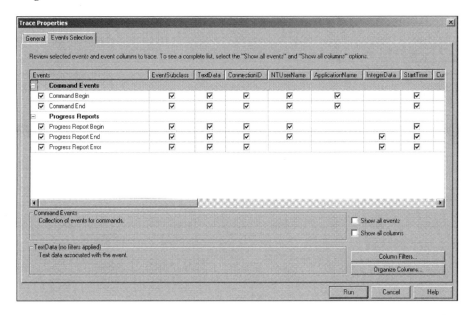

The events chosen in a profiling session are in fact classes of events. For each class there are many actual events that can be generated, and these are shown in the EventSubClass column in Profiler:

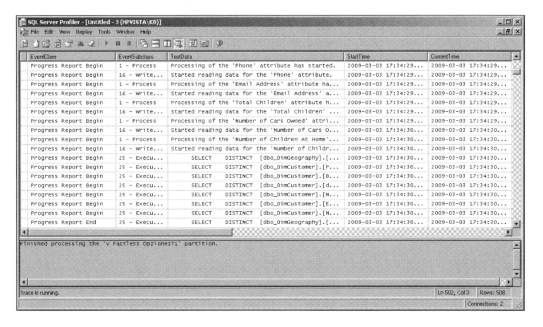

Looking at these events in Profiler itself is not particularly easy, and so saving trace data to a SQL Server table is a good idea since it allows us to query and report on it much more easily. We can save a captured trace session by using the **File | Save As | Trace Table...** menu or we can choose to save a trace session in advance by using the **Save to table** option in the **Trace Properties** dialog box that is shown when we define a new trace session.

The trace events that we are interested in are listed below. Note that event classes and subclasses are identified by an integer value when saved in SQL Server log tables; we have given these integer values in parentheses after the events in the list below and there is a script to insert all these IDs into SQL Server tables available at `http://tinyurl.com/SsasTraceIDs`.

- **Command Begin** (15) / **Command End** (16) – contains only one interesting subclass event:

  - `Batch` (12) contains the XMLA command sent to Analysis Services to process one or more objects.

- **Progress Report Begin** (5) / **Progress Report End** (6) – contains several subclass events that apply to both processing and query operations. Below we list only the subclass events relevant to processing:

  - `Process` (1)
  - `ExecuteSQL` (25)
  - `WriteData` (16)
  - `ReadData` (17)
  - `BuildIndex` (20)
  - `BuildAggsAndIndexes` (28)

It is important to note there is a sort of nesting of events that can be seen in trace data. For example, the `Process` event for a database initiates several other `Process` events for related objects, such as the cubes and dimensions in that database. The outermost events have an execution time (the column **Duration**, in milliseconds) that includes the time taken for all the operations executed within those events. Therefore, the values in the **Duration** column for different events cannot easily be summed, because we have to be careful not to sum events that might include each other. A good approach is to filter rows by event class, event subclass and **ObjectPath** (which uniquely identifies the object that the event refers to). For example, if we want to find how long it took to process the Adventure Works cube, we need to find the row in the trace that has the event class **Progress Report End**, the event subclass 1 `Process` and the object path *ServerName.Adventure Works DW 2008. Adventure Works.*

ASTrace

Using SQL Server Profiler to capture trace data is a good option if we want to create a trace manually, but it is not the best way to automate trace data capture on a production server. A useful tool is ASTrace, which is part of the Microsoft SQL Server Community Samples for Analysis Services, available from `http://sqlsrvanalysissrvcs.codeplex.com`. ASTrace captures an Analysis Services trace and logs it into a SQL Server table.

This utility runs as a Windows service that connects to Analysis Services, creates a trace and logs trace events into a SQL Server table using the SQL Server Profiler format. To customize the trace (for example, to filter on certain events) we can use a standard trace template authored using SQL Server Profiler. Running as a service, this tool does not require a logged in user, unlike SQL Server Profiler.

XMLA

We can also initiate a trace by executing an `XMLA` command. The columns and events used in the trace are defined in the `XMLA` command itself. An example of an `XMLA` script is available here: `http://tinyurl.com/XmlaTrace`.

Flight Recorder

Flight Recorder is a feature of Analysis Services that maintains a log of all events that happened in the recent past that might be useful when investigating crashes or performance problems; it works by running a trace. By default, it doesn't capture all events and only keeps data for a limited time (so as not to fill the disk with trace data), but we can customize it by changing both the length of time it keeps data and the events that it records. We have to remember, though, that Flight Recorder can affect performance: the more events it records, the more I/O operations are required to update the trace files it generates.

Flight Recorder trace files can be opened with SQL Server Profiler and are stored in the `OLAP\Log` folder (usually found at `C:\Program Files\Microsoft SQL Server\MSSQL.2\OLAP\Log`). To customize the trace definition it uses we can use a SQL Profiler template in the same way we did with ASTrace; a description of exactly how to do this is available at `http://tinyurl.com/CustomizeFlightRecorder`.

Flight Recorder and Trace Architecture

A more complete description of the Trace architecture of Analysis Services and the behavior of Flight Recorder is available in Chapter 38 of *Microsoft SQL Server 2008 Analysis Services Unleashed* written by Gorbach, Berger and Melomed.

Monitoring Processing with Performance Monitor counters

In the first part of this chapter we saw how to use Performance Monitor to monitor the operating system. Analysis Services has its own set of Performance Monitor counters too. The most important ones for analyzing Analysis Services processing operations can be found under the **MSOLAP Processing** category. `Total Rows Converted`, `Total Rows Read`, and `Total Rows Written` are, respectively, the count of the number of rows converted, the count of the number of rows read from all relational data sources, and the count of the number of rows written during processing. These values allow us to monitor the amount of data processed, and can be useful for evaluating if the amount of time taken for processing is related to the amount of data processed.

There is another set of performance counters relating to the Memory Manager. These counters are found in the **MSOLAP Memory** category:

- **Cleaner Memory non-shrinkable KB** is the amount of memory that cannot be purged by the Memory Manager
- **Cleaner Memory shrinkable KB** is the amount of memory that can be purged by the Memory Manager
- **Cleaner Memory KB** is the sum of the amount of shrinkable and non-shrinkable memory returned by the two counters above, and this is the total amount of memory controlled by the Memory Manager.
- **Memory Limit High KB** returns the actual amount of memory that corresponds to the threshold set by the `TotalMemoryLimit` property.
- **Memory Limit Low KB** returns the actual amount of memory that corresponds to the threshold set by the `LowMemoryLimit` property.
- **Memory Usage KB** is the total of private virtual memory allocated by Analysis Services and corresponds to `Process\PrivateBytes` counter provided by the operating system. This number should be always greater than or equal to the `CleanerMemoryKB`. We should also look out for any paging caused by Analysis Services virtual memory.

As we previously said in the section Controlling the Analysis Services Memory Manager, it is important to compare the value of `Cleaner Memory KB` to the values of `Memory Limit Low KB` and `Memory Limit High KB`, but also to look for any paging caused by Analysis Services virtual memory. We might consider increasing our memory limits only if there is no paging and there is enough physical RAM available. On the other hand, we might want to decrease our memory limits if paging is having a negative impact on performance (for example, if cache is paged to disk it is much less efficient).

Monitoring Processing with Dynamic Management Views

Dynamic Management Views (DMVs) were introduced in Analysis Services 2008 to track server resources used, and can be queried using a SQL-like syntax. We can run a DMV query in SQL Server Management Studio in an MDX query window. For example, the following query shows the top 10 objects that used most CPU:

```
SELECT TOP 10 *
FROM $System.DISCOVER_OBJECT_ACTIVITY
ORDER BY OBJECT_CPU_TIME_MS DESC
```

The result of this query will display a large number of columns; the following table shows just the first few columns from a sample `Resultset`:

OBJECT_PARENT_PATH	OBJECT_ ID	OBJECT_CPU_ TIME_MS	OBJECT_ READS	OBJECT_ READ_KB
HPVISTA\K8.Databases. Adv Works - DW.Dimensions	Date	62	1011	265
HPVISTA\K8.Databases. Adv Works - DW.Dimensions	Products	62	973	232
HPVISTA\K8.Databases. Adv Works - DW.Dimensions	Employee	46	747	278

> DMV queries support only a subset of standard SQL. We can use WHERE conditions, DISTINCT and ORDER BY, but constructs like GROUP BY, JOIN, LIKE, CAST, and CONVERT are not supported. However, we can also project data using expressions and calling some functions, like **Format**.

Unfortunately, the documentation on DMVs is incomplete, although there is a lot of useful information on Vidas Matelis' blog at http://tinyurl.com/vidasdmv, and on Darren Gosbell's blog at http://tinyurl.com/darrendmv. We can return a list of schema rowsets that can be queried through DMVs by running the following query:

```
SELECT * FROM
$System.Discover_Schema_Rowsets
```

Despite the lack of documentation, DMVs are very useful for monitoring Analysis Services. When we want to monitor processing activity through DMVs, we probably want to see what objects are consuming the most memory and CPU. Each allocation in Analysis Services can be one of two types: shrinkable and non-shrinkable. The shrinkable objects that consume the most memory can be returned using a query like this:

```
SELECT *
FROM $System.DISCOVER_OBJECT_MEMORY_USAGE
ORDER BY OBJECT_MEMORY_SHRINKABLE DESC
```

Shrinkable objects can be purged by Memory Manager if new allocations require memory. However, it can also be useful to take a look at non-shrinkable objects because they cannot be purged, and we might want to know what the most expensive objects are. They will give us an indication of which databases should be moved to another server to reduce resource consumption:

```
SELECT *
FROM $System.DISCOVER_OBJECT_MEMORY_USAGE
ORDER BY OBJECT_MEMORY_NONSHRINKABLE DESC
```

Much of the information provided by DMVs is not available from other sources. For this reason, it is important to know of their existence and to know how to use them in our monitoring infrastructure.

Monitoring query performance

We have already introduced many tools that can be used to get data on processing operations, using trace, performance counters and dynamic management views. The same tools can also be used to monitor query performance, and in this section we'll see how this can be done.

Monitoring queries with trace data

Regardless of the tool we use to collect it (SQL Server Profiler, ASTrace, XMLA, or Flight Recorder), trace data is the most important source of information on query-related operations. Trace data provides information on the internal operations of the Storage Engine and the Formula Engine, for example showing if aggregations are used or not or if calculations are evaluated in bulk mode or not.

The most important trace events for analyzing query performance are as follows (once again, the integer identifier for each event is shown in parentheses after its name):

- **Progress Report Begin (5) / Progress Report End (6)** – there is only one subclass event that is relevant for query operations:
  - ○ **Query** (14) shows when the Storage Engine accesses a partition or aggregation to get data. This will only happen if the data required is not available in the Storage Engine cache.

- **Query Begin (9) / Query End (10)** – are raised at the start and end of query evaluation. They usually contain only one interesting subclass event:
  - ○ MDXQuery (0) shows the MDX statement sent to Analysis Services. For the Query End event, the **Duration** column shows the overall amount of time taken to run the query and return its results back to the client.

- **Calculate Non Empty Begin (72) / Calculate Non Empty End (74)** – have no related subclass events. The Calculate Non Empty events are raised when Analysis Services performs non empty filtering operations, for example when the NonEmpty MDX function or the Non Empty statement is used in a query, and these operations are often the cause of slow query performance. When the value of the **Duration** column for Calculate Non Empty End is large, we should check the IntegerData column to see if it bulk mode is being used or not. When the value of IntegerData is 11, Analysis Services iterates over all the tuples in a set to perform non empty filtering, and this can be very slow. For all other IntegerData values (usually 1), Analysis Services is operating in bulk mode which is usually much faster.

- **Execute MDX Script Begin (78) / Execute MDX Script End (80)** – have no related subclass events. They are raised at the beginning and end of the evaluation of the MDX Script on a cube, which is usually a very quick operation. However, if there are any complex named sets defined on the cube then MDX Script evaluation can take a long time.

- **Get Data From Aggregation (60)** – has no related subclass events. This event is raised when the Storage Engine reads data from an aggregation.

- **Get Data From Cache (61)** – is raised when data is read from cache. There are several subclass events that identify the type of cache used. This event will be seen very frequently on a production server, because after a query has been run all of the data it returns should be kept in cache. If this is not the case, it usually indicates that either there is not enough memory available for caching, or that calculations have been written so that the values they return cannot be cached.

- ° Get data from `measure group` cache (1)
- ° Get data from `flat` cache (2)
- ° Get data from `calculation` cache (3)
- ° Get data from `persisted` cache (4)

- **Query Cube Begin (70) / Query Cube End (71)** – have no related subclass events. After a `Query Begin` event has been raised, in some scenarios the MDX Script of a cube must be evaluated before query evaluation proper can start; in these scenarios `Query Cube Begin` is raised after the Execute MDX `Script End` event and shows when query evaluation actually starts.

- **Query Dimension (81)** – this event is raised when queries retrieve members from dimension hierarchies. These members may or may not be in cache already; if they aren't we would expect to see some I/O read operations executed.
  - ° Cache data (1)
  - ° Non-cache data (2)

- **Query Subcube (11)** – As we saw in Chapter 8, a single MDX query might result in several different subcubes of data being requested from the Storage Engine. A `Query Subcube` event is raised for each of these requests, and may be one of the following types:
  - ° Cache data (1)
  - ° Non-cache data (2)
  - ° Internal data (3)
  - ° SQL data (4)

- **Query Subcube Verbose (12)** – is functionally identical to `Query Subcube`, but it adds more information about the multidimensional space of the subcube that is queried.
  - ° Cache data (1)
  - ° Non-cache data (2)
  - ° Internal data (3)
  - ° SQL data (4)

- **Serialize Results Begin (75) / Serialize Results End (77)** – have no related subclass events. They mark the start and end of query results being sent back to the client. The `Serialize Results Begin` event might be raised before the calculation of all of the cell values in a cellset has been completed, although it often starts just after all calculation is finished (for example, a `Non Empty` statement in an MDX query could force this behavior).

Monitoring queries with Performance Monitor counters

Analysis Services Performance Monitor counters are more useful for monitoring general query behavior than understanding what is happening when individual queries are run. Logging these counters can help us to understand the characteristics of all of the queries our users are running, and therefore help us to find query performance bottlenecks. Here's a list of all of the relevant categories and the important counters in them:

- **MSOLAP: Cache**
  - **CurrentEntries** is the number of entries in the cache
  - **Total Direct Hits** is the number of subcube queries answered from existing cache entries – this number should be compared to Total Misses to evaluate the percentage of subcube queries that are resolved using cache
  - **Total Misses** is the number of cache misses – this number should grow after the cache has been cleared (for example, after the Analysis Services service has been restarted, or after cube processing) and should not grow too much once the cache is warm. If this number continues to grow, we need to evaluate if there is not enough memory for cache or if the queries that are being run cannot take advantage of existing cache.

- **MSOLAP:MDX** contains several counters with very detailed information, the most important of which is:
  - **Total NON EMPTY un-optimized** is the number of Calculate Non Empty operations (as described earlier in the section on trace data) that are using an un-optimized algorithm. If this number continues to grow, there may be MDX queries that are running slowly for this reason and we might want to find them and optimize them.

- **MSOLAP: Memory** – we can use the same counters used to monitor processing operations to monitor query operations.

- **MSOLAP: Storage Engine Query** – contains several counters with detailed information that we can use to measure the workload of Analysis Services; the most generic counter here is:
  - **Total Queries Answered** shows the total number of queries run against Analysis Services; if this number does not increase, no queries are being run.

Monitoring queries with Dynamic Management Views

DMVs are not really useful for finding slow queries or understanding what happens when a query is run; trace data is much more useful for this purpose. That said, the data that DMVs return on memory usage, for example, is very useful for understanding the state of Analysis Services at a given point in time, which will have an impact on query performance.

MDX Studio

As we saw in Chapter 8, MDX Studio is a powerful tool that allows us to analyze MDX expressions, monitor the performance of MDX queries and use trace data to determine whether the Storage Engine or the Formula Engine is the cause of poor query performance. A complete description of MDX Studio and links to download it (for free) are available at: `http://tinyurl.com/MdxStudio`.

Monitoring usage

Apart from monitoring the performance of processing and queries, another important activity is monitoring the overall usage of Analysis Services. At any given point in time we might want to know who is connected to Analysis Services and who is running queries, for example because we might want to warn users that we're about to restart the service for maintenance reasons. Also, in the long term, it is interesting to know which cubes and hierarchies are used and which are not, what type of queries are being run, who the most active users are, which users never use the system, and so on.

To monitor usage we can use the same tools that we've used in previous sections.

Monitoring Usage with Trace Data

Collecting trace data in a SQL Server table can be a very useful way to determine the most active users, or the most frequent or expensive queries, over a long period of time. The most important event to capture is `Query End` / `MDX Query`: The **Duration** column for this event can be used to identify the most expensive queries, and it allows us to see the actual MDX that was run for a query. However, it's very often the case that users will run several very similar MDX queries – for example, they might run the same query but slice by a different date – and it is very difficult to identify this kind of query pattern with just the MDX, so we may also choose to capture lower-level trace events too, such as `Get Data From Aggregation` or even `Query Subcube`.

Another important piece of information in the `Query End` / `MDX Query` event is the **NTUserName** column, which identifies the user who ran the query. The only issue here is that if we are using some form of application-level security, it might be that the same user is used for all Analysis Services queries. In this case, we would need to create a dedicated log at the application level because Analysis Services doesn't have enough information in the trace to identify the end user.

Monitoring usage with Performance Monitor counters

From the Performance Monitor counter point of view, there are specific counters that give us information about current connections and running queries. Of course, the entire **Memory** category of counters we saw earlier also play an important part in any usage monitoring strategy. We may also add the following counters:

- **MSOLAP: Connection**
  - **Current connections** is the number of active client connections at the current point in time.
  - **Current user sessions** is the number of active user sessions; a connection is always tied to a session, but there could be sessions without active user connections.

More detailed information about which connected are available using the DMVs.

Monitoring usage with Dynamic Management Views

DMVs are very useful way to get a snapshot of the current state of Analysis Services. As DMVs can be queried by any client that can connect to Analysis Services, we can build Reporting Services reports that access this information directly, with minimum latency. For example, we can get a detailed list of active client connections by using this command.

```
SELECT *
FROM $System.DISCOVER_CONNECTIONS
```

The result of this query includes the user name, the client application, the date/time when the connection started and the date/time of the last command. For each connection there is always a user session; a list of these sessions can be obtained with the following command.

```
SELECT *
FROM $System.DISCOVER_SESSIONS
```

In the resultset, for each session we can see the last command issued and the current database, the date/time when the connection started and the date/time of the last command.

Finally, we can see a list of all currently executing commands with the following statement.

```
SELECT *
FROM $System.DISCOVER_COMMANDS
```

The resultset will contain non-user-related activity like active traces, queries to metadata information and so on. We will probably want to concentrate our attention on only those commands that are consuming CPU or that are engaged in read/write activity (the columns **COMMAND_CPU_TIME_MS**, **COMMAND_READS**, **COMMAND_READ_KB**, **COMMAND_WRITES** and **COMMAND_WRITE_KB** provide this type of information).

Activity Viewer

A better way to query DMVs is to use a tool specifically designed for this purpose. Unfortunately, SQL Server Management Studio does not have any features to do this for Analysis Services, but there are two versions of a tool called Activity Viewer (one each for Analysis Services 2005 and 2008), that can be used to monitor Analysis Services state.

The first version of Activity Viewer was designed for Analysis Services 2005 and is part of the SQL Server Analysis Services Samples. Strangely enough, it is still part of the Analysis Services community samples available at `http://sqlsrvanalysissrvcs.codeplex.com` even though it doesn't actually work on an Analysis Services 2008 instance.

The second version, Analysis Services Activity Viewer 2008, is available at `http://asactivityviewer2008.codeplex.com`. The following screenshot shows it displaying a list of users currently connected on an instance of Analysis Services. This tool has been improved significantly over the previous version, with new functionality like custom alerts, which can be defined by selecting the **Rules** option in the left-hand pane.

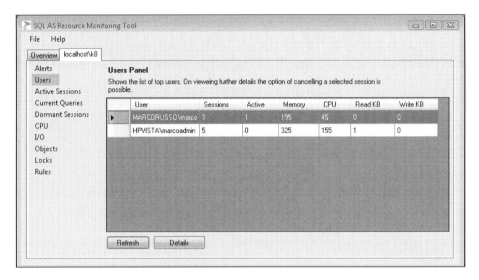

Both these tools allow us to see current connections, sessions and commands. They also allow us to cancel a running query and this single feature makes Activity Viewer a very important addition to any cube administrator's toolkit.

How to build a complete monitoring solution

In this chapter we have seen a set of tools and techniques that we can use to monitor an Analysis Services instance. We already mentioned that it is a good idea to save trace and performance counter information in log files or SQL Server tables, so we can perform more detailed analysis on them. The logical next step would be to build a complete monitoring solution that could provide reports, statistics and detailed information on all aspects of performance and usage, and that would be always running in the background, collecting data.

We could use all of this data as a source for a "performance and usage data mart", and use our favorite tools like Reporting Services and Analysis Services to build a BI solution for ourselves. If we have specific requirements or we have to integrate the monitoring solution with an existing system, designing a custom solution could be a good idea: for example, we might simply build Reporting Services reports that access DMVs, or that query trace data collected using ASTrace and stored in SQL Server. However, if we don't want to start from scratch, we can use the MonitoringSSAS solution that is part of the community samples at `http://sqlsrvanalysissrvcs.codeplex.com`.

This solution automates the collection of performance data from trace, performance counters and **Dynamic Management Views (DMVs)**. Data is collected and stored using several Integration Services packages and other pieces of code, including some T-SQL stored procedures. The solution also includes some Reporting Services reports that perform basic analysis, and show performance counter values at the time when specific queries were run. We suggest customizing this solution rather than trying to build everything ourselves because it includes all the source code and it could save us a lot of time even if we only used a part of it.

Summary

In this chapter we spent most of our time describing the key resources that we have to monitor for Analysis Services: Memory, CPU, and I/O. These resources are controlled by the operating system, and for this reason we looked at how Analysis Services interacts with the operating system and with other processes that may also be competing for resources. We discovered what the most important operating system performance counters are for monitoring an Analysis Services installation, and what tools we have available for accessing them.

After that, we explored various techniques for monitoring processing, query activity and usage of Analysis Services. We focused on using tools like SQL Server Profiler, ASTrace, Activity Viewer and MDX Studio; we also looked at the detailed information provided by traces, performance counters and dynamic management views for each of the monitoring scenarios.

Finally, we discussed building a complete monitoring solution and pointed out that such a solution already exists as part of the SQL Server Community Samples, complete with source code, and that it can be used as a starting point for building our own custom monitoring solution.

Index

Memory Usage KB 321
MSSQLServer OLAP Services 303

N

named set
defining 161
dynamic named sets 163, 164
regular named sets 161-163
New Dimension Wizard, dimension
Enable Browsing option, unchecking 46
key property 45
Name property 46
naming 47
Selection Creation Method step 44
Select Dimension Attributes step 46
Use an existing table option, using 45
using 44-47

O

OLTP database
about 8, 9
common characteristics 8
Online Transactional Processing. *See* **OLTP**
database
operating system
Analysis Service, interacting with 295, 296
Memory management 310
resource consumption monitoring tools 302
SQL Server and Analysis Service,
sharing 315, 316

P

partition, performance-specific design
features
about 194
Analysis Service partitioning 270
and aggregation, monitoring 208
benefits 194
building 195, 196
building, in Integration Service 272-276
building, Query Binding 195
building, Table Binding 195
extra scan, factors 199
generating, in large numbers 198
managing 269, 270

need for 194
relational partitioning 270
Remote Partitions 196
slice property, setting 196
strategy, planning 196, 198
template partition, building 271, 272
unexpected scanning 198
partition processing
add option 280
date option 281
default option 281
full option 280
index option 281
issues 281
options, using 281, 282
unprocess option 281
performance-specific design, features
about 194
aggregation 200
partition 194
Performance Monitor
performance counters 305
PID 2568 303
PID 2768 303
physical database, Analysis Service
data types 28
multiple data sources 28
naming conventions 33
schema, using 33
SQL generated queries 29
subject areas 33
using, instead of DSV 33, 34
views, advantages 34, 35
prefetching 199
Process definition 233
ProcessingGroup property, setting to
ByTable 118
Process ID(PID) 303
processing
dimension processing 277, 278
ErrorConfiguration property used 284, 285
errors, handling 284
Integration Services, benefits 286, 288
Lazy aggregations option, using 283
managing 277
managing, Integration Services
used 286, 288

partition processing 277, 280
proactive caching 289
processingmonitoring, ASTrace tool
   used 320
processingmonitoring, Dynamic
   Management Views used 322
processingmonitoring, Flight Recorder 320
processingmonitoring, Performance
   Monitor counters used 321
processingmonitoring, SQL Server Profiler
   tool 318, 319
processingmonitoring, trace data used 317
processingmonitoring, XMLA
   command 320
processingperformance, monitoring 317
pull-mode processing 289
push-mode processing 289
reference dimension 283, 284
UnknownMember property 284
Profiler
   Get Data From Aggregation event 209
   Progress Report Begin event 209
   Progress Report End event 209
   Query Subcube Verbose events 209
   subcubes 209
   trace results, intepreting 209, 210
   using 208
program counters
   Disk I/O counters, 307
   Disk I/O counters, Current Disk Queue
      Length 307
   Disk I/O counters, Disk Read Bytes/sec
      307
   Disk I/O counters, Disk Write Bytes/ 307
   Disk I/O counters, LogicalDisk 307
   Disk I/O counters, PhysicalDisk 307
   memory counters 305
   memory counters, % Committed Bytes
      in Use 306
   memory counters, Committed Bytes 306
   memory counters, Pages/sec 305
   page file bytes 306
   page file bytes Peak 306
   private bytes 306
   process category, IO Data Bytes/sec 308
   process category, IO Read Bytes/sec 308
   process category, IO Write Bytes/sec 308

Processor category 308
virtual bytes 306
working set 306
working set-peak 306
working set-private 306
property, measures
   AggregateFunction 83
   display folders 81, 82
   format string 80, 81
   setting, points 80, 81

Q

query performance
   and security 264
   cell security 264
   designing 193
   dimension security 264, 265
   dynamic security 265
   MDX calculation performance 215
   optimising 215
   MDX Studio 327
   monitoring 323
   monitoring, DMV used 327
   monitoring, Performance Monitor counters
      used 326
   monitoring, trace data used 323
   MSOLAP
   MSOLAPCache 326
   MSOLAPMDX 326
   MSOLAPMemory 326
   MSOLAPStorage Engine Query 326
   trace events 323
   tuning methodology 192, 193
Query Subcube event 210, 212
Query Subcube Verbose event 210, 211

R

raggged hierarchy
   about 72
   AttributeHierarchyVisible property 73
   HideMemberIf, setting 75, 76
   HideMemberIf, using 77
   modeling 72
   parent/child hierarchy 73, 75
   parent/child hierarchy, limitations 74

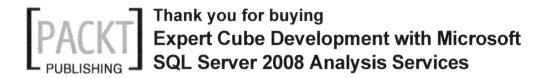

Thank you for buying
**Expert Cube Development with Microsoft
SQL Server 2008 Analysis Services**

About Packt Publishing

Packt, pronounced 'packed', published its first book "*Mastering phpMyAdmin for Effective MySQL Management*" in April 2004 and subsequently continued to specialize in publishing highly focused books on specific technologies and solutions.

Our books and publications share the experiences of your fellow IT professionals in adapting and customizing today's systems, applications, and frameworks. Our solution based books give you the knowledge and power to customize the software and technologies you're using to get the job done. Packt books are more specific and less general than the IT books you have seen in the past. Our unique business model allows us to bring you more focused information, giving you more of what you need to know, and less of what you don't.

Packt is a modern, yet unique publishing company, which focuses on producing quality, cutting-edge books for communities of developers, administrators, and newbies alike. For more information, please visit our website: www.packtpub.com.

Writing for Packt

We welcome all inquiries from people who are interested in authoring. Book proposals should be sent to author@packtpub.com. If your book idea is still at an early stage and you would like to discuss it first before writing a formal book proposal, contact us; one of our commissioning editors will get in touch with you.

We're not just looking for published authors; if you have strong technical skills but no writing experience, our experienced editors can help you develop a writing career, or simply get some additional reward for your expertise.

Learning SQL Server 2008
Reporting Services

A step-by-step guide to getting the most of Microsoft SQL Server Reporting Services 2008

Jayaram Krishnaswamy

PACKT

Learning SQL Server 2008 Reporting Services

ISBN: 978-1-847196-18-7   Paperback: 512 pages

A step-by-step guide to getting the most of Microsoft SQL Server Reporting Services 2008

1. Everything you need to create and deliver data-rich reports with SQL Server 2008 Reporting Services as quickly as possible

2. Packed with hands-on-examples to learn and improve your skills

3. Connect and report from databases, spreadsheets, XML Data, and more

4. No experience of SQL Server Reporting Services required

ASP.NET 3.5
Social Networking

An expert guide to building enterprise-ready social networking and community applications with ASP.NET 3.5

Andrew Siemer

PACKT

ASP.NET 3.5 Social Networking

ISBN: 978-1-847194-78-7   Paperback: 580 pages

An expert guide to building enterprise-ready social networking and community applications with ASP. NET 3.5

1. Create a full-featured, enterprise-grade social network using ASP.NET 3.5

2. Learn key new ASP.NET topics in a practical, hands-on way: LINQ, AJAX, C# 3.0, n-tier architectures, and MVC

3. Build friends lists, messaging systems, user profiles, blogs, message boards, groups, and more

4. Rich with example code, clear explanations, interesting examples, and practical advice – a truly hands-on book for ASP.NET developers

Please check **www.PacktPub.com** for information on our titles

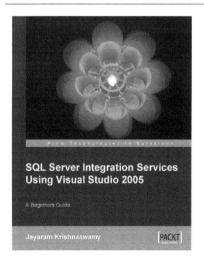

1824331R00192

Made in the USA
San Bernardino, CA
05 February 2013